GLOBALISMS

FACING THE POPULIST CHALLENGE

FOURTH EDITION

D0226310

MANFRED B. STEGER

UNIVERSITY OF HAWAI'I–MĀNOA

AND

WESTERN SYDNEY UNIVERSITY

ROWMAN & LITTLEFIELD
Lanham • Boulder • New York • London

To my family and friends around the world

Executive Editor: Susan McEachern
Assistant Editor: Katelyn Turner
Senior Marketing Manager: Amy Whitaker

Credits and acknowledgments for material borrowed from other sources, and reproduced with permission, appear on the appropriate page within the text.

Published by Rowman & Littlefield
An imprint of The Rowman & Littlefield Publishing Group, Inc.
4501 Forbes Boulevard, Suite 200, Lanham, Maryland 20706
www.rowman.com

6 Tinworth Street, London SE11 5AL, United Kingdom

British Library Cataloguing in Publication Information Available

Library of Congress Cataloging-in-Publication Data Available

Library of Congress Control Number: 2019949256

ISBN 9781538129449 (cloth) | ISBN 9781538129456 (pbk.) | ISBN 9781538129463 (ebook)

Contents

PREFACE

This new edition seeks to update, expand, and revise the arguments of the three previous editions of *Globalisms* in light of significant political and social developments that have occurred in the decade since the publication of the third edition weeks before the 2008–2009 Global Financial Crisis. Still, the basic premise of the book has remained the same: globalization is not merely a set of material processes anchored in economic flows and digital technology but also contains ideologically charged claims about the current compression of the world. The existence of these powerful discourses suggests that globalization also plays itself out in conflicting cultural systems of ideas, moods, and understandings. These meanings circulate in the public realm as more or less coherent stories and narratives that define, describe, and evaluate material processes of globalization.

The present study focuses on these powerful *ideological* aspects of globalization. Many works have been written on objective dimensions of the phenomenon ranging from the consequences of containerization for global trade to the redefining effects of the global intersection of biotechnology and genomic sequencing and DNA editing. By comparison, the subjective domains of globalization have not received the level of attention that has been paid to the material dynamics of global interchange. This is especially true for the study of the ways in which people imagine the world as an interconnected whole. The principal task of this book is to tell the missing half of the globalization story: why and how the ideological dynamics of globalization are just as important as global trade flows, investment transfers, or the transnational movement of goods, technologies, and people.

Thus, this book takes up a suggestion made by prominent social researchers who have called for a more extensive analysis of the production and global circulation of political thought-systems. I contend that this necessary inquiry requires making an analytic distinction between four relevant key concepts. The first is *globalization*, defined in this study as a *matrix of complex processes* pushing toward intensifying interdependence. This "compression of the world" is described by various commentators in different, sometimes contradictory ways. The second term is *globality*, which signifies a *social condition* characterized by tight global economic, political, cultural, and environmental interconnections and flows. Globalization moves us toward the condition of globality, but there is still a long way to go. *Global imaginary*, our third concept, refers to people's growing *global consciousness*. The rising global imaginary has started to unsettle the dominant national imaginary within which people have imagined their communal existence for many generations. The fourth term is *globalisms*, understood as competing *ideologies* that translate and articulate the underlying global imaginary into concrete political agendas, programs, and policies.

This means that *globalism* (the rhetorical package) does not exist in isolation from *globalization* (the multidimensional material process of interconnectivity), *globality* (a possible future condition of intense planetary interrelatedness), and the *global imaginary* (a deep-seated understanding of global interdependence). Ideologies are never idle constructs without foundations in material phenomena. Social institutions, concrete political and economic processes, and the selective ideological interpretation of these processes form an interconnected whole. The distinction between these four concepts sharing the linguistic root "global" helps us to appreciate the considerable role played by ideas, beliefs, language, and symbols in shaping the social world.

My focus on the ideas, discourses, imaginaries, and subjective frames linked to the major forms of globalism allows me to critically analyze the ideological dynamics of globalization unfolding from the 1990s to the present and beyond. Indeed, as I noted in the previous edition, we should not refer to "globalism" in the singular to connote the most influential of these globalization stories—strictly as a market ideology that endows the concept of globalization with neoliberal norms, values, and meanings. It is much more accurate to speak of *globalisms* in the plural, for the dominant discourse of *market globalism* has long been challenged by coherent globalisms on the political Left and Right. Articulating the rising global imaginary into alternative political programs and agendas, these ideologies deserve their own appellations: *justice globalism* and *religious globalism*.

During the second decade of the twenty-first century, we have been witnessing an intensification of this ongoing ideological confrontation. Lately, this expanding battle of ideas has been joined by the unexpectedly powerful surge of an ideological contender whose illiberal leanings stand in tension to pluralist values of liberal democracy: *antiglobalist populism*. Aided by their adroit use of the social media—as well as intrusive psychometric techniques employed by political consulting firms such as Cambridge Analytica—Donald Trump and other national-populist leaders around the world made the term *globalism* a central derogatory foil of their antagonistic politics. Many commentators found themselves unprepared for the remarkable speed and vigor with which right-wing populists in Western democracies exploited this new discontent with those "globalist elites" they held responsible for the growing inequality and the disappearance of "good jobs" in manufacture and the service sector. As antiglobalist populists succeeded at the ballot box beyond their wildest dreams in the late 2010s, mainstream journalists and academics went into crisis mode. Fearing the dismantling of the entire postwar world order, they wondered whether liberal democracy itself was in danger of being obliterated by this "populist explosion."

To be sure, the magnitude of the current ideological challenge of antiglobalist populism to the three established globalisms requires analysis and explanation. To do so is a principal aim of this new edition, which is reflected in its new subtitle: *Facing the Populist Challenge*. At the same time, the book maintains and expands its original mission of offering readers a comprehensive introduction to the evolution of ideologies of globalization over the last three decades. The present study seeks to spell out clearly, and with as many instructive examples as possible:

- how various claims and assumptions made by various globalists articulate, legitimize, reinforce, and defend particular political agendas with global implications;
- how these globalist ideologies have developed over three decades and why they clashed with each other;
- how their core ideological claims have been modified as a result of these confrontations;
- how the recent emergence of antiglobalist populism has impacted the great ideological struggle of the twenty-first century; and
- what the prospects might be for the established globalisms and their national-populist challengers in what promises to be a very tumultuous confronting decade of the 2020s.

Let me end this preface with an important clarification. This study is not about denouncing globalization. Quite to the contrary, as a committed cosmopolitan happily embedded in the Pacific region, I hope that my writings will contribute to the formation of an even more interdependent world. But any socially engaged globalist vision must be predicated upon a critical understanding of current ideologies of globalization that encourages readers to recognize their internal contradictions and biases.

To this end, my approach is situated squarely within the intellectual tradition of *critical theory*. Derived from the Greek verb *krinein* (to discern, to reflect, to judge), "critical" signifies the noble human impulse to contemplate the validity and desirability of social institutions. Guided by the ideal of an equitable and peaceful global order, critical investigations of the global weaken the authoritarian tendency to silence dissent and eliminate freedom of the press and opinion. Ethically and historically informed criticisms represent the lifeblood of all democratic politics—past, present, and future. The critical lens applied in this study seeks to provide readers with an understanding of how dominant beliefs about globalization fashion their own realities and to show that these beliefs can be changed or maintained.

Critical theorists of globalization have consistently challenged the ideological claims of those types of globalism that seem to tolerate growing inequality and social injustice, and, in some instances, justify the use of violence against the weak and marginalized. Although I am sympathetic to the ideological claims of justice globalism, I have not been reluctant to offer constructive criticisms of the existing shortcomings of this ideology. Rather than succumbing to the simplistic notion of an "end of ideology" that was so popular only three decades ago, I hold that critical investigations of today's competing articulations of the global imaginary—and the powerful return of the national imaginary—remind us that different conditions of globality are realizable. With no predetermined outcomes or premature endings, the fate of this beautiful planet depends on engaged human beings willing to journey into unknown territory to make our world a better place.

Acknowledgments

It is a pleasant duty to record my debts of gratitude. First and foremost, I want to thank my colleagues at the University of Hawai'i at Mānoa, particularly those working with me in the Department of Sociology. More thanks go out to my colleagues at the Institute of Culture and Society, Western Sydney University, Australia.

This immensely successful book series would have never seen the light of day without the tremendous engagement of my brilliant coeditor and dear friend, Terrell Carver. I have benefited from his sage advice and unwavering support for many years. Furthermore, I appreciate the opportunity to hone the ideas presented in this book at many invited lectures, academic colloquia, and research seminars around the world.

Many people contributed their efforts to this book. In particular, Paul James, my special Aussie "mate" and close intellectual collaborator at Western Sydney University, offered important suggestions. I would also like to thank Neil Abercrombie, Clyde Barrow, Paul Battersby, Roland Benedikter, Steve Bronner, Franz Broswimmer, Nancie Caraway, Nadège Clitandre, Lane Crothers, Eve Darian-Smith, Mike Douglass, Tommaso Durante, Victor Faessel, Michael Forman, Michael Freeden, Mary Hawkesworth, Manfred Henningsen, Chris Hudson, Mark Juergensmeyer, Isaac Kamola, Hagen Koo, Brad Macdonald, Leo McCann, Phil McCarty, Jim Mittelman, Jamal Nassar, Deane Neubauer, Heikki Patomäki, Steve Rosow, Saskia Sassen, and Amentahru Wahlrab for their perceptive comments on my work.

Susan McEachern, my editor at Rowman & Littlefield, has been a genuine beacon of support and encouragement. Finally, as always, my deepest expressions of gratitude go to my soul mate, Perle Besserman— thanks for everything!

CHAPTER 1

IDEOLOGY AND THE MEANING OF GLOBALIZATION

THE "END OF IDEOLOGY DEBATE"

The global financial system teetering on the edge of total collapse before being rescued by massive taxpayer-funded bailouts. The volatile leaders of powerful nations flirting with large-scale trade wars. The pleas of international scientists to increase funding for climate research being rebuffed by populist governments as a "waste of money." Religious terrorists striking fear into the hearts of people around the globe. Xenophobic voices in prosperous countries calling for drastic measures to keep poor immigrants and political refugees out. The American leader of the "free world" openly disparaging the free press and independent courts. Is this what the "end of ideology" looks like?

Merely three decades ago, the collapse of the Soviet Empire enticed scores of Western commentators to relegate "ideology" to the dustbin of history. Proclaiming a radically new era in human history, they argued that all political belief systems had converged in a single vision: liberal capitalism. But this utopian dream of a universal set of political ideas ruling the world came crashing down in a series of unexpected events unfolding in our young century: the sustained alterglobalization protests from 1999–2001; the 9/11 terrorist attacks; the 2008–2009 Global Financial Crisis and the ensuing European Debt Crisis; and, most recently, the surge of national populism, most stunningly reflected in the Brexit vote and the election victories of Donald Trump in the United States, Rodrigo Duterte in the Philippines, Viktor Orbán in Hungary, and Jair Bolsonaro in Brazil. Looking at this political tumult only two decades into the twenty-first century, it is truly astounding to see how far we have moved away from the globalist triumphalism of the 1990s. Rather than reaching the end of ideology, we find ourselves in the throes of a fierce battle of ideas that threatens to tear our world apart.

The controversy over the fate of ideology goes back some time. It first erupted in the United States and Europe in the 1950s when political pundits on both sides of the Atlantic found themselves embroiled in what came to be known as *the end of ideology debate*. The book that set the terms of this controversy bore the suggestive title *The End of Ideology: On the Exhaustion of Political Ideas in the Fifties*. Widely hailed as a landmark in American social thought, the study was authored by Daniel Bell, a rising intellectual star who postulated the utter exhaustion of Marxist socialism and classical liberalism—two major ideologies of the nineteenth century. The American sociologists argued that their old master concepts, such as the "inevitability of history" or the "self-regulating market," had lost their power to rally modern constituencies who had witnessed the economic desperation of the Great Depression, the horrors of Nazi concentration camps, and the unleashing of nuclear weapons against defenseless civilians in a devastating war of truly global proportions. Most Westerners, Bell insisted, had abandoned simplistic beliefs in nineteenth-century utopias that projected visions of perfect social harmony—be it the classless society of Marxist socialists or the commercial paradise of laissez-faire liberals. At the same time, he thought that the anticolonial ideologies and their "politically naïve" slogans of "national liberation" that had emerged in the newly independent states of Africa and Asia were too parochial and limited to appeal to post–World War II audiences in Europe and the United States.

In spite of its nostalgic tone, Bell's book showed much appreciation for the virtues of a world without ideological battles. He noted that people in the West had become less prone to pledge their allegiance to dangerous forms of political extremism and more accepting of a pragmatic middle way embodied in the class compromise between business and labor that framed the modern welfare state of the 1950s. On one hand, this pragmatic middle way offered the political stability and economic security most people were craving after the traumatic events of the first half of the century. On the other hand, however, its technocratic framework seemed to provide hardly any outlets for political passions and heroic ideals.

Ideology—for Bell largely an emotionally laden and politically dangerous "all-or-none affair"—had become intellectually devitalized and increasingly displaced by a pragmatic reformism built on the virtues of compromise, utility, and scientific objectivity. The preoccupation with administrative solutions for largely technical problems related to the state and national economies had rendered ideology obsolete. Bell cautiously applauded the alleged demise of nineteenth-century ideologies, implying that a "deideologized" politics of the 1950s was facilitating Western progress toward a more rational and less divisive society.[1]

However, as his detractors were quick to point out, Bell's analysis contained a number of uncritical assumptions. For one, in implying a necessary link between the "ideological" and "totalitarianism," he painted the pragmatic mode of empirical problem solving in overly rosy colors. He made the demise of ideology appear as an attempt to refashion a new age of rational moderation—a natural state lost in nearly a century's worth of irrational attempts to put radically utopian ideas into practice. In particular, some commentators interpreted Bell's assertion of a deideologized climate in the United States as a deeply ideological attempt to reclaim objectivity, compromise, and pragmatism as the essential attributes of a superior Anglo-American culture. They considered *The End of Ideology* a sophisticated defense of the "free west" that was itself thoroughly pervaded by the ideological imperatives of the Cold War.

Second, several reviewers argued that Bell was unconsciously trying to substitute technocratic guidance by experts for genuine political debate in society. They charged him with evoking a myth of a popular consensus around basic norms and values in order to forestall a potentially divisive discussion on the remaining inequalities in America. Third, the international tensions produced by the Cold War, together with the sudden upsurge of ideological politics in the 1960s and 1970s, seemed to disprove Bell's thesis entirely. The civil rights movement, the numerous protest movements against the Vietnam War, the feminist movement, and the meteoric rise of environmentalism all pointed to the distinct possibility that at least some of the central norms and values contained in radical, Western nineteenth-century ideologies were still alive and well a century later.

Nearly three decades later, the sudden collapse of communist regimes in Eastern Europe and the Soviet Union unexpectedly resurrected the 1950s end-of-ideology debate. In a seminal 1989 article he later expanded into a book-length study, Francis Fukuyama, then a deputy director of the US State Department's policy-planning staff, argued that the passing of Marxism-Leninism as a viable political ideology marked nothing less than the "end point of mankind's ideological evolution." This end state was "evident first of all in the total exhaustion of viable systematic alternatives to Western liberalism." Fukuyama also postulated the emergence of a deideologized world, but he insisted that this new era would not be characterized by the convergence between liberalism and socialism as predicted earlier by Bell. Rather, Fukuyama asserted that it represented the "unabashed victory of economic and political liberalism." Downplaying the significance of rising religious fundamentalism and ethnic nationalism in the "New World Order" of the 1990s, Fukuyama predicted that the global triumph of the "Western idea" and the spread of its consumerist culture to all corners of the earth would prove to be unstoppable. Driven by the logical development of market forces and the unleashing of powerful new technologies, Western capitalist democracy had emerged as the "final form of human government."[2]

Hence, Fukuyama's vision of a deideologized world only partially overlapped with Bell's similar analysis. While the American political scientist agreed with his colleague on the irrevocable demise of socialism, he disagreed with Bell's bleak assessment of free-market liberalism. Indeed, Fukuyama expected a high-tech realization of the old nineteenth-century free-market utopia. Expressing some discomfort at the coming ideological vacuum at the "end of history," he predicted the rapid marketization of most social relations in a globalized world dedicated to self-interested economic calculation, the endless solving of technological problems, and the satisfaction of ceaseless consumer demands.[3]

It should come as no surprise that this book rejects Fukuyama's influential thesis of a world without ideological competition. Indeed, most political leaders of the twenty-first century have explicitly recognized the staying power of competing political belief systems. For example, in a 2007 televised address to the nation, US President George W. Bush left no doubt that the contest with jihadist Islamism was much more than just a military conflict: "It is the decisive ideological struggle of our time. On one side are those who believe in freedom and moderation. On the other side are extremists who kill the innocent and have declared their intention to destroy our way of life. In the long run, the most realistic way to protect the American people is to provide a hopeful alternative to the hateful ideology of the enemy—by advancing liberty across a troubled region."[4]

A decade later, in his controversial 2018 address to the United Nations, US President Donald J. Trump, too, made ideology the centerpiece of what he called his government's "policy of principled realism": "America is governed by Americans. We reject the ideology of globalism, and we embrace the doctrine of patriotism. Around the world, responsible nations must defend against threats to sovereignty not just from global governance, but also from other, new forms of coercion and domination."[5]

These high-profile acknowledgments of the persistence of ideology bolster the central argument made in this book: *clashing political belief systems are not only very much with us today but also represent just as powerful a force as they did a century ago.* As I see it, far from condemning people to ideological boredom in a world without competing ideas, the opening decades of the twenty-first century have become a teeming battlefield of clashing ideologies. The chief protagonist—the dominant ideology I call "market globalism"—has encountered serious resistance from three ideological challengers—justice globalism, religious globalism, and, most significantly, antiglobalist populism. At the heart of this four-way contest lies the collision of four competing worldviews claiming distinct ideals: *economic freedom, social and environmental justice, religious faith,* and *patriotism.* Each corresponds to an important organizational principle of society: *market, planet, god,* and *nation*. And each ideological camp seeks to universalize its vision at the expense of the others.

At its core, then, the ideological struggle of our time is a battle over *the meaning of globalization*. The current wave of populism demonstrates that the ideological contest over the meaning and shape of globalization has deeply impacted the political landscape of the new century. Far from being an abstract affair playing itself out in the world of concepts, this ideological confrontation impacts the form and direction of material processes of globalization such as international trade or transnational migration. As I will argue in the ensuing chapters, it is highly likely that market globalists will continue to clash with their opponents as each side tries to impress its own ideological agenda on the public mind.

However, before elaborating on these arguments in more detail, let me turn to a brief discussion of the main elements and functions of ideology and clarify their workings in specific thought-systems like market globalism.

ELEMENTS AND FUNCTIONS OF IDEOLOGY: FREEDEN AND CARVER

Ideology can be defined as a *system of widely shared ideas*, patterned beliefs, guiding norms and values, and lofty ideals accepted as "fact" or "truth" by significant groups in society. Codified by social elites, ideologies offer individuals a shared mental map that helps them navigate the complexity of their social environments. These maps assemble a more or less coherent and quite simplified picture of the world not only as it is but also as it should be.

Each ideology is structured around specific concepts and claims that set it apart from other ideologies and endow it with a specific structure or *morphology*. As political theorist Michael Freeden puts it, "Central to any analysis of ideologies is the proposition that they are characterized by a morphology that displays core, adjacent, and peripheral concepts."[6] What makes an ideology "political" is that its concepts and claims select, privilege, or constrict social meanings related to the exercise of power in society. All political belief systems are historically contingent and, therefore, must be analyzed with reference to a particular context that connects their origins and developments to specific times and spaces. Linking belief and practice, ideologies encourage people to act in certain ways that discourage possible alternative actions.

To this end, ideological codifiers construct claims that seek to "lock in" the meaning of their core concepts. Michael Freeden refers to this crucial process as *decontestation*. Although successfully decontested ideas always require ongoing explanation and justification, they are held, for a time, as truth with such confidence that they no longer appear to be assumptions at all. Ultimately, decontested concepts give each ideology its unique fingerprint. As Freeden explains,

> An ideology attempts to end the inevitable contention over concepts by *decontesting* them, by removing their meanings from contest. "This is what justice means," announces one ideology, and "that is what democracy entails." By trying to convince us that they are right and that they speak the truth, ideologies become devices for coping with the indeterminacy of meaning. . . . That is their semantic role. [But] [i]deologies also need to decontest the concepts they use because they are instruments for fashioning collective decisions. That is their political role.[7]

Ideologies can thus be pictured as decontested concepts linked in *truth-claims* that facilitate collective decision making. Their control over language translates directly into political power, including the decision of "who gets what, when, and how."[8] In an excellent essay on the historical development of the concept of ideology from the early nineteenth century to the present, political theorist Terrell Carver also draws attention to this inescapably political function of ideology. He argues that ideology is neither an abstract template against which something is or is not an ideology nor a recipe stating how to put a system of thought together "correctly." "Rather," Carver writes, "it is an agenda of things to discuss, questions to ask, hypotheses to make. We should be able to use it when considering the interaction between ideas and politics, especially systems of ideas that make claims, whether justificatory or hortatory."[9]

Following both Freeden and Carver, one could say that to explore ideologies is to study the heart of politics understood as the *exercise of power* with regard to collective decision making and the regulation of social conflict. After all, politics is the public arena where various "agendas of things to discuss" formulated as "claims whether justificatory or hortatory" and connected to the power interests of particular groups and classes are contested and implemented. Thus, ideology is inextricably linked to the many ways in which power is exercised, justified, and altered in society.

Ideologists speak to their audiences in stories and images whose claims often elicit powerful emotions. They persuade, praise, cajole, convince, condemn, distinguish "truths" from "falsehoods," and separate the "good" from the "bad." Ideology enables people to act while simultaneously constraining their actions by binding them to a particular set of ideas, norms, and values. Hence, ideology constitutes the glue that binds theory and practice by orienting and organizing political action in accordance with general linguistic rules and cultural codes of ethical conduct.

ELEMENTS AND FUNCTIONS OF IDEOLOGY: RICOEUR AND GRAMSCI

In his seminal *Lectures on Ideology and Utopia*, French philosopher Paul Ricoeur integrates the elements and functions of ideology into a comprehensive conceptual framework.[10] Drawing on the insights of Marxist thought, Ricoeur characterizes the first functional level of ideology as *distortion*—that is, the production of contorted and blurred images of social reality. Most importantly, the process of distortion hides the contrast between things as they are envisioned in theory and things as they play themselves out on the plane of material reality. Indeed, all ideologies assemble a picture of the world based on a peculiar mixture that both represents and distorts social processes. Yet Ricoeur disagrees with Karl Marx's notion that distortion explains all there is to ideology. For the French philosopher, distortion is merely one of the three main functions of ideology, representing the surface level of a phenomenon that contains two more functions at progressively deeper levels.

Inspired by the writings of the German sociologist Max Weber, Ricoeur identifies *legitimation* as the second functional level of ideology. Two main factors are involved here: the claim to legitimacy made by the ruling authority and the belief in the authority's legitimacy granted by its subjects. Accepting large parts of Weber's explanation of social action, Ricoeur highlights ideology's function of mediating the gap between belief and claim. In other words, Ricoeur argues that there will always remain some discrepancy between the popular belief in the authority's right to rule and the authority's claim to the right to rule. It is one of ideology's functions to supply the people with additional justification in order to narrow this credibility gap. Ricoeur's model is completed in his description of integration, the third functional level of ideology.

Drawing on the writings of anthropologist Clifford Geertz, who emphasizes the symbolic structure of social action, Ricoeur claims that, on the deepest level, ideology relies on rich symbolic resources that play a mediating or *integrative role*. Thus, ideology provides society with stability as it creates, preserves, and protects the social identity of persons and groups. Performing a constructive function, ideology supplies the symbols, norms, and images that go into the process of assembling and holding together individual and collective identity. Yet this also means that ideology assumes a conservative function in both senses of that word. It preserves identity, "but it also wants to conserve what exists and is therefore already a resistance."[11] Such rigid forms of resistance to change often turn beliefs and ideas into a dogmatic defense of dominant power structures.

Ricoeur's model inspires my own view that the study of ideology yields a better understanding of political action as mediated, structured, and integrated by symbolic systems—most importantly *language* and *images*. Ideologies permeate all societies, with different segments of the population holding particular ideas about power and social order. In no case will a given society be so completely dominated by a single ideology as to have no alternatives available within the system. Even in the "totalitarian" regimes of the past century, pockets of ideological resistance remained despite the governments' efforts to eliminate all opposition. At the same time, however, it must be emphasized that there are periods in modern history when a particular ideology becomes predominant or *hegemonic*.

Made famous by Antonio Gramsci, a leading Italian socialist thinker who died in prison as a victim of Mussolini's fascist regime, *hegemony* can be defined as a power relationship between social groups and classes in which one class exercises control by gaining the active consent of subordinate groups. According to Gramsci, this process involves the internalization on the part of the subordinate classes of the moral and cultural values, the codes of practical conduct, and the worldview of the dominant classes.[12] Submerged in a symbolic universe created by the dominant group, the subordinate groups give their *spontaneous consent* to the social logic of domination that is embedded in hegemonic ideology. This allows dominant groups to maintain a social order favoring their own interests in "informal" ways—that is, largely without having to resort to open coercion.

In his discussion of hegemony, Gramsci also comments on the power of ideology to shape personal and collective identities. As Gramsci scholar William I. Robinson notes, "Under a hegemonic social order, embedded in ideology are definitions of key political, economic, and philosophical concepts and the ideological framework establishes the legitimacy or illegitimacy of the demands placed on the social order."[13]

ELEMENTS AND FUNCTIONS OF IDEOLOGY APPLIED: "THE MARKET 'R' US"

The present study contends that *market globalism* is a political ideology that achieved dominance during the 1990s. Espousing a hegemonic system of ideas that make normative claims about a set of social processes called "globalization," market globalists seek to limit public discussion on the *meaning and character of globalization* to an agenda of things to discuss that supports a specific political agenda.

The following example drawn from the heyday of market globalism in the 1990s provides a first glimpse into the concrete workings of the elements and functions of ideology. The headlines of a *Newsweek* cover story on economic globalization contained the following phrases: "Like It or Not, You're Married to the Market" and "The Market 'R' Us."[14] By equating globalization with marketization, these statements seek to entice their readership to accept a particular representation of social reality as a general truth. A closer analysis of these headlines reveals the following ideological elements and functions.

First, the postulated link between the reader's identity and the impersonal market offers an *explanation of economic globalization*. It is an attempt to *decontest* the concept of *market* by emphasizing its allegedly objective "factuality." Market principles are portrayed as pervading even the most intimate dimensions of our social existence. And there is nothing consumers can do about it. In other words, socially created relations are depicted in a *distorted* way by suggesting that they are exterior, natural forces that are more powerful than human will.

Second, the headlines suggest *standards of normative evaluation*. Although marketization is portrayed as an objective process, there is the implication that its effects are nonetheless beneficial. The concept of "marriage" resonates on a deeply positive note with most *Newsweek* readers and thus contributes to the *legitimation* of markets. After all, who would want to be married to a "bad" person? Who would want to assume the identity of a "bad" person? Thus, the market must be a benign *integrative* force, worthy of becoming our most intimate partner.

Third, the statements serve as a *guide and compass for action*. The *persuasive stories* below the headlines *decontest* markets in a positive way that suggests a natural and superior mode of ordering the world. Hence, they ought to command the reader's approval and support. If "free markets" come under attack by hostile forces, the former should be protected and the latter repelled. Another consequence here is a boost to the *legitimacy* of political regimes that facilitate and defend globalization as understood in market terms.

Fourth, the headlines offer a *simplification of complex social reality*. Most importantly, market interests are presented in a *distorted* way as general interests. Moreover, the clever permutation of a well-known brand name—Toys 'R' Us—serves as an *integrative* marker of positive identity. Lack of choice ("like it or not")—a seemingly undesirable condition—is resolved in a marriage of convenience that appears to harbor great financial opportunity for those who know how to treat their (market) spouse. Finally, the *distorted* gender dynamics at work in these headlines are far from subtle. There is little doubt as to who is the commanding husband in this patriarchal marriage.

Indeed, the two *Newsweek* headlines represent a clear example of how ideological integration contributes to hegemony. For the remainder of this book, I will use the insights into the elements and functions of ideology presented in this chapter in the following ways. In chapter 3, I interpret the normative claims of hegemonic market globalism. Chapter 4 evaluates the responses of justice globalism and jihadist globalism. In chapter 5, I introduce and analyze the ideological challenge of antiglobalist populism.

However, before we can embark on our engagement with the crucial ideological dynamics of our global age, there remains one more preparatory step. It is essential that we familiarize ourselves with the most influential perspectives and views expressed in a lively academic debate over globalization from the 1990s to the present.

Chapter 2

The Academic Debate over Globalization

※

THE BLIND SCHOLARS AND THE ELEPHANT

The ancient Buddhist parable of six blind scholars and their encounter with an elephant illustrates the nature of the ongoing academic debate on globalization. Because the blind scholars did not know what the elephant looked like and had never even heard its name, they resolved to obtain a mental picture and thus the knowledge they desired by touching the animal. Feeling its trunk, one blind man argued that the elephant was like a lively snake. Another man, rubbing along its enormous leg, likened the animal to a rough column of massive proportions. The third person took hold of its tail and insisted that the elephant resembled a large, flexible brush. The fourth man felt its sharp tusks and declared it to be like a great spear. The fifth man examined its waving ear and was convinced that the animal was some sort of fan. Occupying the space between the elephant's front and hind legs, the sixth

13

blind scholar groped in vain for a part of the elephant. Consequently, he accused his colleagues of making up fantastic stories about nonexistent things, asserting that there were no such beasts as "elephants" at all. Each of the six blind scholars held firmly to his story of what he knew an elephant to be. Because their scholarly reputation was riding on the veracity of their respective findings, the blind men eventually ended up arguing and fighting about which story contained the correct definition of the elephant. As a result, their entire community was riven asunder. Suspicion and general distrust became the order of the day.[1]

The parable of the blind scholars and the elephant contains many valuable lessons. First, one might conclude that reality is too complex to be grasped fully by imperfect human beings. Second, although each observer correctly identified one aspect of reality, the collective mistake of the blind men lay in their attempts to reduce the entire phenomenon to their own partial experience. Third, the maintenance of communal peace and harmony might be worth much more than the individual sense of superiority that comes with stubbornly clinging to one's— often one-sided—understanding of the world. Fourth, it would be wise for the blind scholars to return to the elephant and exchange their positions to better appreciate the whole of the elephant as well as the previous insight of each man.

Representing a contemporary version of this ancient parable, the previously separate popular and academic discourses on globalization converged in the 1990s, in the process triggering what came to be known as the *globalization debate*. Influencing the public perception of what "globalization" meant, the lively scholarly exchange on the subject contributed to the formation of the three main variants of "globalism." Over the ensuing two decades, there has been an explosion in the number of books and articles on the subject published by both academic and trade outlets. Consulting the electronic database *Factiva*, which holds some 8,000 newspapers, magazines, and reports worldwide, the global historian Nayan Chanda showed that the number of items mentioning globalization grew from a mere two in 1981 to a high of 57,235 in 2001. In the ensuing years, it stabilized at an annual average of about 45,000.[2] The *Expanded Academic ASAP* database produced 7,737 results with "globalization" in the title, including 5,976 journal articles going back to 1986, 1,404 magazine articles going back to 1984, and 355 news items going back to 1987. The *ISI Web of Knowledge* shows a total of 8,970 references with "globalization" in the title going back to 1968. The *EBSCO Host Database* yields 17,188 results reaching back to 1975. *Proquest Newspaper Database* lists 25,856 articles going back to 1971. Moreover, we can now track relevant writings on globalization through such "big data" mechanisms as the search engine *Ngram*, Google's mammoth database collated from over five million digitized books available free to the public for online searches.[3]

Many of the principal participants in the academic debate reside and teach in the wealthy countries of the Northern Hemisphere, particularly the United States, the United Kingdom, Western Europe, and Australia. Their disproportionate intellectual influence reflects not only existing power relations in the world but also the global dominance of Anglo-American ideas. Although they share a common intellectual framework, these scholars hold radically different views regarding the definition of globalization and its scale, chronology, impact, and policy outcomes. Part of the reason that there is so much disagreement is that globalization itself is a fragmented, incomplete, uneven, and contradictory set of social processes. James N. Rosenau, for example, has defined globalization in terms of what he calls *fragmegrative dynamics* to "underscore the contradictions, ambiguities, complexities, and uncertainties that have replaced the regularities of prior epochs."[4]

As the parable of the blind scholars and the elephant suggests, academics often respond to theoretical challenges by trying to take possession of globalization—as though it were something "out there" to be captured by the "correct" conceptual framework. Indeed, as Stephen J. Rosow points out, many researchers approach globalization as if they were dealing with a process or an object without a meaning of its own prior to its constitution as a conceptual "territory."[5] Moreover, because it falls outside the boundaries of established academic disciplines, the study of globalization has invited armies of social scientists, scholars in the humanities, and even natural scientists to leave their mark on an intellectual terra incognita.

As a result, various scholars have invoked the concept of globalization to describe a variety of changing social processes that are alleged to have accelerated since the 1980s. But only very broad definitions of globalization have achieved general recognition such as "increasing global interconnectedness," "the rapid intensification of worldwide social relations," "the compression of time and space," "distant proximities," "a complex range of processes, driven by a mixture of political and economic influences," and "the swift and relatively unimpeded flow of capital, people, and ideas across national borders."[6] A number of researchers call for perennial refinement of those characterizations, and a few go so far as to deny the utility of the concept altogether. Still, the last decade has witnessed growing areas of consensus, most of them emerging from within the new academic framework of *global studies*.

A transdisciplinary field of scholarly inquiry exploring the many dimensions of globalization, global studies both embraces and exudes a certain mentality identified in the previous chapter as the *global imaginary*—a term referring to a consciousness of the social whole that frames our age as one shaped by the intensifying forces of globalization.[7] A growing number of researchers working in this field suggest giving objective and subjective aspects equal consideration. This means that enhanced interconnectivity does not merely happen in the world "out there" but also operates through our consciousness "in here." Drawing on thematic and methodological resources from the social sciences and humanities, global studies now encompasses about three hundred undergraduate and graduate programs in the United States alone. New journals, book series, textbooks, academic conferences, and professional associations such as the Global Studies Consortium and the Global Studies Association have embraced the novel umbrella designation of "global studies."

It is the aim of this chapter to introduce the reader to the *major theoretical approaches to globalization* expressed in the pertinent academic debate over the last three decades. These range from the suggestion that globalization is little more than "globaloney" to interpretations of globalization as an economic, political, or cultural process. Indeed, our exploration of the academic debate over globalization is indispensable for gaining a better understanding of "globalisms," which, after all, constitute the focus of this book. The principal voices in the academic globalization debates can be divided into three intellectual "camps": *globalizers*, *skeptics*, and *modifiers*. Let us examine the principal arguments of these three groups in more detail before we turn to an overview of influential literature on the *four main dimensions of globalization*.

GLOBALIZERS

Most academic participants in the globalization debate fall into the category of *globalizers*. They argue that globalization is a profoundly transformative set of social processes that is moving human societies toward unprecedented levels of interconnectivity.[8] Emphasizing that globalization is not a single monolithic process but a complex and often contradictory and uneven dynamic of simultaneous social integration and fragmentation, they insist that empirical research clearly points to the intensification of significant worldwide flows that can be appropriately subsumed under the general term *globalization*. While committed to a big picture approach, globalizers nonetheless tend to focus their research efforts on one of the principal dimensions of globalization.

For example, some globalizers suggest that a quantum change in human affairs has taken place in the last decades as the flow of large quantities of trade, investment, and technologies across national borders has expanded from a trickle to a flood. In addition to these issues, perhaps the two most important aspects of economic globalization relate to the changing nature of the production process and the increasing power of transnational organizations.

Other globalizers approach their subject often from the perspective of *global governance*. Representatives of this group analyze the role of various national and multilateral responses to the fragmentation of economic and political systems and the transnational flows permeating through national borders. Some of these researchers argue that political globalization might facilitate the emergence of democratic transnational social forces emerging from a thriving sphere of *global civil society*.[9] This topic is often connected to discussions focused on the impact of globalization on human rights and vice versa.[10] For example, Martin Shaw emphasizes the role of global political struggles in creating a "global revolution" that would give rise to an internationalized, rights-based state conglomerate symbolically linked to global institutions. Thus, he raises the fascinating prospect of "state formation beyond the national level."[11]

Political scientists such as David Held articulate in their respective writings the need for effective global governance structures as a consequence of various forces of globalization. Held portrays globalization as diminishing the sovereignty of national governance, thereby reducing the relevance of the nation-state. In his view, neither the old Westphalian system of sovereign nation-states nor the postwar global system centered on the United Nations offers a satisfactory solution to the enormous challenges posed by political globalization. Instead, he predicts the emergence of a multilayered form of democratic governance based on Western cosmopolitan ideals, international legal arrangements, and a web of expanding linkages between various governmental and nongovernmental institutions. Rejecting the charge of utopianism often leveled against his vision, Held provides empirical evidence for the existence of a tendency inherent in the globalization process that seems to favor the strengthening of supranational bodies and the rise of a global civil society. He predicts that democratic rights will ultimately become detached from their narrow relationship to discrete territorial units.[12]

A number of academic critics have challenged the idea that globalization is fueling a development toward *cosmopolitan democracy*. Most of their criticism boils down to the charge that optimists like Held indulge in an abstract idealism that fails to engage with current political developments on the level of policy. Some critics argue that the emergence of private authority has increasingly become a factor in the post–Cold War world. In their view, global collective actors like religious terrorists and organized criminals are not merely symptoms of the weakening nation-state, but their actions also dim the prospects for the rise of cosmopolitan democracy.[13] Other critics raise the suspicion that cosmopolitan thinkers like Held do not explore in sufficient detail the cultural feasibility of global democracy. As cultural patterns become increasingly interlinked through globalization, critics argue, the possibility of resistance, opposition, and violent clashes becomes just as real as the cosmopolitan vision of mutual accommodation and tolerance of differences.[14]

Some globalizers located at the extreme end of their camp could be labeled *hyperglobalizers*, for they see globalization as the main driver of nearly all social change today and often adopt quite deterministic perspectives situated within economistic frameworks. For example, the influential Japanese management guru Kenichi Ohmae celebrates new forms of techno-economic interconnectivity as the indispensable central nervous system of a hypercompetitive *borderless world*.

He envisions transnational investment and commodity flows directed by globally interlinked electronic stock markets operating 24/7 as the catalysts for the imperative jettisoning of the last vestiges of antiquated trade protectionism. He expresses the hope that "outdated" nationalist sentiments at the core of crucial modern legal notions such as "state sovereignty" will soon be eclipsed by the border-traversing logic of global capitalism.[15]

More moderate globalizers, however, caution against such "misleading simplifications" and "uncritical generalizations" in the study of globalization. Accusing hyperglobalizers for the "general thinness" of their empirical evidence, moderates call instead for "middle-range approaches" that focus on particular aspects of globalization.[16] Serving as a warning to extreme globalization proponents, such empirically based accounts would break the concept of globalization into smaller, more manageable parts that contain a higher analytical value because they can be more easily associated with "real-world" processes.

Still, both of these two globalizer subgroups are united in their conviction that the contemporary phase in the expansion and intensification of social relations is transformative and truly global in its reach and impact. For this reason, globalizers are also referred to as *transformationalists*. To reiterate, this camp contains the bulk of contemporary globalization scholars.

SKEPTICS

The second camp in the ongoing globalization debate is inhabited by *skeptics* who acknowledge some forms and manifestations of globalization while also emphasizing its limited nature. This perspective is perhaps best reflected in the writings of Robert Wade, Paul Hirst, and Grahame Thompson.[17] In their detailed historical analysis of economic globalization, Hirst and Thompson claim that the world economy is not a truly global phenomenon, but one centered on Europe, East Asia, Australia, and North America. The authors emphasize that the majority of economic activity around the world still remains primarily national in origin and scope. Presenting relevant data on trade, foreign direct investment, and financial flows, the authors warn against drawing premature conclusions from increased levels of economic interaction in advanced industrial countries. Ultimately, their argument against the existence of economic globalization is linked to their criticism of the general misuse of the concept. Without a truly global economic system, they insist, there can be no such thing as globalization: "[A]s we proceeded [with our economic research] our skepticism deepened until we became convinced that globalization, as conceived by the more extreme globalizers, is largely a myth."[18] Buried under an avalanche of quantitative data, one can detect a critical-normative message in the Hirst–Thompson thesis: exaggerated accounts of an "iron logic of economic globalization" tend to produce disempowering political effects. For example, the authors convincingly demonstrate that certain political forces have used the thesis of an inexorable economic globalization to propose national economic deregulation and the reduction of welfare programs. Obviously, the implementation of such policies stands to benefit neoliberal interests.

There also remain several problems with the Hirst–Thompson thesis. For example, as several critics have pointed out, the authors set overly high standards for the economy in order to be counted as "fully globalized."[19] Second, their construction of an abstract model of a perfectly globalized economy unnecessarily polarizes the topic by pressuring the reader to either completely embrace or entirely reject the concept of globalization. Third, as critics like William Robinson have pointed out, Hirst and Thompson collect and make sense of their data from within their nation-state–centric framework of analysis that prevents them "from interpreting facts in new ways that provide greater explanatory power with regard to novel developments in the late twentieth- and early twenty-first-century world."[20]

But the most serious problem with the Hirst–Thompson thesis lies in its attempt to counteract neoliberal ideological determinism with a good dose of *economic determinism*. Their argument implicitly assumes that globalization is primarily an economic phenomenon. As a result, they portray all other dimensions of globalization—culture, politics, and ideology—as reflections of deeper economic processes. While paying lip service to the multidimensional character of globalization, their own analysis ignores the logical implications of this assertion. After all, if globalization is truly a complex, multilevel phenomenon, then economic relations constitute only one among many globalizing tendencies. It would therefore be entirely possible to argue for the significance of globalization even if it can be shown that increased transnational economic activity appears to be limited to advanced industrial countries.

A small subgroup of skeptics could be called *rejectionists*, because they contend that existing accounts of globalization are incorrect, imprecise, or exaggerated. They note that just about everything that can be linked to some transnational process is cited as evidence for globalization and its growing influence. Considering globalization a prime example of a "big idea resting on slim foundations," they claim that the term is so broad and hazy that it could be associated with "anything from the Internet to a hamburger."[21] Claiming that such generalizations often amount to little more than *globaloney*, rejectionists dismiss the utility of the concept "globalization" for scientific academic discourse.[22] They also emphasize that the world is not nearly as integrated as many globalizers believe. In their view, the term *globalization* does not constitute an accurate label for the actual state of affairs. However, as empirical studies in the last decade have provided more evidence for the existence of significant globalization dynamics, the number of rejectionists has dramatically dwindled.

MODIFIERS

The third camp in the contemporary globalization debates consists of *modifiers* who acknowledge the power of globalization but dispute its novelty and thus the innovative character of globalization theory. They, therefore, seek to *modify and assimilate globalization theory* to tried and tested approaches in international relations (IR), international political economy, and other related fields, claiming that a new conceptual framework called "globalization" is unwarranted. Implying that the term has been used in a historically imprecise manner, modifiers embrace current globalization theories that highlight the longevity of the phenomenon. Robert Gilpin, for example, cites relevant data collected by the prominent American economist Paul Krugman to note that the world economy in the late 1990s appeared to be even less integrated in a number of important respects than it was prior to the outbreak of World War I. Even if one were to accept the most optimistic assessment of the actual volume of transnational economic activity, the most that could be said is that the postwar international economy has simply restored globalization to approximately the same level that existed in

1913. Gilpin also points to two additional factors that seem to support his position: the globalization of labor was actually much greater prior to World War I, and international migration declined considerably after 1918. Warning his readers against accepting the arguments of hyperglobalizers, the political economist insists that such ahistorical short-term thinking requires serious modifications.[23]

Similar calls for adapting globalization theory to previous perspectives come from the proponents of *world-systems analysis*—a generic label for various explanations of long-term, large-scale social change favoring the emergence of a single world-system rooted in structural components of the world economy. World-systems theory was pioneered in the 1970s by neo-Marxist scholars such as Immanuel Wallerstein, Andre Gunder Frank, Giovanni Arrighi, and Christopher Chase-Dunn. They argue that globalization theory should be adapted to fit their own framework, which suggests that the modern capitalist economy in which we live today has been global since its inception five centuries ago.[24] They contend that, driven by the exploitative logic of capital accumulation, the capitalist world-system has created global inequalities based on the domination of modernizing Western *core countries* over non-Western *peripheral areas*. States are crucial subentities within the capitalist world-system with the capacity to coordinate and reproduce the core-periphery hierarchy. These structural forms of exploitation were inscribed in nineteenth-century systems of colonialism and imperialism and have persisted in the twentieth and twenty-first centuries in different forms. World-systems analysts object, therefore, to the use of the term *globalization* as referring exclusively to the relatively recent phenomenon of the last few decades. Instead, they emphasize that globalizing tendencies have been proceeding along the continuum of modernization for a long time. As Wallerstein puts it, "The proponents of world-systems analysis . . . have been talking about 'globalization' since long before the word was invented—not, however, as something new but as something that has been basic to the modern world-system ever since it began in the sixteenth century."[25]

The greatest virtue of the world-system critique of globalization lies in its historical sensitivity. Any general discussion of globalization should include the caution that cross-regional transfers of resources, technology, and culture did not start only in the past few decades. Indeed, the origins of globalizing tendencies can be traced back to the political and cultural interactions that sustained the ancient empires of Persia, China, and Rome. On the downside, however, a world-system approach to globalization suffers from the same weaknesses as the Marxist economic-determinist view pointed out previously in my discussion of the Hirst–Thompson thesis. Wallerstein leaves little doubt that he considers global integration to be a process driven largely by economic forces whose essence can be captured by economistic analytical models. Accordingly, he assigns to culture and ideology merely a subordinate role as "idea systems" dependent on the "real" movements of the capitalist world economy.[26]

However, more studies produced by dissenting world-system scholars acknowledge that the pace of globalization significantly quickened in the last few decades of the twentieth century. Ash Amin, for example, has suggested that much of the criticism of globalization as a new phenomenon has been based on quantitative analyses of trade and output that neglect the qualitative shift in social and political relations. This qualitative difference in the globalizing process, he argues, has resulted in the world capitalist system's new configuration as a complex network of international corporations, banks, and financial flows. Hence, these global developments may indeed warrant a new label.[27] In their efforts to gauge the nature of this qualitative difference, world-system theorists such as Barry K. Gills focus more closely on the interaction between dominant-class interests and cultural transnational practices.[28] In so doing, they have begun to raise important normative questions, suggesting that the elements of the "ideological superstructure"— politics, ideas, values, and beliefs—may, at times, neutralize or supersede economic forces. Leslie Sklair, for example, highlights the importance of what he calls the *culture-ideology of global consumerism*.[29]

Overall, then, all three groups of globalization critics make an important contribution to the academic debate on the subject. The insistence of skeptics and modifiers on a more careful and precise usage of the term forces globalizers to hone their analytical skills and pay attention to larger temporal frames. Moreover, their critical intervention serves as an important reminder that some aspects of globalization may neither constitute brand-new developments nor reach to all corners of the earth. However, by focusing too narrowly on abstract issues of terminology, the critics of the globalizer camp tend to downplay the significance and extent of today's intensifying connectivities.

Finally, skeptics and modifiers are inclined to conceptualize globalization mostly along economic lines, thereby often losing sight of its multidimensional character.

From the 1990s forward, the participants in the academic globalization debate recognized the difficulty of developing a comprehensive theoretical framework that presented the compression of the world as a differentiated set of processes that could not be reduced to a single dynamic, yet remained attentive to its manifestations in specific aspects of social life. In most cases, the first step in resolving this conundrum consisted of assembling a "lay of the land" by identifying the most pivotal *dimensions* or *domains* of the phenomenon. These discrete aspects were supposed to be brought together again in the holistic depiction of globalization as a "highly differentiated phenomenon involving various domains of social activity and interactions as diverse as the political, military, economic, cultural, migratory, and environmental. Each of these domains involves different patterns of relations and activities."[30]

This "rebundling" of multiple domains under the signifier *multidimensional* served two important objectives. First, it made it easier for globalization researchers to accomplish their analytical task of breaking up the phenomenon's enormous proportions. Second, it allowed them to work collectively on the overarching project of understanding globalization in its totality while at the same time bringing each researcher's special academic expertise to bear on its specific domains.

Let us then turn to the next section of this chapter, which offers a general overview of these inquiries into the *four main dimensions of globalization: economics, politics, culture, and ecology*.

THE MAIN DIMENSIONS OF GLOBALIZATION: ECONOMICS

The widespread scholarly emphasis on the *economic dimension of globalization* derives partly from its historical development as a subject of academic study. Some of the earliest writings on the topic explore in much detail how the evolution of international markets and corporations led to an intensified form of global interdependence. These studies point to the growth of international institutions such as the European Union, the North American Free Trade Association, and other regional trading blocs.[31] Economic accounts of globalization convey the notion that the essence of the phenomenon involves "the increasing linkage of national economies through trade, financial flows, and foreign direct investment . . . by multinational firms."[32] Thus, expanding economic activity is identified as both the primary aspect of globalization and the engine behind its rapid development. Many scholars who share this economic perspective thus argue that the central task of globalization research should be the close examination of the evolving structure of global economic markets and their principal institutions.

Studies of economic globalization are usually embedded in thick historical narratives that trace the gradual emergence of the new postwar world economy to the 1944 Bretton Woods Conference. Pressured by the United States, the major economic powers of the West decided to reverse the protectionist policies of the interwar period (1918–1939) by committing themselves to the expansion of international trade. The major achievements of the Bretton Woods Conference include the limited liberalization of trade and the establishment of binding rules on international economic activities.

In addition, the Bretton Woods participants agreed on the creation of a stable currency exchange system in which the value of each country's currency was pegged to a fixed gold value of the US dollar. Within these prescribed limits, individual nations were free to control the permeability of their borders, which allowed them to set their own economic agendas, including the implementation of extensive social welfare policies. Bretton Woods also set the institutional foundations for the establishment of three new international economic organizations. The International Monetary Fund was created to administer the international monetary system. The International Bank for Reconstruction and Development, or World Bank, was initially designed to provide loans for Europe's postwar reconstruction. Beginning in the 1950s, its purpose was expanded to fund various industrial projects in developing countries around the world. In 1947, the General Agreement on Tariffs and Trade (GATT) became the global trade organization charged with fashioning and enforcing multilateral trade agreements. Founded in 1995, the World Trade Organization emerged as the successor organization to GATT. As will be shown in later chapters of this book, both the philosophical purpose and the neoliberal policies of this new international body became the focal points of intense ideological controversies over the effects of economic globalization starting in the late 1990s.

During its operation for almost three decades, the Bretton Woods system contributed greatly to the establishment of what is often described as the *golden age of controlled capitalism*. According to this interpretation, existing mechanisms of state control over international capital movements made possible full employment and the expansion of the welfare state. Rising wages and increased social services secured in the wealthy countries of the global North a temporary class compromise. Most scholars of economic globalization trace the accelerating integrationist tendencies of the global economy to the collapse of the Bretton Woods system in the early 1970s. In response to profound changes in the world economy that undermined the economic competitiveness of US-based industries, President Richard Nixon decided in 1971 to abandon the gold-based fixed-rate system. The combination of new political ideas and economic developments—high inflation, low economic growth, high unemployment, public-sector deficits, and two major oil crises within a decade—led to the spectacular election victories of conservative parties in the United States and the United Kingdom. These parties spearheaded the neoliberal movement toward the expansion of international markets (a dynamic supported by the deregulation of domestic financial systems), the gradual removal of capital controls, and an enormous increase in global financial transactions. Within the next three decades, neoliberal economic ideas and policies spread rapidly from the Anglo-American center to the rest of the world. These diffusionist dynamics were greatly facilitated by increasingly interdependent state behavior.[33] During the 1980s and 1990s, neoliberal efforts to establish an integrated global market were further strengthened through comprehensive trade-liberalization agreements that increased the flow of economic resources across national borders. The rising neoliberal paradigm received further legitimation with the 1989–1991 collapse of command-type economies in Eastern Europe.

Shattering the postwar economic consensus on Keynesian principles, free-market theories pioneered by Friedrich Hayek and Milton Friedman established themselves as the new economic orthodoxy, advocating the reduction of the welfare state, the downsizing of government, and the deregulation of the economy. A strong emphasis on "monetarist" measures to combat inflation led to the abandonment of the Keynesian goal of full employment in favor of establishing more "flexible" labor markets. In addition, the dramatic shift from a state-dominated to a market-dominated world was accompanied by technological innovations that lowered the costs of transportation and communication. Thus, the total value of world trade increased from $57 billion in 1947 to an astonishing $19.5 trillion in 2018.

In addition to the issue of free trade, perhaps the two most important aspects of economic globalization relate to the changing nature of the production process and the liberalization and internationalization of financial transactions. Indeed, many analysts consider the emergence of a transnational financial system the most fundamental economic feature of our time. Its key components include the deregulation of interest rates, the removal of credit controls, and the privatization of government-owned banks and financial institutions. As sociologist Manuel Castells points out, the process of financial globalization accelerated dramatically in the late 1980s as capital and securities markets in Europe and the United States were deregulated. The liberalization of financial trading allowed for the increased mobility among different segments of the financial industry, with fewer restrictions and a global view of investment opportunities.

Moreover, advances in data processing and information technology contributed to the explosive growth of tradable financial value. New satellite systems and fiber-optic cables provided the nervous system of Internet-based technologies that further accelerated the liberalization of financial transactions. As captured by the snazzy title of Microsoft founder Bill Gates's best-selling book at the turn of the twenty-first century, many people conducted "business at the speed of thought."[34] Millions of individual investors utilized global electronic investment networks and e-retailers like amazon.com not only to place their orders but also to receive valuable information about relevant economic and political developments. However, a large part of the money involved in expanding markets had little to do with supplying capital for productive investment—putting together machines, raw materials, and employees to produce salable commodities and the like.

Most of the growth occurred in the purely money-dealing currency and securities markets that trade claims to draw profits from future production. Aided by new digital communication technologies, global rentiers and speculators earned spectacular incomes by taking advantage of weak financial and banking regulations in the emerging markets of developing countries. However, whereas these international capital flows can be reversed swiftly, they are capable of creating artificial boom-and-bust cycles that endanger the social welfare of entire regions. The 1997–1998 Southeast Asia crisis was one such economic disaster created by unregulated speculative money flows, followed by similar debacles in Russia (1998), Brazil (1999), Argentina (2000–2003), and, of course, the Global Financial Crisis (2008–2009) and the ensuing Eurozone Debt Crisis, both of which I will discuss in more detail in later chapters.

While the creation of international financial markets represents a crucial aspect of economic globalization, another important economic development of the past three decades also involves the changing nature of global production. Powerful firms with subsidiaries in several countries, transnational corporations (TNCs) became the primary engines of production. Their numbers skyrocketed from 7,000 in 1970 to more than 100,000 in 2018. Consolidating their global operations in an increasingly deregulated global labor market, enterprises such as Walmart, General Motors, ExxonMobil, Mitsubishi, and Siemens belong to the two hundred largest TNCs, which account for over half the world's industrial output. A comparison of gross domestic product (GDP) and corporate sales in 2018 reveals that forty-two of the world's one hundred largest economies were corporations; fifty-eight were countries. The availability of cheap labor, resources, and favorable production conditions in developing countries enhanced both the mobility and the profitability of TNCs. Accounting for more than 70 percent of world trade, these gigantic enterprises expanded their global reach as their direct foreign investments rose approximately 15 percent annually during the 1990s.[35]

Their ability to *outsource manufacturing jobs*—that is, to cut labor costs by dispersing economic production processes into many discrete phases carried out by low-wage workers in the global South—is often cited as one of the hallmarks of economic globalization. In the last two decades, outsourcing, combined with automation, has threatened white-collar jobs in the global North as well. Job insecurity and precarious work have been on the rise—an ominous development often camouflaged in neoliberal discourse as "job flexibility." For example, transnational law firms headquartered in the United States have outsourced low-level office work, such as the drafting of research memos and the surveying of laws under different jurisdictions, to lawyers and paralegals in India who are paid between $6 and $8 per hour—about one-third of what their American counterparts are paid.[36] In manufacturing, the formation of such *global commodity chains* allows huge corporations such as Walmart, Nike, and General Motors to produce, distribute, and market their products on a global scale.[37] Transnational production systems augment the power of global capitalism by enhancing the ability of TNCs to bypass the nationally based political influence of trade unions and other workers' organizations in collective wage-bargaining processes.

THE MAIN DIMENSIONS OF GLOBALIZATION: POLITICS

The economic dimensions of globalization can hardly be assessed apart from an analysis of political processes and institutions. As I mentioned in the previous discussion of the three camps, most of the debate on *political globalization* involves the weighing of conflicting evidence with regard to the fate of the modern nation-state. In particular, two questions have moved to the top of the research agenda. First, what are the political causes for the massive flows of capital, money, and technology across territorial boundaries? Second, do these flows constitute a serious challenge to the power of the nation-state? These questions imply that economic globalization might be leading to the reduced control of national governments over economic policy. The latter question, in particular, involves an important subset of issues pertaining to the principle of state sovereignty, the growing impact of intergovernmental organizations, and the prospects for global governance.

An influential group of scholars considers political globalization as a process intrinsically connected to the expansion of markets. In particular, steady advances in computer technology and communication systems such as the World Wide Web are seen as the primary forces responsible for the creation of a single global market.[38] As Richard Langhorne puts it, "Globalization has happened because technological advances have broken down many physical barriers to worldwide communication which used to limit how much connected or cooperative activity of any kind could happen over long distances."[39] According to even more extreme technological-determinist explanations, politics is rendered powerless in the face of an unstoppable and irreversible technoeconomic juggernaut that will crush all governmental attempts to reintroduce restrictive policies and regulations. Economics is portrayed as possessing an inner logic apart from and superior to politics. According to this view, it is this combination of economic self-interest and technological innovation that is responsible for ushering in a new phase in world history in which the role of government will be reduced to that of a handmaiden to free-market forces. As Lowell Bryan and Diana Farrell assert, the role of government will ultimately be reduced to serving as "a superconductor for global capitalism."[40]

As noted previously, hyperglobalizers such as Kenichi Ohmae have celebrated the rise of a "borderless world" brought on by the irresistible forces of capitalism. In their view, the nation-state has already lost its role as a meaningful unit of participation in the global economy. As territorial divisions are becoming increasingly irrelevant to human society, states are less able to determine the direction of social life within their borders. Because the workings of genuinely global capital markets dwarf their ability to control exchange rates or protect their currency, nation-states have become vulnerable to the discipline imposed by economic choices made elsewhere over which states have no practical control. In the long run, the process of political globalization will lead to the decline of territory as a meaningful framework for understanding political and social change. No longer functioning along the lines of discrete territorial units, the political order of the future will be one of regional economies linked in an almost seamless global web that operates according to free-market principles.[41]

It is important to note that many neo-Marxist scholars also share such an economistic interpretation of political globalization. Caroline Thomas, for example, portrays politics merely as a consequence of global processes driven by a reinvigorated capitalism that has entered the stage wherein accumulation is taking place on a global rather than a national level. Consequently, she insists that the concept of globalization "refers broadly to the process whereby power is located in global social formations and expressed through global networks rather than through territorially-based states."[42]

Other scholars dispute the view that large-scale economic changes simply happen to societies in the manner of natural phenomena such as earthquakes and hurricanes. Instead, they highlight the central role of politics—especially the successful mobilization of political power—in unleashing the forces of globalization.[43] This view rests on a philosophical model of active human agency. If the shape of economic globalization is politically determined, then shifting political preferences are capable of creating different social conditions. Daniel Singer, for example, argues that at the root of the rapid expansion of global economic activity lies neither a "natural law of the market" nor the development of computer technology but political decisions made by governments to lift the international restrictions on capital: "Once the decisions were implemented in the 1980s, the technology came into its own. The speed of communication and calculation helped the movement of money to reach astronomical proportions."[44] The clear implication of Singer's view is that nation and territory still do matter—even in a globalized context.

Hence, this group of scholars argues for the continued relevance of conventional political units, operating in the form of either modern nation-states or "global cities."[45] At the same time, most proponents of this view understand that the development of the past few decades has significantly constrained the set of political options open to states, particularly in developing countries. Jan Aart Scholte, for example, points out that globalization refers to gradual processes of "relative deterritorialization" that facilitate the growth of "supraterritorial" relations between people.[46] Scholte emphasizes, however, that his concession to deterritorialization does not necessarily mean that nation-states are no longer the main organizing forces in the world. Equipped with the power to regulate economic activities within their sphere of influence, states are far from being impotent bystanders to the workings of global forces. If concrete political decisions were responsible for changing the international context in the direction of deregulation, privatization, and the globalization of the world economy, then different political decisions could reverse the trend in the opposite direction.[47]

To be sure, it took the 2008–2009 Global Financial Crisis—a calamity of gigantic proportions brought on by neoliberal market ideologists—to provide states with new incentives to make their boundaries less permeable to transnational flows. Still, even this catastrophic scenario did not lead to permanent reversal of seemingly irresistible globalizing tendencies. The core message of this group of academics focusing on the political dimensions of globalization is loud and clear: politics is the crucial category on which rests a proper understanding of globalization.

THE MAIN DIMENSIONS OF
GLOBALIZATION: CULTURE

Any account of the academic globalization debate would be woefully inadequate without an examination of its cultural dimension. A number of prominent scholars have emphasized the centrality of culture for globalization. As sociologist John Tomlinson puts it, "Globalization lies at the heart of modern culture; cultural practices lie at the heart of globalization."[48] The thematic landscape traversed by scholars of *cultural globalization* is vast, and the questions they raise are too numerous to be completely fleshed out in this short survey. Rather than presenting a long laundry list of relevant topics, this section focuses on two central questions raised by scholars of cultural globalization. First, does globalization increase cultural homogeneity, or does it lead to greater diversity and heterogeneity? Or, to put the matter into less academic terms, does globalization make people more alike or more different? And, second, how does the dominant culture of consumerism impact the natural environment?

Most commentators preface their response to the first question with a general analysis of the relationship between the globalization process and contemporary cultural change. Tomlinson, for example, defines cultural globalization as a "densely growing network of complex cultural interconnections and interdependencies that characterize modern social life." He emphasizes that global cultural flows are directed by powerful international media corporations that utilize new communication technologies to shape societies and identities. As images and ideas can be more easily and rapidly transmitted from one place to another, they profoundly impact the way people experience their everyday lives. Culture no longer remains tied to fixed localities such as town and nation but acquires new meanings that reflect dominant themes emerging in a global context. This interconnectivity caused by cultural globalization challenges parochial values and identities because it undermines the linkages that connect culture to fixity of location.[49]

A number of scholars argue that these processes have facilitated the rise of an increasingly homogenized global culture underwritten by an Anglo-American value system. Referring to the global diffusion of American values, consumer goods, and lifestyles as *Americanization*, these authors analyze the ways in which such forms of "cultural imperialism" are overwhelming more vulnerable cultures. The American sociologist George Ritzer, for example, coined the term *McDonaldization* to describe the wide-ranging process by which the principles of the fast-food restaurant are coming to dominate more and more sectors of American society as well as the rest of the world. On the surface, these principles appear to be rational in their attempts to offer efficient and predictable ways of serving people's needs. Only toward the end of his study does Ritzer allow himself to address the normative ramifications of this process: when rational systems serve to deny the expression of human creativity and cultural difference, they contribute to the rise of irrationality in the world. In the long run, McDonaldization leads to the eclipse of cultural diversity and the dehumanization of social relations.[50]

The late American political theorist Benjamin R. Barber warned his readers against the cultural imperialism of what he calls "McWorld"—a soulless consumer capitalism that is rapidly transforming the world's diverse population into a blandly uniform market. For Barber, McWorld is a product of a superficial American popular culture assembled in the 1950s and 1960s and driven by expansionist commercial interests: "Its template is American, its form style . . . [m]usic, video, theater, books, and theme parks . . . are all constructed as image exports creating a common taste around common logos, advertising slogans, stars, songs, brand names, jingles, and trademarks."[51]

Much to its credit, Barber's analysis moves beyond offering a neutral, "scientific" account of the forces of McWorld. His insightful account of cultural globalization contains the important recognition that the colonizing tendencies of McWorld provoke cultural and political resistance in the form of *jihad*—the parochial impulse to reject and repel Western homogenization forces wherever they can be found. Fueled by the furies of ethnonationalism and/or religious fundamentalism, jihad represents the dark side of cultural particularism. Barber sees jihad as the "rabid response to colonialism and imperialism and their economic children, capitalism and modernity." Guided by opposing visions of homogeneity, jihad and McWorld are dialectically interlocked in a bitter cultural struggle for popular allegiance. Barber insists that both forces ultimately work against a participatory form of democracy, for they are equally prone to undermine civil liberties and thus thwart the possibility of a global democratic future.[52]

As might be expected, Barber's dialectical account received a lot of public attention after the events of 9/11. They also helped to resurrect Samuel Huntington's 1993 thesis of a *clash of civilizations* involving primarily the West and Islam. This rather crude argument relies on overly broad definitions and generalizations that divide the post-1990 world into nine "major contemporary civilizations."[53] Within a year of the terrorist attacks, dozens of books offered endless permutations of the arguments first presented by Barber and Huntington. For example, legal scholar Amy Chua and philosopher Roger Scruton warned their readers that "the global spread of markets and democracy is a principal, aggravating cause of group hatred and ethnic violence throughout the non-Western world" and that "globalization has plunged the Islamic world into crisis by offering the spectacle of a secular society maintained in being by man-made laws, and achieving equilibrium without the aid of God."[54] For such commentators, the lessons drawn from this clash between the "West and the rest" were obvious: "In the face of this [religious violence] we in the West must . . . do what we can to reinforce the nation-state. . . . This means that we must constrain the process of globalization, so as to neutralize its perceived image as threat from the West to the rest."[55]

Proponents of the *cultural homogenization thesis* offer ample empirical evidence for their interpretation. They point to Amazonian Indians wearing Nike sneakers, denizens of the southern Sahara purchasing Texaco baseball caps, and Palestinian youths proudly displaying their Chicago Bulls sweatshirts in downtown Ramallah. Documenting the spread of Anglo-American culture facilitated by the deregulation and convergence of global media and electronic communication systems, some commentators even go so far as to insist that there no longer exist any viable alternatives to the Americanization of the world. For example, French political economist Serge Latouche argues that the media-driven, consumerist push toward *planetary uniformity* according to Anglo-American norms and values will inevitably result in a world-wide "standardization of lifestyles."[56]

The cultural homogenization thesis also relies to some extent on arguments that point to the power of the Anglo-American culture industry to make English the global lingua franca of the twenty-first century. And yet it would be too simplistic to conclude that the globalization of English is inevitable. As political scientist Selma

Sonntag puts it, "Global English represents globalization-from-above, but it also contains the possibility of globalization-from-below, most plausibly in terms of a subaltern resistance to linguistic hegemony. Globalization pushes forward global English hegemony, but in doing so it creates its own antithesis."[57]

Given these highly complex global interactions, research in this area frequently yields contradictory conclusions. Unable to reach a general agreement, experts in the field have developed several different hypotheses. One model posits a clear correlation between the growing global significance of a few languages—particularly English, Chinese, and Spanish—and the declining number of other languages around the world. Another model suggests that the globalization of language does not necessarily mean that our descendants are destined to utilize only a few tongues. Still another thesis emphasizes the power of the Anglo-American culture industry to make English—or what some commentators call *Globish*—*the* "global lingua franca of the 21st century."[58]

Hence, it is one thing to acknowledge the powerful cultural logic of global capitalism, but it is quite another to assert that the cultural diversity existing on our planet is destined to vanish. In fact, several influential academics offer contrary assessments that link globalization to new forms of cultural diversity.[59] Roland Robertson has famously argued that global cultural flows often reinvigorate local cultural niches. Contending that cultural globalization always takes place in local contexts, Robertson predicts a pluralization of the world as localities produce a variety of unique cultural responses to global forces. The result is not increasing cultural homogenization but *glocalization*—a complex interaction of the global and local characterized by cultural borrowing.[60] These interactions lead to a complex mixture of both homogenizing and diversifying impulses.

Often referred to as *hybridization* or *creolization*, the processes of cultural mixing are reflected in music, film, fashion, language, and other forms of symbolic expression. Sociologist Jan Nederveen Pieterse, for example, argues that exploring hybridity amounts to "mapping no man's land." For Nederveen Pieterse, the hybridity concept "does not preclude struggle but yields a multifocus view on struggle and by showing multiple identity on both sides, transcends the 'us versus them' dualism that prevails in cultural and political arenas."[61] Ulf Hannerz, too, emphasizes the complexity of an emerging *global culture* composed of new zones of hybridization. In these regions, meanings derive from different historical sources that were originally separated from one another in space but have come to mingle extensively. Hence, rather than being obliterated by Western consumerist forces of homogenization, local difference and particularity evolve into new cultural constellations and discourses.[62]

In addition to addressing the question of whether globalization leads to cultural homogeneity or diversity, cultural globalization scholar Arjun Appadurai identifies five conceptual dimensions or "scapes" that are constituted by global cultural flows: *ethnoscapes* (shifting populations made up of tourists, immigrants, refugees, and exiles), *technoscapes* (development of technologies that facilitate the rise of TNCs), *finanscapes* (flows of global capital), *mediascapes* (electronic capabilities to produce and disseminate information), and *ideoscapes* (ideologies of states and social movements). Each of these scapes contains the building blocks of the new "imagined worlds" that are assembled by the historically situated imaginations of persons and groups spread around the globe.[63] Suspended in a global web of cultural multiplicity, more and more people become aware of the density of human relations. Their enhanced ability to explore and absorb new cultural symbols and meanings coexists in uneasy tension with their growing sense of *placelessness*. Focusing on the changing forms of human perception and consciousness brought on by global cultural flows, Appadurai discusses subjective forms of cultural globalization that are often neglected in more common analyses of objective relations of interdependence.

Sociologist Martin Albrow uses the concept of *globality* to describe a new condition where people and groups of all kinds refer to the globe as the cultural framework for their beliefs and actions. Analyzing the complex web of interactions underlying this epochal shift in people's consciousness, he concludes that a dawning *global age* is slowly supplanting the old conceptual framework of modernity. A proper understanding of this new era demands that researchers revise dogmatic Enlightenment ideas of progress and science and instead embrace a more cautious and pragmatic universalism that explicitly recognizes the uncertainties and contingencies of the global age. Albrow speaks of a new condition of globality that is profoundly different from modernity in that there is no presumption of centrality of control. In short, the project of modernity has ended.[64]

On this issue, then, the debate on cultural globalization has linked with the long-standing controversy in political and social theory over whether our present age should be understood as an *extension of modernity* or whether it constitutes a new condition of *postmodernity* characterized by the loss of a stable sense of identity and knowledge.[65] Indeed, scholars of cultural globalization have shown more willingness to engage in sustained investigations of the norms and values underlying globalization than their colleagues in political science or economics.

THE MAIN DIMENSIONS OF GLOBALIZATION: ECOLOGY

The same is true for those researchers who have explored the connection between cultural globalization and ecology, especially in light of today's escalating environmental problems. After all, how people view their natural environment depends to a great extent on their cultural milieu. For example, cultures steeped in Taoist, Buddhist, and various animist religions often emphasize the interdependence of all living beings—a perspective that calls for a delicate balance between human wants and ecological needs. Nature is not considered a mere "resource" to be used instrumentally to fulfill human desires. The most extreme manifestations of this anthropocentric paradigm are reflected in the dominant values and beliefs of consumerism. The US-dominated culture industry seeks to convince its global audience that the meaning and chief value of life can be found in the limitless accumulation of material possessions.

The two most ominous ecological problems connected to the global spread of consumer culture are human-induced *global climate change*, such as *global warming*, and the worldwide destruction of *biodiversity*. The rapidly intensifying dynamic of global climate change, in particular, has intensified academic interest in the *ecological dimension of globalization*. The rapid buildup of gas emissions, including carbon dioxide, methane, and chlorofluorocarbons in our planet's atmosphere, has greatly enhanced Earth's capacity to trap heat. The resulting *greenhouse effect* is responsible for raising average temperatures worldwide. Indeed, the US Union of Concerned Scientists has presented data suggesting that the global average temperature increased from about 53.3°F in 1880 to 57.9°F in 2000. Further increases in global temperatures could lead to partial meltdowns of the polar ice caps, causing global sea levels to rise by up to three feet by 2100—a catastrophic development that would threaten the many coastal regions of the world. Indeed, the impact of such drastic rises in temperature would be massive rises in sea levels, which in turn would lead to the extinction of species such as the polar bear and also the disappearance of many small Pacific islands. This in turn creates a host of economic, social, and political problems as displaced populations seek refuge in countries not as affected by global warming. Changes to weather patterns and temperatures would also have a significant impact on food production and availability and access to water. Those most likely to be affected are people in the global South, who are least responsible for the processes that have contributed to bringing the world to this point of environmental crisis.

To be sure, the precise effects of global warming are difficult to calculate. Drawing on data collected by the National Oceanic and Atmospheric Administration and the UN's Intergovernmental Panel on Climate Change (IPCC), a 2016 National Defense Council report predicts that global average temperatures in 2100 will be up to 8°F warmer than today, should global emissions continue on their current path. Evidence shows that the decade from 2000 to 2010 was hotter than any other decade in the last 1,300 years. A special 2018 report issued by the IPCC calculated the serious impacts of global warming of 1.5°C above preindustrial levels, which could happen as early as the mid-twenty-first century.[66]

Indeed, the *Stern Report*, commissioned by the UK government, demonstrated that as early as 2007 average global temperatures had risen by at least 0.5°C based on preindustrialization temperatures. These significant increases in global temperatures have also led to melt-downs of large chunks of the world's major ice reserves. The polar ice caps have melted faster in the last twenty years than in the last 10,000. The large Greenland ice sheet is shrinking the fastest, and its complete melting would result in a global rise of sea levels of up to twenty-two feet. However, even a much smaller sea level rise would spell doom for many coastal regions around the world. The small Pacific island nations of Tuvalu and Kiribati, for example, would disappear. Large coastal cities such as Tokyo, New York, London, and Sydney would lose significant chunks of their urban landscapes. Higher temperatures are also worsening many kinds of extreme weather events, including intense storms, catastrophic wildfires, floods, and droughts. And such disasters caused by global climate change not only endanger human lives, but also cause trillions of dollars of damage.

With regard to the *loss of biodiversity*, many biologists today believe that we are now in the midst of the fastest mass extinction of living species in the 4.5-billion-year history of the planet. Environmental sociologist Franz Broswimmer concedes that this problem is not new in natural history, but he points out that human beings in our age of globalization have managed to destroy species and their natural habitat at an alarming rate. Broswimmer fears that up to 50 percent of all plant and animal species—most of them in the global South—will disappear by the end of the twenty-first century.[67]

The central feature of all these potentially disastrous environmental problems is that they are "global," thus making them serious problems for all sentient beings inhabiting our magnificent blue planet. Indeed, transboundary pollution, global warming, climate change, and species extinction are challenges that cannot be contained within national or even regional borders. They do not have isolated causes and effects, for they are caused by aggregate collective human actions and thus require a coordinated global response. There has been much discussion among scholars of ecological globalization about the severity of climate change and the best ways for the global community to respond to it. Yet, while much has been written and spoken about this issue, few coordinated measures have been implemented. Most international environmental treaties still lack effective enforcement mechanisms. For the most part, political efforts in favor of immediate change have been limited. The most significant obstacles to the creation and implementation of an effective global environmental agreement has come from the unwillingness of China and the United States—the world's two largest polluters—to lead the global community into an ecologically sustainable future.

Despite this litany of bad ecological news, one might find reason for cautious optimism in the bright side of globalization—the rising number of international treaties and agreements on the environment. Some rich countries in the EU managed to impose a national carbon tax on emitters. But poor countries argue that they should not be bound by the same carbon measures or trading schemes as developed countries. They make this argument for two reasons. First, they need to build up their industries and infrastructures in order to pull themselves out of poverty. Placing significant carbon emissions restrictions on their industries would seriously impede their economic development. Second, they argue that poor countries have not been responsible for the production of most of the greenhouse gases that have caused the current problem. Identifying developed countries as the primary producers of greenhouse gases, they suggest that the major burden for limiting the production of greenhouse gases should fall on the developed world—at least until developing countries have pulled their populations out of extreme poverty.

After a series of unsuccessful international negotiations, the UN Framework Convention on Climate Change summit held in Paris in December 2015 appeared to be a turning point for action to limit climate change with the expressed objective of moving to a *zero carbon world* within the foreseeable future. Uniting all of the world's nations in a single agreement on tackling climate change for the first time in history, the Paris *global climate deal* was composed of a number of key elements. First, the parties committed themselves to arrest the rise of global temperatures. Second, they pledged to limit the amount of greenhouse gases emitted by human activity to the same levels that trees, soil, and oceans can absorb naturally, beginning at some point between 2050 and 2100. Third, countries agreed to review each other's contribution to cutting emissions every five years so as to scale up the challenge. Finally, rich countries promised to help poorer nations by providing "climate finance" to adapt to climate change and switch to renewable energy. While the final signing of the Paris Agreement in 2016 constitutes an important milestone in the global struggle for environmental sustainability, the long road to a zero carbon world suffered a major setback in 2017 when the new Trump administration announced the US withdrawal from the treaty.

In their comprehensive study, the Australian globalization scholars Peter Christoff and Robyn Eckersley have identified five deep-seated and interlocking problems that stand in the way of an effective global environmental treaty system. First, states have failed to integrate environmental and economic governance at the national level. Second, states have failed to integrate environmental and economic governance at the international level. Third, powerful social forces continue to resist or co-opt efforts to transform economies and societies in a more ecologically sustainable direction. Fourth, the neoliberal economic discourse remains globally dominant, undermining sustainable development and ecological modernization discourses and practices. Fifth, all of the above persists because national and international accountability mechanisms remain weak and inadequate in a globalizing world.[68]

Unfortunately, the 2015 Paris agreement only addresses some of these points. Moreover, not all of the provisions of the treaty are legally binding, which means that international peer pressure constitutes the most effective form of enforcement available for addressing domestic activities that are protected by national sovereignty. Thus, the negotiations over climate change serve as an instructive example for how the various dimensions of globalization intersect. In this case, political globalization simply has not kept up with the demands of ecological globalization. But time is of the essence. Confronted with the ill health of our Mother Earth in the second decade of the twenty-first century, it has become abundantly clear to many people that the contemporary phase of globalization has been the most environmentally destructive period in human history. As I will discuss in the next chapter, much depends on challenging a powerful global ideology that is rooted in the utopia of unfettered markets and the desire for the unlimited accumulation and consumption of material things.

CONCLUDING REMARKS ON THE IDEOLOGICAL DIMENSION OF GLOBALIZATION: TOWARD A CRITICAL EXAMINATION OF GLOBALISM

This chapter has introduced the three major theoretical camps in the academic debate on globalization and linked them to an overview of the four main dimensions of globalization. Still, this overview does not encompass all topics of the ever-expanding discourse on the subject. In addition to exploring the economic, political, cultural, and ecological dimensions of globalization, many scholars have raised a number of additional topics, such as the structure and direction of transnational migration flows, the emergence of transnational social movements such as the women's movement, the spread of global diseases, transnational crime, and the globalization of military technology linked to a transnationalization of defense production.

Rather than providing a full account of every conceivable aspect of the debate, the purpose of this chapter has been to show that there exists no single conceptual framework for the study of globalization. Academics remain divided on the validity of available empirical evidence for the existence and extent of globalization, not to mention its normative and ideological implications. For this reason, globalization scholars such as Fredric Jameson have questioned the utility of forcing such a complex social phenomenon as globalization into a single analytical framework. He aptly characterizes the new field of global studies as generating an academic "space of tension" framed by multiple disagreements in which the very problematic of globalization itself is being continuously produced and contested.[69]

The persistence of academic divisions on globalization notwithstanding, it is important to acknowledge some emerging points of scholarly agreement in recent years.[70] Moreover, there is much value in the intellectual advances brought about by analytical research programs for the study of globalization. No serious scholar would wish to disavow the importance of conceptual clarity and precise formulations. But the impulse to separate the social-scientific study of globalization from ideological and normative matters often serves to further perpetuate stale disputes over definitions and methodological differences. As Ian Clark puts it, "While there can be no objection to a precise definition of globalization, definitions should not be permitted to resolve the underlying issues of substance and historical interpretation."[71]

Any overly objectivist approach to globalization is bound to overlook the insight that all social-scientific concepts are simultaneously analytical and normative. This dual status of concepts means that they never merely describe that to which they refer but are also necessarily engaged in a normative process of meaning construction.[72] Yet many scholars believe that the normative and ideological nature of the globalization debate that takes place in the public arena actually interferes with and obstructs the formulation of more *objective* or *value-free* accounts of globalization. This instinctive scholarly fear of ideological "contamination" derives partly from the historic mission of academic institutions. Like their nineteenth-century predecessors, today's universities subscribe to the belief that the world is, in principle, knowable and controllable through a balanced operation of human rationality. This means that scholars are encouraged to conduct their research within established parameters of objectivity and neutrality in order to reach a clear understanding of the phenomenon in question. Matters of ideology—particularly one's own political and moral preferences—are seen as compromising the scientific integrity of the research project. Therefore, the normative dimension of ideology is often excluded from academic attempts to understand globalization.

In fact, a discussion of the normative and ideological dimension of the phenomenon is often seen as unscientific "journalism." However, this argument misses the dynamics of globalization as a public discourse. The popular debate over globalization that occurs largely outside the walls of academia represents an important aspect of the phenomenon itself. As several empirical studies have shown, the term *globalization*, in the media, "appears to be associated with multiple ideological frames of reference, including 'financial market,' 'economic efficiency,' 'negative effect,' and 'culture.'"[73] If a researcher wants to understand the material and ideal stakes raised in the debate, then these "multiple ideological frames of reference" generating public judgments regarding the meanings and likely consequences of globalization represent an important subject of study. Thus, the researcher must enter the value-laden arena of ideology. The task can no longer be limited to an objective classification of the constitutive parts of the elephant called "globalization," but a critical assessment of the language about globalization that shapes the very phenomenon itself. Rather than being rejected as a confusing cacophony of subjective assertions, the exhibited normative preferences and the rhetorical and polemical maneuvers performed by the main participants in the public debate on globalization become the focus of the researcher's critical task.

In my view, it is virtually impossible for globalization scholars to interpret the popular discourse on the subject apart from their own ideological and political framework. In spite of the obvious dangers inherent in this move, the inclusion of one's own beliefs and values does not necessarily invalidate one's research project. As the German philosopher Hans-Georg Gadamer has pointed out, the motivations and prejudices of the interpreter condition every act of understanding.[74] Hence, it would be a mistake to consider the researcher's values and preconceptions solely as a hindrance to a proper understanding of social processes. In fact, the interpreter's inescapable normative involvement enables the very act of understanding. Thus, the study of globalization as a real-life phenomenon must include an investigation of the ideological projects that I have called *globalisms*.

Fortunately, the tendency of the academic discourse to separate ideological and normative matters from analytical concerns has been subjected to criticism from a variety of scholars who reject a narrow scientistic approach to the study of globalization. For example, the writings of Stephen Gill and Robert W. Cox probe the extent to which neoliberal conceptions of the market have been shaping the popular debate on globalization.[75] My own work also is anchored in a more interpretive approach to understanding social phenomena that does not shy away from normative and ideological matters. As I noted previously, I seek to avoid a general discussion of globalization (the material process) without a proper recognition that the former is inextricably intertwined with the various globalisms (the ideological package). Hence, I argue that academic efforts to capture the nature of globalization apart from the ongoing ideological claims made in the public arena reinforce, intentionally or not, the dominant market-globalist project that alternately masks and transmits a neoliberal worldview, thus making it easier for existing power interests to escape critical scrutiny.

As Alan Scott notes, the separation of analytical concerns from ideological and normative matters harbors the danger that the ethos of scientific detachment might unintentionally serve politically motivated attempts to provide "people with persuasive arguments to the effect that little can be done in the face of these enormous economic, political and social developments."[76] Seeking to avoid this danger of *depoliticization*, the next chapter of this book discusses not only the rise of market globalism to world dominance in the 1990s, but also critically analyzes its core concepts and major ideological claims.

Chapter 3

The Dominance of Market Globalism in the 1990s

MARKET GLOBALISM AND NEOLIBERALISM

After the collapse of Soviet-style communism in 1989, Anglo-American proponents of the nineteenth-century utopia of the *self-regulating market* found in the concept of "globalization" a new guiding metaphor for their neoliberal message. The central tenets of *neoliberalism* include the primacy of economic growth, the importance of free trade to stimulate growth, the unrestricted free market, individual choice, the reduction of government regulation, and the advocacy of an evolutionary model of social development anchored in the Western experience and applicable to the entire world.

Neoliberalism is an economic perspective rooted in the *classical liberal ideals* of British philosophers such as Adam Smith (1723–1790), David Ricardo (1772–1823), and Herbert Spencer (1820–1903). Smith is often credited with creating the Scottish Enlightenment image of

Homo economicus—the view that people are isolated individuals whose actions reflect mostly their economic self-interest. In Smith's view, economic and political matters are largely separable, with economics claiming a superior status because it supposedly operates best without government interference under a harmonious system of natural laws. The market is seen as a self-regulating mechanism tending toward equilibrium of supply and demand, thus securing the most efficient allocation of resources. Any constraint on free competition is said to interfere with the natural efficiency of market mechanisms. Composed of small buyers and sellers, the market's "invisible hand" translates individual pursuit of self-interest into optimal public benefit. Attacking the seventeenth-century economic doctrine of mercantilism—absolute control of the economy by a powerful state with the objective of building up large gold reserves—Smith argued vigorously in favor of "liberating" markets from intrusive state regulation. His classical understanding of liberalism defends freedom as a person's right to be "left alone" by social demands so that the individual may act in the market as *Homo economicus* unencumbered by social regulations. This early vision of economic liberty still forms the backbone of contemporary neoliberal doctrine. Smith complemented his *laissez-faire market ideal* with a defense of free trade and its principles of laissez-passer, most importantly the elimination of tariffs on imports and other barriers to trade and capital flows between nations.

But it was Ricardo's nineteenth-century *theory of comparative advantage* that became the gospel of modern free traders. Ricardo argued that free trade amounted to a win-win situation for all trading partners involved because it allowed each country to specialize in the production of those commodities for which it had a comparative advantage. For example, if Italy could produce wine more cheaply than England and England could produce cloth more cheaply than Italy, then both countries would benefit from specialization and trade. In fact, Ricardo even went so far as to suggest that benefits from specialization and trade would accrue even if one country had an absolute advantage in producing all the products traded. Politically, Ricardo's theory amounted to a powerful argument against government interference with trade and was used by later liberals such as Richard Cobden as a formidable ideological weapon in the struggle to repeal the protectionist Corn Laws in nineteenth-century England.[1]

Perhaps the most influential formulation of classical liberalism appears in Herbert Spencer's justification of the "natural dominance" of Western laissez-faire capitalism over the rest of the world by drawing on Charles Darwin's *theory of evolution by natural selection*. Writing in the late nineteenth century, Spencer argued that free-market economies constitute the most civilized form of human competition in which the "fittest" would "naturally" rise to the top. Establishing himself as the leading proponent of early industrial capitalism, Spencer did not support imperialist policies but limited the required tasks of the state to protecting individuals against internal and external forms of aggression. Any interference with the workings of private enterprise would inevitably lead to cultural and social stagnation, political corruption, and the creation of large, inefficient state bureaucracies.

Spencer denounced socialism, trade unions, and even rudimentary forms of social regulation such as factory safety laws as examples of "over-regulation" inimical to rational progress and individual freedom. In his early study *Social Statics*, he enshrined laissez-faire capitalism as the final system toward which all societies were evolving under the economic and cultural leadership of Anglo-American countries. Spencer's elevation of free-market competition as the natural source of humankind's freedom and prosperity proved to be extremely influential with the commercial interests of Victorian England. Toward the end of his life, the reported total sales of his books approached 400,000 copies. No doubt, Spencer's theories greatly contributed to the hegemony of free-market economic doctrine in nineteenth-century Britain.[2]

The intensification of European and American *imperialism* in the 1890s, the collapse of world trade during World War I, and the economic crises and conflicts during the interwar years caused free-market ideas to lose much of their appeal. Virulent forms of nationalism and trade protectionism emerged as extreme reactions to *laissez-faire capitalism*, and it was not until the end of World War II that modified versions of liberalism reappeared on the political agenda of Western countries. Until the 1970s, even the most pro-market political parties in Europe and the United States embraced rather extensive forms of state interventionism propagated by British economist John Maynard Keynes in the 1930s and 1940s. Culminating in the creation of the modern welfare state, Keynes's advocacy of a *social market* engineered by a pragmatic government represented the impressive attempt to combine some redeemable values of socialism with the virtues of liberalism in a system of mixed economy and political pluralism that balanced capitalist markets with demands for greater social equality.[3]

However, the rise of neoliberal ideas in the late 1970s found a favorable economic context as inflation, high unemployment, and other structural problems plagued Western industrialized countries. Making a strong case for the return to free-market policies of the past, neoliberal politicians drew on the neoclassical laissez-faire economic theories of European and American economists such as Friedrich Hayek and Milton Friedman. In the early 1980s, British Conservatives under the intellectual leadership of Keith Joseph and Margaret Thatcher implemented what some commentators have called *turbo-capitalism*.[4] Their social conservatism combined with neoliberal economic policies to create a strange hybrid often referred to as *neoconservatism*—a position favoring the weakening of the power of labor unions and initiating drastic market-oriented reforms while opting for a hawkish foreign policy, especially toward the Soviet Union and other adversaries of Western democracies. By the late 1980s, British Prime Minister Margaret Thatcher and US President Ronald Reagan were both revered and reviled as the founding figures of a new market paradigm. After the collapse of communism in Eastern Europe, President Bill Clinton and Prime Minister Tony Blair could afford to drop the tough foreign policy stance of their predecessors and expand the neoliberal project into a full-blown market ideology.

As this chapter suggests, the dominance of market globalism was established during what American Nobel Prize–winning economist Joseph Stiglitz calls the *Roaring Nineties*.[5] The public interpretation of globalization fell disproportionately to global power elites enamored with the philosophical and economic principles of the Thatcher–Reagan revolution. This global phalanx consisted mostly of corporate managers, executives of large transnational corporations, corporate lobbyists, prominent journalists and public-relations specialists, cultural elites and entertainment celebrities, academics writing for large audiences, high-level state bureaucrats, and political leaders.[6] They marshaled their considerable material and ideological resources to sell to the public the alleged benefits of the liberalization of trade and the global integration of markets: rising living standards, reduction of global poverty, economic efficiency, individual freedom and democracy, and unprecedented technological progress. Ideally, the state should only provide the legal framework for contracts, defense, and law and order. Public policy initiatives should be confined to those measures that liberate the economy from social constraints: privatization of public enterprises, deregulation instead of state control, liberalization of trade and industry, massive tax cuts, strict control of organized labor, and the reduction of public expenditures. Other models of economic organization were discredited as being "protectionist" or "socialist." As noted in chapter 1, the stunning collapse of Soviet-style communism proved to be a particularly useful trump card in the rhetorical arsenal of these market globalists.

Seeking to enshrine their neoliberal paradigm as the self-evident and universal order of our global era, the ideological claims of market globalists articulated the overarching global imaginary as concrete political programs and agendas. They asserted that all peoples and states were equally subject to the logic of globalization, which was, in the long run, beneficial and inevitable, and that societies had no choice but to adapt to this world-shaping force.

GLOBALIZATION AS "MARKETS-PLUS-TECHNOLOGY" AND THE MYTH OF THE NEOLIBERAL CONSENSUS

Throughout the 1990s, the dominant interpretation of globalization as driven by the irresistible forces of the market and technology was frequently expressed in quasi-religious language that bestowed almost divine wisdom on the market.[7] A growing number of influential free-market advocates were making great strides in their efforts to sell liberalism's promise of the good life. Influential journalists and intellectuals such as Thomas Friedman, Martin Wolf, Jagdish Bhagwati, Paul Krugman, and Joseph Stiglitz, together with powerful international corporate and political elites who gathered annually at the World Economic Forum in Davos, Switzerland, had perfected their sales pitch. It boiled down to the endless intonation of the mantra, *the globalization of markets*, popularized a decade earlier by Theodore Levitt, then dean of the Harvard Business School.[8] Building on the familiar theme of unstoppable modernization in the image of the West, this shibboleth was meant to evoke a providential dynamism destined to reach the farthest corners of the earth. Amplified in the corporate media, the steady stream of hegemonic globalization talk provided the discursive glue that held together the applied neoliberal policy project of deregulating economies, opening up trade, privatizing public enterprises, cutting marginal tax rates, emasculating labor unions, and creating "flexible" labor markets—both offshore and at home. Soon, the new social structure of neoliberal capitalist accumulation acquired the stability and authority required to promote corporate profitability and stable expansion during the 1990s and beyond.[9]

The "globalization of markets" also served as the central metaphor for a refurbished version of the old laissez-faire utopia of social harmony established by the invisible hand. Economically, this claim of general agreement was presented in the neoliberal formula of *globalization as markets-plus-technology:* a peerless New Economy powered by new technologies such as the Internet. Its associated culture of consumerism was celebrated as a homogenizing global force that enabled people everywhere to experience the exhilarating freedom of increased buying choices. As Pulitzer Prize–winning journalist Daniel Yergin asserted, the neoliberal success of decamping the state from the commanding heights of the economy marked the great divide between the twentieth and twenty-first centuries.[10]

Politically, the dominant *myth of the neoliberal consensus* was promoted as a global *pax mercatus*—an American-led market peace that drastically reduced the likelihood of large-scale conflicts between states. The global integration of markets was portrayed as *the* democratic medium of social harmony because it was said to express the popular will more accurately and more meaningfully than the messy political process controlled by privileged elites who were detached from ordinary people and their everyday concerns.[11] Indeed, the political dimension of neoliberalism received a catchy expression in Margaret Thatcher's famous TINA slogan: "There Is No Alternative." Embraced and swiftly spread across the globe by the global corporate media, Thatcher's rhetorical one-way street was a potent weapon in the larger neoliberal effort to delegitimize dissenting worldviews while reinforcing ongoing efforts to depoliticize the public sphere and foster new forms of rationality that reached ever more deeply into the microstructures of self and identity.[12] Hailed as creative "entrepreneurs," working people were encouraged to shed their old class-based self-image of passive industrial cogs in the exploitative capitalist machine and imagine themselves instead as proactive "human capital." Reinvented as a "flexible work force," they could be more easily motivated to invest their labor power in the perfection of their own personal "brand."

Technologically, the neoliberal myth of benign social convergence found its expression in the neoliberal formulation of *globalization as markets-plus-technology*. Starting in the 1990s, the public discourse became rife with quasi-religious public invocations of the countless blessings of the information and communications technology (ICT) revolution, especially the Internet's delivery of worldwide simultaneity and instantaneity. The daily glorification of digital technology served to legitimize and naturalize the economic imperatives of what later commentators would call "cybercapitalism" or "platform capitalism."[13] Combining the language of technological determinism with established neoliberal practices of profit extraction, cybercapitalism fed on the growing influence of giant oligopolistic corporations such as Microsoft, Sony, Intel, and Apple. Joined some years later by Google, Amazon, Verizon, Facebook, and Twitter, these transnational media conglomerates incessantly promoted free-market policies as the only way to realize their techno-utopian vision of an automated, carefree future that promised receptive consumers.

SELLING GLOBALIZATION IN THE 1990S

Let us take a concrete example to illustrate the selling of market globalism in the 1990s by neoliberal acolytes. At the end of the decade, the American magazine *BusinessWeek* featured a cover story on globalization that contained the following statement: "For nearly a decade, political and business leaders have struggled to persuade the American public of the virtues of globalization." Citing the results of a national poll on globalization conducted in April 2000, the article goes on to report that most Americans were of two minds on the subject. On the one hand, about 65 percent of the respondents thought that globalization was a "good thing" for consumers and businesses in both the United States and the rest of the world. On the other hand, they were afraid that globalization might lead to a significant loss of American jobs. In addition, nearly 70 percent of those polled believed that free-trade agreements with low-wage countries were responsible for driving down wages in the United States. The article ends on a rather combative note by issuing a stern warning to American politicians and business leaders not to be "caught off guard" by the arguments of "antiglobalist" forces. In order to assuage people's increasing anxiety on the subject, American "decision makers" ought to be more effective in highlighting the benefits of globalization. After all, the article concludes, the persistence of public fears over globalization might result in a significant backlash, jeopardizing the health of the international economy and "the cause of free trade."[14]

This cover story contained two important pieces of information with regard to the dominance of market globalism in the 1990s. First, there was the author's open admission that political and business leaders were actively engaged in selling their preferred market version of globalization to the public. In fact, he saw the construction of arguments and images that portray globalization in a positive light as an indispensable tool for the realization of a global order based on free-market principles. No doubt, such favorable visions of globalization pervaded public opinion and political choices at the time. Whereas language and ideas mattered in the ongoing struggle to persuade the global public of the virtues of globalization, neoliberal decision makers had to become expert designers of an attractive ideological container for their market-friendly political agenda. Given that the exchange of commodities constitutes the core activity of all market societies, the discourse on globalization itself turned into an extremely important commodity destined for public consumption.

Second, the polling data presented in the *BusinessWeek* cover story revealed the existence of a remarkable cognitive dissonance between the American people's normative orientation toward globalization and their personal experiences in the globalizing world. How else can one explain that a sizable majority of respondents were afraid of the negative economic impact of globalization on their lives while at the same time deeming globalization to be a "good thing"? One obvious answer is ideology. Pro-market visions of globalization shaped a large part of public opinion, even if people's daily experiences reflected a less favorable picture. For example, the same *BusinessWeek* article also told the harrowing story of a factory worker employed by the Goodyear Tire & Rubber Company in Gadsden, Alabama. Having lost his job after Goodyear shifted most of its tire production to low-wage jobs in Mexico and Brazil, the worker had been only recently rehired by the same company for much less money. Still, the article concluded this disturbing story by reaffirming the overall positive impact of economic globalization: "Polls have shown for years that a solid majority of Americans believe that open borders and free trade are good for the economy."[15]

BusinessWeek is only one among dozens of magazines, journals, newspapers, and electronic media that, during the 1990s, fed global audiences a steady diet of market-globalist claims that served concrete political purposes. The dominant media presented globalization in such a way as to advance the material and ideal interests of those groups in society who benefited the most from the liberalization of the economy, the privatization of ownership, a minimal regulatory role for government, efficient returns on capital, and the devolution of power to the private sector. Like all ideologists, market globalists engaged continuously in acts of simplification, distortion, legitimation, and integration in order to cultivate in the public mind the conviction that the globalization of markets is a "good thing." When people accepted the claims of market globalism, they simultaneously embraced as authority large parts of the comprehensive political, economic, and intellectual framework of neo-liberalism. Thus, the ideological reach of market globalism went even beyond the crucial task of providing the public with an explanation of the meaning of globalization. Most importantly, it was a compelling story that sold an overarching worldview, thereby creating collective meanings and shaping personal and collective identities.

Hence, market globalism and its associated neoliberal framework became in the Roaring Nineties what some social and political thinkers call a "strong" or "dominant" discourse."[16] In this context, "discourse" refers to the communicative practices through which ideology is exercised. Any hegemonic discourse is notoriously difficult to resist and repel because it has on its side powerful social forces that have already preselected what counts as "real" and, therefore, shape the world accordingly. As American social philosopher Judith Butler notes, the constant repetition, public recitation, and "performance" of an ideology's central claims and slogans frequently have the capacity to produce what they name.[17] As more neoliberal policies are enacted, the claims of globalism become even more firmly planted in the public mind. They solidify into what French social philosopher Michel Foucault calls a solid "ground of thinking."[18] The political realization of the neoliberal agenda, in turn, leads to the further weakening of those political and social institutions that subject market forces to public control. Neoliberal policies are made to appear as the most rational response to inevitable, but efficient, market forces. Growing global disparities in wealth and well-being are shrugged off as mere temporary dislocations on the sure path to a brighter future.

EXAMINING THE CORE CONCEPTS AND IDEOLOGICAL CLAIMS OF MARKET GLOBALISM

Having explored market globalism's rise to dominance in the 1990s on the macrolevel of economics, politics, and technology, let us now explore this ideology on the microlevel of ideas and concepts following Michael Freeden's approach to ideology discussed in chapter 1. I subject key utterances, speeches, and writings of influential advocates of market globalism to a particular form of *critical discourse analysis*, which I call *morphological discourse analysis* (MDA). Ideological morphologies can be pictured as patterned ideas serving the *representation* of reality as well as discursive practices engaged in the *construction* of reality.

Originally developed by Freeden and refined by the present author, MDA is designed to systematically explore and map the concepts and claims of ideologies.[19] The key difference between Freeden's morphological analysis of ideology and mine concerns MDA's more fluid conceptualization of basic ideological units that carry meanings. In addition to following Freeden's method of disaggregating ideational systems into relatively static elements according to levels of decreasing contestation from core concepts to adjacent concepts to peripheral concepts, I also evaluate the morphological status of ideologies on the basis of their ability to arrange concepts of roughly equal significance into meaningful "decontestation chains" or "central ideological claims."[20] While these claims rarely appear verbatim in texts, they nonetheless represent realistic composites of linked concepts in the form of mininarratives. This expansion of Freeden's methodological approach better captures the dynamic and changeable character of thought-systems as well as the narrative process of concept formation and contextual responsiveness.

Focusing on pertinent texts in the public domain, this method is particularly suited to help researchers comprehend the role played by language use in producing and reinforcing asymmetrical power relations that sustain certain forms of social and political identity.[21] It takes seriously the ideational and linguistic dimensions of globalization while at the same time recognizing the importance of material factors such as politics and economics. The central idea behind MDA is "to conceive of language as a communicative set of interactions, through which social and cultural beliefs and understandings are shaped and circulated."[22]

In the next three chapters, I employ MDA to identify and analyze the *core concepts*, and, more importantly, the *central ideological claims* of the three competing globalisms as well as their right-wing "antiglobalist" populist challenger. Ideological claims arrange core concepts into powerful meanings that undergo ceaseless contestation in the public arena. Ultimately, the winning ideology in this ceaseless struggle enjoys the temporary advantage of making its assertions into the dominant framework of understanding. Thus, the core claims of market globalism serve as an important source of collective and individual identity as well as significant political power.[23] In the case of market globalism in the 1990s, global power elites functioned as ideological codifiers who imbued the concept "globalization" with values, beliefs, and meanings that supported the global spread of free-market principles.

Some critics might object to morphological discourse analysis as a biased attempt to present the audience with a greatly exaggerated account of the claims of market globalism. Others might object to my approach as a project of building up a straw person that can be easily dismantled. In his critical study of economic globalization, Michael Veseth responds to the same objections by pointing out that this "artificial straw person" is actually the product of the codifiers' own making.[24] In other words, market globalists themselves construct these claims to sell their political agenda. It may be true that no single market globalist speech or piece of writing contains all the assertions discussed below. But all of them contain some of these claims.

CLAIM NUMBER ONE: GLOBALIZATION IS ABOUT THE LIBERALIZATION AND GLOBAL INTEGRATION OF MARKETS

This first claim of market globalism is anchored in the neoliberal ideal of the self-regulating market as the normative basis for a future global order. According to this perspective, the vital functions of the free market—its rationality and efficiency as well as its alleged ability to bring about greater social integration and material progress—can only be realized in a democratic society that values and protects individual freedom. For Friedrich Hayek and his neoliberal followers, the free market represents a state of liberty because it is "a state in which each can use his knowledge for his own purpose."[25] Thus, the preservation of individual freedom depends on the state's willingness to refrain from interfering with the private sphere of the market. Liberal thinkers such as Isaiah Berlin refer to this limitation on governmental interference as "negative liberty." This concept defends the protection of a private area of life within which one "is or should be left to do or be what he is able to do or be, without interference by other persons."[26] Because neoliberals allege that the free market relies on a set of rational rules applying equally to all members of society, they consider it both just and meritocratic. While the existence of the market depends on human action, its resulting benefits and burdens are not products of human design. In other words, the concrete outcomes of market interactions are neither intended nor foreseen but are the result of the workings of what Adam Smith famously called the *invisible hand.*

Opposing the expansion of governmental intervention in the economy that occurred in Western industrialized nations during the first three-quarters of the twentieth century, globalists in the 1990s called for the *liberalization of markets*—that is, the *deregulation* of national economies. In their view, such neoliberal measures would not only lead to the emergence of an integrated global market but also result in greater political freedom for all citizens of the world. As Milton Friedman notes, "The kind of economic organization that provides economic freedom directly, namely competitive capitalism, also promotes political freedom because it separates economic power from political power and in this way enables the one to offset the other."[27] This citation highlights the crucial neoliberal assumption that politics and economics are separate realms. The latter constitutes a fundamentally nonpolitical, private sphere that must remain sheltered from the imposition of political power. Governments ought to be limited to providing an appropriate legal and institutional framework for the fulfillment of voluntary agreements reflected in contractual arrangements.

A short passage in a 1999 *BusinessWeek* editorial implicitly conveys this neoliberal suspicion of political power in defining globalization in market terms: "Globalization is about the triumph of markets over governments. Both proponents and opponents of globalization agree that the driving force today is markets, which are suborning the role of government. The truth is that the size of government has been shrinking relative to the economy almost everywhere."[28] Claiming that it is the liberalization of markets that "makes globalization happen," the British *Financial Times* reporter Martin Wolf conveyed a similar perspective to his mass readership. He argued that globalization "marks the worldwide spread of the economic liberalization that began nearly fifty years ago in western Europe with the Marshall Plan." Celebrating the most "precious right of democracy, the right to be left alone," the British journalist Peter Martin took Wolf's argument a step further: "The liberal market economy is by its very nature global. It is the summit of human endeavor. We should be proud that by our work and by our votes we have—collectively and individually—contributed to building it."[29] In short, market globalist voices in the 1990s presented globalization as a natural economic phenomenon whose essential qualities are the liberalization and integration of global markets and the reduction of governmental interference in the economy. *Privatization, free trade*, and *unfettered capital movements* are portrayed as the best and most natural way for realizing individual liberty and material progress in the world.

Market globalists in the 1990s usually conveyed their assertion that globalization is about the liberalization and global integration of markets in the form of moral demands and rational imperatives. President Bill Clinton's US Trade Representative Charlene Barshefsky, for example, admonished her audiences in both the United States and the global South to realize that globalization requires a rational commitment "to restructure public enterprises and accelerate privatization of key sectors—including energy, transportation, utilities, and communication—which will enhance market-driven competition and deregulation."[30] Asserting that the realization of "open, dynamic economies" constitutes "the very essence of globalization," International Monetary Fund (IMF) managing director Michael Camdessus argued that in order "to optimize the opportunities and reduce the risks of globalization, we must head towards a world with open and integrated capital markets."[31]

Perhaps the most eloquent exposition of the neoliberal claim that globalization is about the liberalization and global integration of markets can be found in Thomas Friedman's 1999 best-seller, *The Lexus and the Olive Tree: Understanding Globalization*. Indeed, many commentators of the day saw Friedman as the "official narrator of globalization" in the United States.[32] Although the award-winning *New York Times* correspondent claimed that he does not want to be considered as "a salesman of globalization," he eagerly admonished his readers to acknowledge the factuality of existing global realities and "think like globalists."[33] For Friedman, this meant that people ought to accept the following "truth" about globalization:

> The driving idea behind globalization is free-market capitalism—the more you let market forces rule and the more you open your economy to free trade and competition, the more efficient your economy will be. Globalization means the spread of free-market capitalism to virtually every country in the world. Therefore, globalization also has its own set of economic rules—rules that revolve around opening, deregulating, and privatizing your economy, in order to make it more competitive and attractive to foreign investment.[34]

Asserting that, for the first time in history, "virtually every country in the world has the same basic hardware—free-market capitalism," Friedman predicted that globalization would result in the creation of a single global marketplace. He informed his readers that this feat would be achieved by means of the "Golden Straitjacket"—the "defining political–economic garment of this globalization era."[35] Stitched together by Anglo-American neoliberal politicians and business leaders, the Golden Straitjacket would force every country in the world to adopt the same economic rules:

> [M]aking the private sector the primary engine of its economic growth, maintaining a low rate of inflation and price stability, shrinking the size of its state bureaucracy, maintaining as close to a balanced budget as possible, if not a surplus, eliminating and lowering tariffs on imported goods, removing restrictions on foreign investment, getting rid of quotas and domestic monopolies, increasing exports, privatizing state-owned industries and utilities, deregulating capital markets, making its currency convertible, opening its industries, deregulating its economy to promote as much domestic competition as possible, eliminating government corruption, subsidies and kickbacks as much as possible, opening its banking and telecommunications systems to

private ownership and competition and allowing its citizens to choose from an array of competing pension options and foreign-run pension and mutual funds. When you stitch all of these pieces together you have the Golden Straitjacket.[36]

Friedman concluded his pitch for the liberalization and global integration of markets by pointing out that the global market system of the 1990s was the result of "large historical forces" that gave birth to a new power source in the world—the "Electronic Herd." Made up of millions of faceless stock, bond, and currency traders sitting behind computer screens all over the globe, the Electronic Herd also included the executive officers of large transnational corporations (TNCs) who shifted their production sites to the most efficient, low-cost producers. In order to succeed in the new era of globalization, countries not only had to put on the Golden Straitjacket but also had to please the Electronic Herd. Friedman explained, "The Electronic Herd loves the Golden Straitjacket, because it embodies all the liberal, free-market rules the herd wants to see in a country. Those countries that put on the Golden Straitjacket are rewarded by the herd with investment capital. Those that don't want to put it on are disciplined by the herd—either by the herd avoiding or withdrawing its money from that country."[37]

A critical discourse analysis of the market globalist claim that globalization is about the liberalization and global integration of markets might begin by contrasting the neoliberal rhetoric of liberty with Friedman's depiction of globalization proceeding by means of the Golden Straitjacket. If the liberalization of trade and markets depends on coercive measures employed by the United States and its allies, then this form of liberty comes dangerously close to Jean-Jacques Rousseau's famous idea that only in obeying the *general will*—even under duress—is a person truly free. Yet, for the French philosopher, in order to count as a truly universal expression, the general will must come from all citizens and not merely from a partisan Electronic Herd or the government of a superpower that seeks to impose its ideology on the rest of the world.

In selling their *particular will* as the *general will*, market globalists condemn alternative ways of organizing the economy. Their project of "opening up economies" is advocated as an endeavor of universal applicability, for it supposedly reflects the dictates of human freedom in general. However, such efforts to stitch together a neoliberal economic straitjacket—one-size-fits-all countries—are hardly compatible with a process of globalization that is alleged to contribute to the spread of freedom, choice, and openness in the world.

Second, as Friedman concedes, the message of liberalizing and globally integrating markets is realizable only through the political project of engineering free markets. In order to advance their enterprise, market globalists must be prepared to utilize the powers of government to weaken and eliminate those social policies and institutions that curtail the market. Whereas only strong governments are up to this ambitious task of transforming existing social arrangements, the successful liberalization of markets depends on the intervention and interference of centralized state power. The assertion that governments can best contribute to the process of market liberalization by simply getting out of the way represents, therefore, a clear example of ideological distortion. Such remarks reflect a neoliberal idealization of the limited role of government, which stands in stark contrast to government's role in the actual social arena. In truth, market globalists do expect governments to play an extremely active role in implementing their political agenda. The activist character of neoliberal administrations in the United States, the United Kingdom, Australia, and New Zealand during the 1980s and 1990s attests to the importance of strong governmental action in engineering free markets.[38] Indeed, pro-market governments serve as indispensable catalysts of "globalization-from-above." In their pursuit of market liberalization and integration, both neoliberal and neoconservative power elites violate their own principles of decentralization, limited government, and negative liberty.

Finally, the neoliberal claim that globalization is about the liberalization and global integration of markets serves to solidify as "fact" what is actually a contingent political initiative. In the 1990s, market globalists largely succeeded because they persuaded the public that their neoliberal account of globalization represented an objective or at least neutral diagnosis rather than a direct contribution to the emergence of the very conditions it purported to analyze. To be sure, neoliberals may indeed be able to offer some "empirical evidence" for the "liberalization" of markets. But did the spread of market principles really happen because there existed an intrinsic, metaphysical connection between globalization and the expansion of markets? Or did it occur because market globalists had the political and discursive power to shape the world, largely according to their ideological formula:

liberalization + integration of markets = globalization

However, this economistic-objectivist representation of globalization detracts from the multidimensional character of the phenomenon. Ecological, cultural, and political dimensions of globalization are discussed only as subordinate processes dependent on the movements of global markets. Even if one were to accept the central role of the economic dimension of globalization, there is no reason to believe that these processes must necessarily be connected to the deregulation of markets. As we shall see, an alternative view offered by justice globalists instead suggested linking globalization to the creation of a global regulatory framework that would make markets more accountable to international political institutions.

The setting of a successful political agenda always occurs simultaneously with concerted efforts to sell to the public the general desirability of a particular system of ideas. Market globalism is no exception. Like all ideologies, its values and beliefs are conveyed through a number of justificatory claims, usually starting with one that establishes what the phenomenon is all about. As international relations expert Edward Luttwak pointed out, there was a good reason that the spectacular advance of "turbo-capitalism" in the 1990s was accompanied by so much talk about globalization in the public arena. The presentation of globalization as an enterprise that liberates and integrates global markets as well as emancipates individuals from governmental control was the best way of enlisting the public in the market-globalist struggle against those laws and institutions these dominant elites found most restrictive.[39] By engineering popular consent with the help of the corporate global media, they only rarely resorted to open forms of coercion. The Golden Straitjacket would do splendidly to keep dissent to a minimum. For those who remained skeptical, market globalists had another ideological claim up their sleeves: Why doubt a process that proceeds with historical inevitability?

CLAIM NUMBER TWO: GLOBALIZATION
IS INEVITABLE AND IRREVERSIBLE

At first glance, the belief in the historical inevitability of globalization seems to be a poor fit for a globalist ideology based on neoliberal principles. After all, throughout the twentieth century, liberals and conservatives consistently criticized Marxism for its determinist claims that devalued human free agency and downplayed the ability of noneconomic factors to shape social reality. In particular, neoliberals attacked the Marxist notion of history as a teleological process that unfolded according to "inexorable laws" that hastened the demise of capitalism, ultimately leading to the emergence of a classless society on a global scale.

However, a close study of the utterances of influential market globalists in the 1990s reveals their reliance on a similar monocausal, economistic narrative of historical inevitability. While disagreeing with Marxists on the final goal of historical development, they nonetheless share with their ideological opponents a fondness for such terms as *irresistible*, *inevitable*, and *irreversible* to describe the projected path of globalization. As Ulrich Beck pointed out, "In a way, neoliberal globalism thus resembles its archenemy: Marxism. It is the rebirth of Marxism as a management ideology."[40] By focusing on the "logic" of technology and markets, market globalists minimized the role of human agency and individual choice, which, ironically, served as the centerpiece of liberal thought from John Locke and John Stuart Mill to Milton Friedman.

According to the market-globalist perspective, globalization reflects the spread of irreversible market forces driven by technological innovations that made the global integration of national economies inevitable. In fact, market globalism is almost always intertwined with the deep belief in the ability of markets to use new technologies to solve social problems far better than any alternative course.[41] Governments, political parties, and social movements allegedly had no choice but to "adjust" to the inevitability of globalization. Their sole remaining task is to facilitate the integration of national economies in the new global market. States and interstate systems should, therefore, serve to ensure the smooth working of market logic.[42] Indeed, the multiple voices of market globalism in the 1990s conveyed to the public their message of inevitability with tremendous consistency. Below are some examples.

In a speech on US foreign policy, President Clinton told his audience, "Today we must embrace the inexorable logic of globalization—that everything from the strength of our economy to the safety of our cities, to the health of our people, depends on events not only within our borders, but half a world away."[43] On another occasion he emphasized that "globalization is irreversible. Protectionism will only make things worse."[44] Deputy Secretary of the Treasury Stuart Eizenstat echoed the assessment of his boss: "Globalization is an inevitable element of our lives. We cannot stop it any more than we can stop the waves from crashing on the shore. The arguments in support of trade liberalization and open markets are strong ones—they have been made by many of you and we must not be afraid to engage those with whom we respectfully disagree."[45]

Frederick W. Smith, chair and CEO of FedEx Corporation, suggested that "globalization is inevitable and inexorable and it is accelerating. . . . Globalization is happening, it's going to happen. It does not matter whether you like it or not."[46] Thomas Friedman came to a similar conclusion: "Globalization is very difficult to reverse because it is driven both by powerful human aspiration for higher standards of living and by enormously powerful technologies which are integrating us more and more every day, whether we like it or not."[47] But Friedman simply argued by asserting that there was something inherent in technology that required a neoliberal system. He never considered that, for example, new information technologies could just as easily be used to enhance public-service media as utilized in commercial, profit-making enterprises. The choice always depends on the nature of the political will exerted in a particular social order.

Neoliberal elites in non-Western countries faithfully echoed the market-globalist language of inevitability. For example, Rahul Bajaj, a leading Indian industrialist, insisted that "we need much more liberalization and deregulation of the Indian economy. No sensible Indian businessman disagrees with this. . . . Globalization is inevitable. There is no better alternative." He added that "India and Indian companies have to recognize that the forces of globalization are irreversible. I think the agenda for India is not whether globalization is on, but what to do about it, what are the implications of networking and alliances."[48] Manuel Villar Jr., Speaker of the House of Representatives in the Philippines, agreed: "Of course, we cannot simply wish away the process of globalization.

It is a reality of a modern world. The process is irreversible."⁴⁹ Masaru Hayami, governor of the Bank of Japan, concurred: "The essence of globalization is the integration of markets worldwide and the deepening of various interdependent relations. . . . Thus, the move toward globalization is an inevitable reality, and not likely to be reversed."⁵⁰

This neoliberal portrayal of globalization as some sort of natural force, like the weather or gravity, made it easier for market globalists to convince people that they had to adapt to the discipline of the market if they were to survive and prosper. Hence, the claim of inevitability serves a number of important political functions. For one, it neutralizes the challenges of alterglobalist opponents by depoliticizing the public discourse about globalization: neoliberal policies are above politics because they simply carry out what is ordained by nature. This view implies that, instead of acting according to a set of choices, people merely fulfill world-market laws that demand the elimination of government controls. Nothing can be done about the natural movement of economic and technological forces; political groups ought to acquiesce and make the best of an unalterable situation. Since the emergence of a world based on the primacy of market values reflects the dictates of history, resistance would be unnatural, irrational, and dangerous.

As John Malott, former US ambassador to Malaysia, put it, "Some people think that the debate about globalization is whether it is good or bad. To me, globalization just is. We cannot stop it; we have to accept it, and adjust to it. Those countries, those companies, those people who adjust to a changing world will do better. Those who resist will suffer." For Malott, "adjustment" referred to the implementation of deregulatory policies that allow for "less rather than more government control and influence over business decision-making."⁵¹ Thus, market globalists utilized the idea of the historical inevitability of globalization in order to better advance their thoroughly political project of implementing neoliberal economic policies. For the masses, however, market globalists prescribed an attitude of political passivity in the face of inevitability. This made it easier for them to admonish the general public to "share the burdens of globalization." In short, market-globalist ideology constitutes high politics while presenting itself in nonpolitical garb.

By turning the market into a natural force, market globalists suggested that human beings were at the mercy of external imperatives they cannot control. As the neoliberal economist Alain Lipietz emphasized, the modern market economy was an autonomous realm "defined by immutable economic laws, behaviors and tendencies."[52] The strategy seemed to be working exceedingly well in the 1990s. Even prolabor voices, such as AFL-CIO director of public policy David Smith, accepted the globalist claims of inevitability and irreversibility: "Globalization is a fact. . . . We're not going to turn these tides back. We shouldn't want to turn these tides back; even if we wanted to, we couldn't."[53]

Finally, the claim that globalization is inevitable and irresistible was inscribed within a larger evolutionary discourse that assigned a privileged position to those nations that are in the forefront of "liberating" markets from political control. For example, Lorenzo Zambrano, the Mexican CEO of CEMEX Corporation, the world's largest cement producer, strongly supported this idea: "I agree that globalization is inevitable and that it may be inherent to the evolution of a civilization and that it has been brought about by progress in telecommunications allowing instantaneous contact to be established."[54]

Some American globalists were even more culturally explicit than Zambrano. For them, the United States and its philosophy of free-market capitalism was spearheading the inevitable historical progress toward the creation of a global "market civilization." Francis Fukuyama represented an exemplary perspective on this issue. He insisted that globalization was really a euphemism that stood for the irreversible Americanization of the world: "I think it has to be Americanization because, in some respects, America is the most advanced capitalist society in the world today, and so its institutions represent the logical development of market forces. Therefore, if market forces are what drives globalization, it is inevitable that Americanization will accompany globalization."[55] Friedman, too, ended his 1999 best-seller with a celebration of America's unique role in a globalizing world: "And that's why America, at its best, is not just a country. It's a spiritual value and role model. . . . And that's why I believe so strongly that for globalization to be sustainable America must be at its best—today, tomorrow, all the time. It not only can be, it must be, a beacon for the whole world."[56]

These statements reveal the existence of a strong link between the market-globalist claim of inevitability and the American pursuit of global cultural hegemony. As John Gray observed, neoliberal forces have successfully "appropriated America's self-image as the model for a universal civilization in the service of a global free market."[57] In other words, history looked kindly on the "shining city on the hill" because it was listening to the voice of the market. As a reward, objective market forces chose the United States to point all other nations in the right direction. In what appeared to be the market-globalist version of the old American theme of manifest destiny, US political and business leaders proclaimed to the rest of the world: adopt our American values and neoliberal policies and you, too, can become "America."

By activating the *ideological function of integration*, market globalists favored the creation of an American-style market identity that was designed to eclipse most other components of personal, group, or class identity. As Steven Kline pointed out, global marketing efforts particularly attempt to provide young people with the identity of the consuming global teenager. Coca-Cola, Levi Strauss & Co., McDonald's, and Disney "have become the source of endless campaigns to enfranchise youth in the globalizing democracy of the market."[58] Why should mere consumers be interested in strengthening civic ties and working for global justice if such endeavors are not profitable? Why show moral restraint and solidarity if "we," the consumers, are incessantly told that we can have it all? As Benjamin Barber emphasized, by broadly endorsing happiness that comes with shopping and consuming, this market identity took on distinct cultural features because "America" and "American culture" are best-selling commodities in the global marketplace. American films, American television, American software, American music, American fast-food chains, American cars and motorcycles, American apparel, and American sports—to name but a few of those cultural commodities—are pervading the world to such an extent that even ordinary Indonesians have become convinced that they also can become "cool" by drinking Coke instead of tea. In Budapest, people are breathlessly watching *Cosby Show* reruns, and the Russian version of *Wheel of Fortune* offers lucky winners Sony DVDs into which they can load their pirated versions of wildly popular American films.[59]

And so it appears that market-globalist forces in the 1990s resurrected the nineteenth-century paradigm of Anglo-American vanguardism propagated by Herbert Spencer and William Graham Sumner. The main ingredients of classical market liberalism are all present in market globalism. We find inexorable laws of nature favoring Western civilization, the self-regulating economic model of perfect competition, the virtues of free enterprise, the vices of state interference, the principle of laissez-faire, and the irreversible, evolutionary process leading up to the survival of the fittest. And yet, market globalists translated a decidedly *global* imaginary into their concrete political agenda. Equipped with a quasi-Marxist language of historical inevitability, market globalists looked forward to the final realization of their *global* free-market utopia. They were confident that human history would end on a positive note—in spite of some undeniable risks and conflicts inherent in the process of globalization.

CLAIM NUMBER THREE: NOBODY IS IN CHARGE OF GLOBALIZATION

Market globalism's deterministic language offers another rhetorical advantage. If the natural laws of "The Market" have indeed preordained a neoliberal course of history, then globalization does not reflect the arbitrary agenda of a particular social class or group. In other words, market globalists merely carry out the unalterable imperatives of a transcendental force much larger than narrow partisan interests. People are not in charge of globalization; markets and technology are. Certain human actions might accelerate or retard globalization, but in the last instance (to paraphrase none other than Friedrich Engels), the invisible hand of the market will always assert its superior wisdom. Robert Hormats, vice chair of Goldman Sachs International, agreed: "The great beauty of globalization is that no one is in control. The great beauty of globalization is that it is not controlled by any individual, any government, any institution."[60]

In the early part of *The Lexus and the Olive Tree*, Friedman imagines himself engaged in a spirited debate with the former prime minister of Malaysia, who had accused Western powers of manipulating markets and currencies during the 1997–1998 Asian crisis in order to destroy the vibrant economies of their overseas competitors. Friedman tells his readers how he would respond to Prime Minister Mahatir Mohamad's charge:

> Ah, excuse me, Mahatir, but what planet are you living on? You talk about participating in globalization as if it were a choice you had. Globalization isn't a choice. It's a reality. . . . And the most basic truth about globalization is this: No one is in charge. . . . We all want to

believe that someone is in charge and responsible. But the global marketplace today is an Electronic Herd of often anonymous stock, bond and currency traders and multinational investors, connected by screens and networks.[61]

Of course, Friedman was right in a formal sense. There was no conscious conspiracy orchestrated by a single evil force to disempower Asian nations. But does this mean that nobody is in charge of globalization? Is it really true that the liberalization and integration of global markets proceed outside the realm of human choice? Does globalization, therefore, absolve businesses and corporations from social responsibility? Our morphological discourse analysis of Friedman's statement reveals how he utilizes a realist narrative to sell to his audience a neoliberal version of globalization. Indeed, he implied that anyone who thinks that globalization involves human choice is either hopelessly naïve or outright dangerous. Such persons might as well apply for permanent residence on Prime Minister Mohamad's alien planet.

For Friedman, the real player in the global marketplace was the Electronic Herd. But he never offered his readers a clear picture of the Herd's identity. Throughout his book, he portrayed the Herd as a faceless crowd of individual profit maximizers whose human identity remained hidden behind dim computer screens. Apparently, these traders and investors were solely interested in moneymaking; they didn't seem to be part of any politically or culturally identifiable group. Although they wielded tremendous power, they were not in charge of globalization. *Ah, excuse me, Tom, but where is the "realism" in your description?*

Writing about the importance of unfettering financial markets in the emerging global economic order, Steward Brand, the cofounder of California-based Global Business Network, also asserted that *nobody is in charge of globalization.* According to Brand, there existed "no policy body nor even an agreed-on body of theory to constrain the activity of world markets; the game continues to evolve rapidly, with none of the players ever quite sure what the new rules are."[62] Notice how this statement denies the existence of alterglobalist challengers who propose the regulation of markets. Moreover, Brand's argument implies that the "players" of the globalization "game" did not make the rules themselves. Presumably, they merely adjusted to the new rules dictated to them by the impersonal logic of evolving markets.

Neo-Marxist thinkers Michael Hardt and Antonio Negri remind their readers that it is important to be aware of the two extreme conceptions of global authority that reside on opposite ends of the ideological spectrum. One is the market-globalist notion that nobody is in charge because globalization somehow rises spontaneously out of the natural workings of the hidden hand of the world market. The other is the idea that a single evil power dictates to the world its design of globalization according to a conscious and all-seeing conspiratorial plan.[63] Both conceptions are distortions.

Still, even some neoliberal commentators conceded that the market-globalist initiative to integrate and deregulate markets around the world was sustained by asymmetrical power relations. Backed by powerful states in the North, international institutions such as the World Trade Organization, the IMF, and the World Bank enjoyed the privileged position of making and enforcing the rules of the global economy. In return for supplying much-needed loans to developing countries, the IMF and the World Bank demanded from their creditors the implementation of neoliberal policies that further the material interests of the global North.

Unleashed on developing countries in the 1990s, these policies are often referred to as the *Washington Consensus*. It consisted of a ten-point program that was originally devised and codified by John Williamson, an IMF adviser in the 1970s. The program was directed mostly at countries with large remaining foreign debts from the 1970s and 1980s, with the purpose of reforming the internal economic mechanisms of these countries so that they would be in a better position to repay the debts they had incurred. In practice, the terms of the program spelled out a new form of colonialism. The ten areas of the Washington Consensus, as defined by Williamson, required Third World governments to enforce the following reforms:

1. A guarantee of fiscal discipline and a curb to budget deficits
2. A reduction of public expenditure, particularly in the military and public administration
3. Tax reform, aiming at the creation of a system with a broad base and with effective enforcement
4. Financial liberalization, with interest rates determined by the market

   5. Competitive exchange rates to assist export-led growth
   6. Trade liberalization, coupled with the abolition of import licensing and a reduction of tariffs
   7. Promotion of foreign direct investment
   8. Privatization of state enterprises, leading to efficient management and improved performance
   9. Deregulation of the economy
  10. Protection of property rights[64]

That this program is called the "Washington Consensus" is no coincidence. The United States is by far the most dominant economic power in the world, and the world's largest TNCs are headquartered in the United States. As the British journalist Will Hutton pointed out, one of the principal aims of the Economic Security Council set up by President Clinton in 1993 was to open up ten countries to US trade and finance. Most of these "target countries" are located in Asia and the Middle East.[65] Again, this is not to say that the United States was in complete control of global financial markets and, therefore, ruled supreme over this gigantic process of globalization. But it does suggest that both the substance and the direction of economic globalization were, indeed, to a significant degree shaped by American foreign and domestic policy. As we shall see in the next chapter, this is especially true after the 9/11 attacks. Substantiation of increasing US hegemony comes from no less an observer than Friedman, who, in later passages of his book, surprisingly contradicted his previous account of a leaderless, anonymous Electronic Herd. Speaking in glowing terms about the global leadership of the United States, he suddenly acknowledged the existence of a captain at the helm of the global ship:

> The Golden Straitjacket was made in America and Great Britain. The Electronic Herd is led by American Wall Street Bulls. The most powerful agent pressuring other countries to open their markets for free trade and free investments is Uncle Sam, and America's global armed forces keep these markets and sea lanes open for this era of globalization, just as the British navy did for the era of globalization in the nineteenth century.[66]

Toward the end of his book, Friedman became even more explicit: "Indeed, McDonald's cannot flourish without McDonnell Douglas, the designer of the U.S. Air Force F-15. And the hidden fist that keeps the world safe for Silicon Valley's technologies to flourish is called the U.S. Army, Air Force, Navy, and Marine Corps. And these fighting forces and institutions are paid for by American taxpayer dollars."[67] In other words, global neoliberalism did not rely blindly on a hidden hand of the self-regulating market. When the chips were down, globalism seemed to prefer the not-so-hidden fist of US militarism.

Yet Friedman was not the only globalist who oscillates between the claim that "nobody is in charge" and the admission that "America is in control" (or that it should be). After telling a US congressional subcommittee that globalization proceeded in a neutral arena that allowed access to "many players," Joseph Gorman, chair and CEO of TRW Inc., a large Cleveland-based manufacturing and service company of high-tech products, urged his political audience to strengthen the leadership role of the United States. His ten-page statement was divided into sections that bear the following titles:

- "To win in the global economy, the United States must lead liberalization efforts."
- "International trade and investment agreements are still needed to open foreign markets for American companies and their workers."
- "If the United States is not at the table, it can't play and it can't win."
- "Success in the global economy is critical for the American economy, its companies, and its workers."
- "The global economy is real, and the United States is part of it."
- "Because the United States is the world's most competitive nation, we have the most to gain from the global economy and from trade and investment liberalization."
- "Developing countries in particular hold huge promise."[68]

The interpretive possibilities arising from a morphological discourse analysis of Gorman's testimony are almost limitless. Images of the world as a gambling table that can be accessed only by the best "players" are as telling as his neo-imperialist desire to cash in on "promising" developing nations. As far as the integrative, identity-giving function of ideology is concerned, Gorman's testimony sought to persuade its audience that one's loyalty to market principles allows one to be both a patriot defending American interests and a market globalist. Although class conflicts continue to be a very real phenomenon in the daily world of commodity production, Gorman's market rhetoric nonetheless conjured up a harmonious common identity. Businesspeople, workers, and farmers of the world unite around your consumer identity!

But if nobody is in control of globalization, why did Gorman try so hard to make a case for US leadership? One obvious answer is that the claim of a leaderless globalization process did not reflect social reality. Rather, the idea that nobody is in charge served the neoliberal political agenda of defending and expanding American global hegemony. Like the market-globalist rhetoric of historical inevitability, the portrayal of globalization as a leaderless process sought to both depoliticize the public debate on the subject and demobilize global justice movements. The deterministic language of a technological progress driven by uncontrollable market laws turned political issues into scientific problems of administration. Once large segments of the population accepted the globalist image of a self-directed juggernaut that simply runs its course, it became extremely difficult to challenge what Antonio Gramsci called the "power of the hegemonic bloc." As ordinary people ceased to believe in the possibility of choosing alternative social arrangements, market globalism gained strength in its ability to construct passive consumer identities. This tendency was further enhanced in the 1990s by assurances that globalization would bring prosperity to all parts of the world.

CLAIM NUMBER FOUR: GLOBALIZATION BENEFITS EVERYONE

This claim lies at the very core of market globalism because it provides an affirmative answer to the crucial normative question of whether globalization represents a "good" or a "bad" phenomenon. Market globalists in the 1990s frequently connected their arguments in favor of the integration of global markets to the alleged benefits resulting from the liberalization and expansion of world trade. At the 1996 G-7 Summit in Lyon, France, the heads of state and government of the seven major industrialized democracies issued a joint communiqué that contains the following passage:

> Economic growth and progress in today's interdependent world is bound up with the process of globalization. Globalization provides great opportunities for the future, not only for our countries, but for all

others too. Its many positive aspects include an unprecedented expansion of investment and trade; the opening up to international trade of the world's most populous regions and opportunities for more developing countries to improve their standards of living; the increasingly rapid dissemination of information, technological innovation, and the proliferation of skilled jobs. These characteristics of globalization have led to a considerable expansion of wealth and prosperity in the world. Hence we are convinced that the process of globalization is a source of hope for the future.[69]

The dominant discourse on globalization reverberated with such generalizations. Here are some more examples. In 1999, US Secretary of the Treasury Robert Rubin asserted that free trade and open markets provided "the best prospect for creating jobs, spurring economic growth, and raising living standards in the United States and around the world."[70] Denise Froning, trade-policy analyst at both the Center for International Trade and Economics and the Heritage Foundation, suggested that "societies that promote economic freedom create their own dynamism and foster a wellspring of prosperity that benefits every citizen."[71] Alan Greenspan, chair of the US Federal Reserve Board, insisted that "there can be little doubt that the extraordinary changes in global finance on balance have been beneficial in facilitating significant improvements in economic structures and living standards throughout the world."[72]

However, not one of these speakers addressed the ideological assumptions behind their key concepts. Who exactly is "every citizen"? What does "great opportunities" mean? As discussed in more detail in the ensuing chapter, dissenting voices argued that income disparities between nations were actually widening at a quicker pace than ever before in recent history. Two of the most thorough scientific assessments of changes in global income distribution in the 1990s arrived at sharply conflicting results. Columbia University economist Xavier Sala-i-Martin argued that his evidence showed that inequality across the world's individuals was declining, but according to World Bank economist Branko Milanovic, global inequality had risen slightly.[73] Jay Mazur, the president of the US Union of Needletrades, Industrial, and Textile Employees, argued that "the benefits of the global economy are reaped disproportionately by the handful of countries and companies that set rules and shape markets. . . . Of the 100 largest economies in the world, 51 are corporations. Private financial flows have long since surpassed public-development aid and remain remarkably concentrated."[74]

Already in the 1990s, there were many indications that the global hunt for profits actually made it more difficult for poor people to enjoy the benefits of technology and scientific innovations. Consider the following story. A group of US scientists warned the public that economic globalization might be the greatest threat to preventing the spread of parasitic diseases in sub-Saharan Africa. They pointed out that US-based pharmaceutical companies were stopping production of many antiparasitic drugs because developing countries could not afford to buy them. For example, the US manufacturer for a drug to treat bilharzia, a parasitic disease that caused severe liver damage, stopped production because of declining profits—even though the disease was thought to affect more than two hundred million people worldwide. Another drug used to combat damage caused by liver flukes was not produced because the "customer base" in the Third World did not wield enough "buying power."[75]

While some market globalists acknowledged the existence of unequal global distribution patterns, they nonetheless insisted that the market itself would eventually correct these "irregularities." As John Meehan, chair of the US Public Securities Association, put it, while such "episodic dislocations" were "necessary" in the short run, they would eventually give way to "quantum leaps in productivity."[76] Although he admitted that problems of global and domestic inequality created by such dislocations constituted a "legitimate concern," the flamboyant Speaker of the House of Representatives, Newt Gingrich, was quick to add that the "reality" of globalization was made visible in "a rising general standard of living for everybody." Ignoring the glaring contradiction arising from his recognition of global inequality while at the same time including "everybody" in the pool of globalization's beneficiaries, Gingrich launched into a masterpiece of market-globalist distortion:

> That is why people overall are generally better off than they have ever been—but in the short run, in a period of great transition those who are more successful pull away, and get even wealthier faster. But the historical pattern is that everybody else begins to catch up over time,

and I think if you know what you are doing you don't become a "have not," and if you don't know what you are doing transferring welfare to you does not solve the problem. We've got to find a way to have more people understand the information age and participate in it.[77]

In the end, Gingrich justified the real human costs of globalization as the short-term price of economic liberalization. Such ideological statements were disseminated in the 1990s to large audiences by what Benjamin Barber called the profit-oriented *infotainment telesector*. Television, radio, and the Internet frequently placed existing economic, political, and social realities within a neoliberal framework, sustaining the claim that globalization benefited everyone through omnipresent affirmative images and sound bites. As a popular television commercial suggested, "the whole world is Ford country." Market-globalist ideology appeared as "videology," the product of popular culture driven by commercial interests that incessantly instills in its audience the values, needs, and desires required for the expansion of markets.[78] The alleged benefits of globalization were also touted on television, on the Internet, and in film. Mega-shopping malls and theme parks glorified the new global market as enhancing consumer choice and facilitating individual self-realization. The 1990s also saw an enormous expansion of the celebrity "gossip market," which presented viewers and readers with the riveting private lives and heartrending troubles of global celebrities such as Paris Hilton, Lindsay Lohan, Britney Spears, and Martha Stewart. These stories became more real and newsworthy than the persistence of poverty, inequality, displacement, and environmental degradation.

Actual economic and social conditions mattered little; global media TNCs that controlled global information and communications could conjure up an ideal world of the global village inhabited by beautiful people who lived long and fulfilling lives as mindless consumers. In fact, market globalists such as Friedman even pretended to know beyond the shadow of a doubt that the poor in developing countries were itching to assume the identity of Western consumers: "[L]et me share a little secret I've learned from talking to all these folks [in the Third World]: With all due respect to revolutionary theorists, the 'wretched of the earth' want to go to Disney World—not the barricades. They want the Magic Kingdom, not *Les Misérables*."[79]

CLAIM NUMBER FIVE: GLOBALIZATION FURTHERS
THE SPREAD OF DEMOCRACY IN THE WORLD

This final market-globalist claim is anchored in the neoliberal assertion that freedom, free markets, free trade, and democracy are synonymous terms. Persistently affirmed as common sense, the compatibility of these core concepts usually went unchallenged in the public discourse of the 1990s. The most obvious strategy by which neoliberals and neo-conservatives generated popular support for the equation of democracy and the market was discrediting traditionalism and socialism. The contest with both precapitalist and the anticapitalist forms of tradition-alism, such as feudalism, had been won rather easily because the political principles of popular sovereignty and individual rights had been enshrined as the crucial catalyst for the technological and scientific achievements of modern market economies. The battle with socialism turned out to be a much tougher case. As late as the 1970s, socialism provided a powerful critique of the elitist, class-based character of liberal democracy, which asserted that a substantive form of democracy had not been achieved in capitalist societies. Since the collapse of Soviet communism in the early 1990s, however, the ideological edge shifted decisively to the defenders of a neoliberal perspective who emphasized the relationship between economic liberalization and the emergence of democratic political regimes.

Francis Fukuyama, for example, asserted that there exists a clear correlation between a country's level of economic development and successful democracy. While globalization and capital development did not automatically produce democracies, "the level of economic development resulting from globalization is conducive to the creation of complex civil societies with a powerful middle class. It is this class and societal structure that facilitates democracy."[80] But Fukuyama's argument hinges on a limited definition of democracy that emphasizes formal procedures such as voting at the expense of the direct partici-pation of broad majorities in political and economic decision making. This "thin" definition of democracy is part of what William I. Robinson identified as the Anglo-American neoliberal project of *promoting polyar-chy* in the developing world. For Robinson, the concept of polyarchy differed from the concept of "popular democracy" in that the latter posited democracy as both a process and a means to an end—a tool for devolving political and economic power from the hands of elite minorities to the masses. Polyarchy, on the other hand, represented an elitist and regimented model of "low-intensity" or "formal" market democracy. Polyarchies not only limit democratic participation to voting in elections but also require that those elected be insulated from popular pressures so that they may "effectively govern."[81]

This focus on the act of voting—in which equality prevails only in the formal sense—helps to obscure the conditions of inequality reflected in existing asymmetrical power relations in society. Formal elections provide the important function of legitimating the rule of dominant elites, thus making it more difficult for popular movements to challenge the rule of elites. The claim that globalization furthers the spread of democracy in the world was, therefore, based largely on a narrow, formal-procedural understanding of "democracy." Neoliberal economic globalization and the strategic promotion of polyarchic regimes in the Third World were two sides of the same ideological coin. They represented the systemic prerequisites for the legitimation of a full-blown world market. The promotion of polyarchy provided market globalists with the ideological opportunity to advance their neoliberal projects of economic restructuring in a language that ostensibly supported the *democratization of the world.*

Friedman's discussion of the democratic potential of globalization represented another clear example of such ideological maneuvering. Assuring his readers that globalization tended to impose democratic standards (like voting) on undemocratic countries, he argued that the integration of countries such as Indonesia and China into the global capitalist system showed that the global market forced on authoritarian regimes the rules-based business practices and legal standards they could not generate internally. Friedman coined the term *globalution* to refer to the "revolutionary process" by which the powerful Electronic Herd contributed to building the "foundation stones of democracy":

> The Electronic Herd will intensify pressures for democratization generally, for three very critical reasons—flexibility, legitimacy, and sustainability. Here's how: The faster and bigger the herd gets, the more greased and open the global economy becomes, the more flexible you need to be to get the most out of the herd and protect yourself from it. While one can always find exceptions, I still believe that as a general

rule the more democratic, accountable, and open your governance, the less likely it is that your financial system will be exposed to surprises.[82]

It is not difficult to notice the instrumentalist tone of Friedman's argument. Devoid of any moral and civic substance, democracy represented for Friedman merely the best shell for the imperatives of the market. His use of the term *accountability* hardly resonated with the idea of participatory democracy. Rather, he equated accountability with the creation of social and economic structures conducive to the business interests of the Electronic Herd. Moreover, he used "flexibility" as a code word for deregulatory measures and privatization efforts that benefited capitalist elites but threatened the economic security of ordinary citizens. Granted, the "flexibility" of labor markets may well be an important factor in attracting foreign investment, but it is hardly synonymous with the successful creation of popular-democratic institutions in developing nations.

To amplify its deeply depoliticizing effects, the market-globalist claim of democracy supercharged by globalization relied heavily on the glorification of digital technology. Innovations like the World Wide Web and mobile phones, it was asserted, would put free markets, not governments, in charge of democratization. Turbocharged by the microchip, ceaseless global flows of goods and information would empower ordinary people to improve their lives by plugging into multiplying networks capable of connecting the global to the local in both physical space and cyberspace. Leading acolytes of cybercapitalism such as Thomas Friedman lionized the new digital technologies as the cutting-edge democratic models of communication that played a crucial role in imparting "digital literacy" on a global citizenry. As the world was becoming flatter, the *New York Times* columnist asserted, the democratic ideals of accountability and transparency could be more easily achieved.[83]

CONCLUSION

Exploring the rise of market globalism, this chapter employed morphological discourse analysis to identify and analyze its five central ideological claims. Neoliberal globalization talk became canonical, solidifying into the dominant ideology of the 1990s. To sustain its claims, the market-globalist alliance of advanced economies headed by the United States habitually turned a blind eye to hard empirical data suggesting that the results of neoliberal capitalism had been highly uneven, both socially and geographically. Its institutional forms and sociopolitical consequences varied significantly across spatial scales and among major different zones of the globalizing economy. East and South Asia, for example, enjoyed impressive growth rates and rising living standards while vast regions in Africa and other parts of the global South stagnated or declined. Moreover, the dominant phalanx of market-globalist forces routinely ignored mounting evidence that corporate-led globalization was producing social inequalities at an alarming rate—both within and among nations. They also paid little attention to the troubling ecological "externalities" of neoliberal capitalism, which were most spectacularly reflected in escalating global climate change and rapid loss of biodiversity. Indeed, these ominous developments at the end of the twentieth century received only scant scrutiny from the global corporate media.

Overall, then, market globalists in the Roaring Nineties experienced little pushback to their overarching ideological vision of the economy, society, democracy, and history. They asserted that globalization would secure, once and for all, the universal rule of freedom, rights, property, and mobility enshrined in the American-led neoliberal world order. Furthermore, globalization opened up countless new economic opportunities for ordinary people, rhetorically invoked in the dominant discourse as the "hundreds of millions lifted out of poverty," rather than the top 0.1 percent of elites whose wealth had been exploding during the 1990s. Social actors critical of global capitalism were denigrated as "globalization losers"—a catchall category meant to shame those bold enough to dissent, thus disparaging any form of political resistance to an allegedly historically ordained neoliberal project. Finally, globalization was said to propel humanity toward a harmonious "Future Perfect" where rational individuals pursued their material interests largely free from government intervention; enjoyed instant access to unlimited digitalized information; and overcame the age-old tyranny of distance through new technologies of interconnectivity and hypermobility operating in both geographic and cyberspace.[84]

However, to argue that market globalism had achieved a hegemonic status by the end of the 1990s does not mean that it enjoyed undisputed ideological dominance. Gradually, there arose appealing alternative stories about globalization that also aimed to provide authoritative accounts of what the phenomenon was all about. As a result, globalism's central claims became contested both by the emerging ideologies of *justice globalism* on the political Left and by *religious globalism* on the political Right. It is the task of the next chapter to examine their respective counterarguments—and the response of market globalists to these formidable challenges.

CHAPTER 4

FIRST-WAVE CHALLENGERS IN THE 2000S

JUSTICE GLOBALISM AND RELIGIOUS GLOBALISM

In the first chapter of this book, I suggested that ideologies represent systems of ideas, values, and beliefs that make simplified claims about politics. Putting before the public a specific agenda of things to discuss (and not to discuss), various groups in society seek to advance their particular interests. I also emphasized that ideology should not be reduced to a nebulous construct floating in thin air above more material political or economic processes. Ideals, power interests, and physical entities all converge in concrete social practices that are both ideational and material. At the onset of the global age, market globalism—and its modified imperial version—emerged as the dominant ideology, chiseling into the minds of many people around the world a particular understanding of globalization, which, in turn, was sustained and re-confirmed by pro-market governments.

But no single ideational system ever enjoys absolute dominance. Battered by persistent gales of socioeconomic change and political dissent, the small fissures and ever-present inconsistencies in all political ideologies threaten to turn into major cracks and serious contradictions. Growing gaps between the assertions of the ideologues and the lived experience of ordinary people usher in long-term crises for the hegemonic paradigm. At the same time, however, such systemic crises also represent a golden opportunity for disadvantaged social groups to propagate new ideas, beliefs, practices, and institutions.

At the end of the Roaring Nineties, arguments critical of market globalism began to receive more play in the public discourse on globalization. This development was aided by a heightened awareness of how extreme corporate profit strategies were leading to widening global disparities in wealth and well-being. Market globalism encountered a serious challenger on the *political Left* in the form of *justice globalism*. Aware of the power of discourse, justice globalists attacked market globalism by branding it *corporate globalization* and *globalization-from-above*.

But the first decade of the new century also saw the rise of another challenger of market globalism from the *political Right* in the form of *religious globalism*. While this fledgling thought-system is not tied to one specific religion, the Islamist *salafi* variant of religious globalism—a strict orthodox doctrine advocating a return to the early Islam of the Qur'an propagated by al Qaeda that gained tremendous publicity in the wake of the 9/11 attacks—emerged as perhaps the most significant manifestation of religious globalism. However, this chapter's focus on jihadist globalism is neither meant to downplay the diversity of ideational currents within Islamism nor to present this particular strain as its most representative or authentic manifestation. Rather, my selection of jihadist globalism as articulated by groups such as al Qaeda, ISIS, al-Shabab, Boko Haram, the Taliban, Jemaah Islamiyah, and others simply reflects the tremendous influence of their doctrine around the world.

Before we survey the pertinent political context of the 2000s and analyze the ideational morphologies of both justice globalism and jihadist globalism in more detail, let us briefly reflect on the enduring significance of the ideological distinction between the political Left and Right.

THE SIGNIFICANCE OF THE
LEFT-RIGHT DISTINCTION

The distinction between the political Left and Right originated in the *French National Assembly* at the outset of the revolutionary period in the late eighteenth century. Those representatives favoring radical change in the direction of more equal social arrangements congregated on the left side, or "wing," of the chamber, whereas those arguing for the traditional status quo gathered on the right wing. Deputies supporting only moderate change sat in the center. The world's political landscape has changed dramatically since 1789, and reliance on the old Left-Right metaphor as an indicator for contemporary ideological differences has undergone growing criticism, especially after the collapse of the Soviet Union in 1991.

Consciously linking his reappraisal of the Left-Right divide to this momentous event, Anthony Giddens suggested in the early 1990s that these traditional labels "Right" and "Left" had come to mean different things in different social and geographical contexts. In particular, the British sociologist maintained that it was very problematic to refer to market globalism as a "right-wing ideology." After all, he noted, neoliberal programs tend to undermine the sanctity of tradition and custom by supporting radical processes of change stimulated by the incessant expansion of markets. On the other hand, neoliberalism did depend on the persistence of some traditional values for its legitimacy. Its attachment to conservative norms was particularly obvious in the areas of religion, gender, and the family.[1]

Likewise, Giddens continued, the fuzzy boundary between the political Left and Right was also reflected in the eclectic value structures of new social movements such as environmentalism and feminism. Hence, he concluded that the Left-Right metaphor retained only limited validity in the contemporary political discourse:

> No doubt, the differentiation of left and right—which from the beginning has been a contested distinction in any case—will continue to exist in the practical contexts of party politics. Here its prime meaning, in many societies at least, differs from what it used to be, given that the neoliberal right has come to advocate the rule of markets, while the left favors more public provision and public welfare: straddling the ground

of left and right, as we know, is a diversity of other parties, sometimes linked to social movements. But does the distinction between left and right retain any core meaning when taken out of the mundane environment of orthodox politics? It does, but only on a very general plane. On the whole, the right is more happy to tolerate the existence of inequalities than the left, and more prone to support the powerful than the powerless. This contrast is real and remains important. But it would be difficult to push it too far, or make it one of overriding principle.[2]

Around the same time Giddens made these comments, however, Norberto Bobbio published a celebrated defense of the continued significance of this political distinction in *Left and Right*, an enormously successful book that sold hundreds of thousands of copies in Europe. The seasoned Italian political thinker argued that it was the attitude of political groups toward the ideal of equality that constituted the most important criterion in distinguishing between the Left and the Right. According to Bobbio, members of the political Left had historically shown support for the idea that political and social institutions are socially constructed. Hence, they emphasized the power of human reason to devise workable schemes for the reduction of social inequalities such as power, wealth, educational opportunity, and so on. But, according to Bobbio, this did not mean that all members of the Left favored the complete elimination of all forms of inequality; only extreme leftists embraced such a radical position.

Representatives of the political Right, on the other hand, were more reluctant to support policies that reduce existing social inequalities. Bobbio argued that they consider many of these inequalities legitimate because they saw them as anchored in a largely unalterable "natural order" anchored in religious beliefs. Skeptical of the power of reason to change social arrangements without seriously undermining social stability, the Right affirmed existing social arrangements based on custom, tradition, and the force of the past. Only extremist members of the Right were opposed to all social change; others supported change, provided that it occurs in a slow, incremental fashion over a long period of time. Thus, Bobbio suggested that the distinction between Left and Right was based on deep-seated values, whereas the contrast between extremism and moderation pertains to the method of social change.[3]

Although the Italian thinker conceded that the line dividing the Left and the Right always shifted with changing historical circumstances, he nonetheless emphasized that this distinction—anchored in two fundamentally different perspectives on *equality*—retained its significance even in our postcommunist era of globalization:

> The communist left was not the only left; there was—and still is—another left within the capitalist horizon. The distinction has a long history which goes back long before the contrast between capitalism and communism. The distinction still exists, and not, as someone jested, simply on road signs. It pervades newspapers, radio, television, public debates, and specialized magazines on economics, politics, and sociology in a manner which is almost grotesque. If you look through the papers to see how many times the words "left" and "right" appear, even just in headlines, you will come up with a good crop.[4]

In 2008, Alain Noël and Jean-Philippe Therien published a sophisticated defense of the Left-Right distinction that extended Bobbio's thesis to *global politics*. Drawing on the 1999–2001 World Values Survey—a worldwide database covering cultural and political trends in seventy-eight countries—the Canadian political scientists found that the Left-Right scheme was not only consistently evoked in the global public sphere but also corresponded to clearly distinct perspectives on equality, justice, and social protection. Thus, they concluded that this ideological divide had survived the transformation of class structures of the past two centuries as well as the more recent rise of new postmaterialist values in advanced democracies. In short, this binary has endured into the age of globalization and continues to help people around the world integrate into coherent patterns their attitudes and ideas about politics.[5]

In this chapter, I follow the lead of Bobbio as well as Noël and Therien by classifying market globalism's challengers according to this enduring Left-Right distinction. I particularly agree with these authors' central contention that today's conflicting political worldviews—especially on the issues of *global justice and equality*—justify the drawing of this distinction. In our global age, the existing differences between these two camps has remained significant enough to distinguish between justice globalists on the political Left and jihadist globalists on the political Right.

As I will explain in chapter 5, *national populists* also constitute a significant group of right-wing critics of market globalism. However, unlike justice globalists and jihadist globalists, they fail to draw on the rising *global imaginary* in their ideological articulation of a concrete political agenda. Clinging to a destabilizing *national imaginary*, national populists represent a growing group of detractors with genuinely *antiglobalization* views—rather than the *alterglobalization* perspectives of justice globalists and religious globalists.

THE POLITICAL CONTEXT OF
JUSTICE GLOBALISM IN THE 2000s

In the early 1990s, left-wing social activists around the world reacted to the collapse of communism with a mixture of despair, embarrassment, and relief. Although most of them were glad to see the authoritarian Soviet regime exit the world stage for good, they had hoped that Mikhail Gorbachev's *perestroika* (economic restructuring) and *glasnost* (openness) reforms would result in the transformation of Russian totalitarianism into a Scandinavian-style social democracy. When it became clear that the successor states of the Soviet Empire would be subjected to a humiliating capitalist shock therapy administered by neoliberal elites in the United States and Europe, the democratic Left found itself searching for new ideas and engaged in what social movement expert Sidney Tarrow calls *global framing*—a flexible form of "global thinking" that connected local or national grievances to the larger context of *global justice, global inequalities*, and *world peace*. Tarrow argues that most of these left-wing activists could be characterized as *rooted cosmopolitans* because they remained embedded in their domestic environments while at the same time developing a global consciousness as a result of vastly enhanced contacts to like-minded individuals and organizations across national borders.[6]

Most of these would later point to a number of events in the 1990s that had a galvanizing impact on the formation of a "global justice movement" (GJM) that began to cohere ideologically through its opposition to market globalism. The first event was the 1994 uprising of the Zapatista Army of National Liberation in their native province of Chiapas in southern Mexico against the initiation of the North American Free Trade Agreement (NAFTA). The "Zapatistas" stitched together an interpretive framework that presented their rebellion as an act of popular resistance against their government's free-trade policies. Engaging in effective global framing, their leader, Subcomandante Marcos, announced to the world that the local struggle in Chiapas was of global significance: "[W]e will make a collective network of all our particular struggles and resistances. An intercontinental network of resistance against neoliberalism, an intercontinental network of resistance for humanity."[7] Keeping their promise, the Zapatistas managed to get their message out to other progressive forces around the world. Their efforts culminated in the 1996 First Intercontinental Meeting for Humanity and Against Neoliberalism held in the jungles of Chiapas and attended by more than 4,000 participants from nearly thirty countries. The conference set into motion further initiatives that sensitized millions of people to the suffering of poor peasants in the global South caused by market-globalist policies. Indeed, the creation of the global "Zapatista solidarity network" served as a model for dozens of other alliances that vowed to challenge "neoliberal" globalization "from below."

A second significant catalyst in the formation of justice globalism was the devastating Asian economic crisis of 1997. In the early 1990s, the governments of Thailand, Indonesia, Malaysia, South Korea, and the Philippines had gradually abandoned their control over the domestic movement of capital in order to attract foreign direct investment. Intent on creating a stable monetary environment, they raised domestic interest rates and linked their national currency to the value of the US dollar. The ensuing influx of foreign investments translated into soaring stock and real estate markets all over Southeast Asia. However, by 1997, many investors realized that prices had become inflated far beyond their actual value. They panicked and withdrew a total of $105 billion from these countries within days, forcing governments in the region to abandon the dollar peg. Unable to halt the ensuing free fall of their currencies, those governments used up nearly all their foreign exchange reserves. As a result, economic output fell, unemployment increased, and wages plummeted. Foreign banks and creditors reacted by declining new credit applications and refusing to extend existing loans. By the end of 1997, the entire region found itself in the throes of a financial crisis that threatened to wreak havoc on the global economy. Disaster was narrowly averted by a combination of international bailout packages and the immediate sale of

Southeast Asian commercial assets to foreign corporate investors at rock-bottom prices. In addition to wrecking the regional economy for years to come, the crisis also caused serious ideological damage. Power elites and ordinary citizens alike had been treated to an ominous preview of the 2008 Global Financial Crisis: what a world run on unfettered market-globalist principles might look like.

Finally, the formation of justice globalism owed much to a spectacular series of strikes that hit France and other parts of Europe from 1995 to 1998. Protesting government policies that had driven up unemployment while reducing social services, the striking workers and public employees received tremendous support from these new Left networks. Lasting alliances between unions and environmentalists were forged, and many new multi-issue coalitions were born. One of these novel organizational networks was the *Association pour une taxation des transactions financiers pour l'aide aux citoyens* (Association for the Taxation of Financial Transactions for the Aid of Citizens [ATTAC]). ATTAC began to draft comprehensive proposals for the elimination of offshore corporate tax havens, the blanket forgiveness of developing countries' debts, and the radical restructuring of the major international economic institutions, including the International Monetary Fund (IMF) and the World Trade Organization (WTO). But its core demand was the leveling of a *Tobin Tax*, named after its inventor, the Nobel Prize–winning economist James Tobin, on international short-term financial transactions, with proceeds going to the global South. If introduced globally, a tax from 0.1 to 0.25 percent on these transactions might have raised up to US$250 billion. Within a few years, ATTAC grew into an impressive alliance with tens of thousands of members and autonomous branches in more than fifty countries.

This potent combination of growing global activism and spectacular market failures in Asia and Europe created larger discursive and political openings for the fledgling GJM, which had become confident enough to call on its mass membership to organize protests at official international meetings of high-profile market-globalist institutions like the IMF, the World Bank, the G-7 (after 1998, the G-8), the World Economic Forum (WEF), or the WTO. The first large-scale confrontation between the forces of market globalism and its challengers on the Left came in late 1999, when 50,000 people representing labor, human rights, and environmental groups took part in the anti-WTO protests in Seattle, Washington.

In spite of the predominance of North American participants, there was also a significant international presence. In fact, the transnational character of the Seattle demonstrations was a central feature that distinguished it from other mass protests in the recent past. Activists such as José Bové, a charismatic French sheep farmer who became an international celebrity for trashing a McDonald's outlet, marched shoulder to shoulder with Indian farmers and leaders of the Philippines' peasant movement. Clearly articulating justice-globalist concerns, this eclectic alliance criticized the WTO's neoliberal position on agriculture, multilateral investments, and intellectual property rights.[8] The ensuing street clashes between demonstrators and with the police—dubbed the *Battle of Seattle*—received extensive news coverage, ultimately making headlines both in the United States and abroad.

The Battle of Seattle—and the series of similar demonstrations that followed in the early 2000s—had a number of significant impacts. First, buoyed by the street demonstrators, many WTO delegates of developing countries refused to support the neoliberal agenda that had been drafted behind closed doors by the major economic powers led by the United States. While emphasizing the "obvious benefits of free trade and globalization," even the pro-market Clinton administration admitted that the WTO needed to implement "some internal reforms." For example, US Trade Representative Charlene Barshefsky conceded that "we found that the WTO has outgrown the processes appropriate to an earlier time. . . . We needed a process which had a greater degree of internal transparency and inclusion to accommodate a larger and more diverse membership."[9]

Second, the large-scale GJM protests of the early 2000s showed that many of the new technologies hailed by market globalists as the true hallmark of globalization could also be employed in the service of justice-globalist forces and their political agenda. For example, the Internet enabled the organizers of the Seattle protest to arrange for new forms of protests, such as a series of demonstrations held in concert in various cities around the globe. Justice-globalist groups and networks all over the world learned to utilize the Internet to readily and rapidly recruit new members, establish dates, share experiences, arrange logistics, and identify and publicize targets—activities that only a decade earlier would have demanded much more time and money. Other new technologies such as sophisticated cell phones allowed demonstrators not only to maintain close contact throughout an event but also to react quickly and effectively to shifting police tactics. This enhanced ability to arrange and coordinate protests without the need of a central command, a clearly defined leadership, a large bureaucracy, and significant financial resources added an entirely new dimension to the nature of justice-globalist street demonstrations. Moreover, cheap and easy access to global information raised the protesters' level of knowledge and sophistication. Justice-globalist teach-ins and street-theater performances, organized by various groups via the Internet, were particularly successful in recruiting college students for international anti-sweatshop campaigns.

Third, the new wave of justice-globalist demonstrations also vindicated the old egalitarian vision of forging nonhierarchical alliances among progressive groups—even among those who shared a rather antagonistic history. Perhaps the best example of this new spirit of coalition building on the Left was the willingness of labor unions and environmental groups to advance a common justice-globalist agenda. There were many signs of this new cooperation among protesters in major world cities. For example, union leaders learned a crucial lesson: the best way of challenging the established framework of market globalism was to build a broad international support network that includes workers, environmentalists, consumer advocates, and human-rights activists.[10]

Finally, the alterglobalization demonstrations at the turn of the twenty-first century also served as a vital catalyst in the 2001 creation of the World Social Forum (WSF) in Porto Alegre, Brazil. Indeed, the WSF has become a central organizing space for tens of thousands of justice globalists who delighted in their annual "counter-summit" to the January meeting of the market-globalist WEF in the exclusive Swiss ski resort of Davos. Designed as an "open meeting place," the WSF encouraged and facilitated a free exchange of ideas among scholars and activists dedicated to challenging the neoliberal framework of globalization-from-above. In particular, the WSF sought to accomplish two fundamental tasks. The first was ideological, reflected in concerted efforts to undermine the premises of the reigning market-globalist worldview. WSF member organizations constructed and disseminated alternative articulations of the global imaginary based on the anti-neoliberal core principles of the WSF. The second task was political, manifested in the attempt to realize these principles by means of mass mobilizations and nonviolent direct action aimed at transforming the core structures of market globalism: international economic institutions such as the WTO and the IMF, transnational corporations and affiliated NGOs, and large industry federations and lobbies. Academic observers such as Mary Kaldor related the rise of the WSF to what they saw as the birth of a *global civil society*—"groups, networks and movements which comprise the mechanisms through which individuals negotiate and renegotiate social contracts or political bargains on a global level."[11]

Unfortunately, however, the massive alterglobalization protests all over the world also served as a convenient excuse for neoliberal governments to radicalize their police forces. Worried about their continued viability, market globalists—contrary to their laissez-faire philosophy—increasingly supported the state's coercive power against dissenters. The growing brutality and arbitrariness of police actions became especially evident at the January 2001 WEF meeting in Davos. Determined to prevent a repetition of the "embarrassing events" of the year before, Swiss authorities pledged to keep protesters out of the alpine village. In what has been described as the country's largest security operation since World War II, Swiss border units refused entry to thousands of people—often merely on the suspicion that these individuals might be participating in anti-WEF demonstrations. Police and military units set up dozens of roadblocks on all roads leading to Davos. They halted all train services to the town and placed thousands of police and military troops on alert.[12] But the harsh treatment of peaceful protesters received intense criticism from within Switzerland and abroad.

A second example of this ominous turn toward *hard power* is even more drastic. At the 2001 G-8 Summit in Genoa, the Italian government employed a contingent of over 16,000 police and military troops to "guarantee the safety" of the delegates. As world leaders were feasting on sea bass and champagne aboard a luxury liner safely anchored in the city's harbor, dozens of demonstrators and police were injured in street clashes. Twenty-three-year-old Carlo Giuliani, one of thousands of protesters taking to the streets of the Mediterranean port city, was shot to death by a twenty-year-old *carabinieri*. The official reaction from attending politicians was mixed, with French President Jacques Chirac wondering what was prompting so many people to turn up in the streets. However, the general tenor of the comments was predictable. Expressing his sorrow at this "tragic loss of life," Italian President Azeglio Ciampi urged the demonstrators to "immediately cease this blind violence." Prime Minister Silvio Berlusconi and President George W. Bush quickly followed suit, arguing that both violent and nonviolent protesters embraced "policies that lock poor people into poverty."[13]

The transnational corporate media legitimized these elite views by broadcasting images from Genoa that focused not on police brutality but almost entirely on the unruly behavior of relatively few hard-core anarchists. It seemed to be of little concern to the powerful media voices of neoliberalism that the overwhelming majority of those people who participated in the series of justice-globalist demonstrations from Seattle to Genoa were firmly committed to nonviolent means of protest. Nor was it big news when Italian Green Party Senator Francisco Martone told the BBC that he had credible evidence for the Italian government's use of infiltrators and provocateurs both to cement the public image of violent, cobblestone-throwing "Black Bloc" anarchists and to justify extreme police reactions. Finally, there were credible reports of police collusion with radical right-wing organizations, including neofascist groups, not to speak of subsequent political persecution of several protest organizers. And yet, two months later, the Italian parliament approved a report absolving the police of wrongdoing during the G-8 Summit.[14]

After al Qaeda's devastating attacks on the world's most recognized symbols of a US-dominated globalized economy and culture, this new tendency to tolerate or endorse hard-power tactics grew even stronger. In the volatile post-9/11 environment in the United States, President George W. Bush abandoned the mildly isolationist position he espoused during the 2000 election campaign and instead adopted the bellicose views of inveterate hard-power advocates such as Dick Cheney and Donald Rumsfeld. As discussed later in this chapter, their attempts to stabilize the neoliberal model by means of generating fear and demands for greater security were increasingly reflected in market-globalist discourse. Globalizing markets were now portrayed as requiring protection against the violent hordes of irrationalism. In other words, the allegedly "inevitable" and "irreversible" unfolding of self-regulating markets suddenly needed to be helped along by strong law enforcement measures that would "beat back" the enemies of democracy and the free market.

In the first few months following the 9/11 attacks, even dyed-in-the-wool justice globalists like the Canadian progressive journalist Naomi Klein worried that the cataclysmic events of that day might have a negative effect on the size and strength of the GJM. Suddenly, she noted, obituaries of the movement appeared in newspapers around the world, proclaiming that "anti-globalization is so yesterday."[15] Indeed, most demonstrations planned for September and October 2001 were canceled in deference to the mood of mourning and out of fear of stepped-up police violence. Moreover, the November 2001 WTO meeting had been arranged in remote Doha, the capital of the tiny Persian Gulf state of Qatar. Only a handful of carefully picked representatives of nongovernmental organizations was allowed into the country.

As the initial shock of 9/11 slowly wore off in 2002, justice-globalist protesters returned to various meetings of international economic organizations, although their numbers were generally smaller than before the attacks. At the same time, the continuation of worldwide terrorist attacks throughout the 2000s facilitated the convergence of the neoconservative security agenda and the market-globalist economic project. However, the American drive toward war in Iraq backfired and led to the accelerating merger of the anti–Global War on Terror movement and the GJM. The rapid growth of a united Left front against market globalism and militarism was particularly apparent at the October 2002 IMF and World Bank meeting in Washington, DC. More than fifteen thousand protesters carried signs and chanted slogans such as "No more wars, no more corporate exploitation" or "Drop the debt, not bombs." This blending of peace issues and the antiglobalist agenda culminated in early 2003 when it became clear that the Bush administration was set on a collision course with Iraq. On February 15, 2003, an estimated fifteen to twenty million people in over sixty countries—a remarkable conglomerate of peace activists and justice globalists—took to the streets to register their firm opposition to a US-led war against Iraq. Cities like London and Barcelona registered the largest crowds of protesters in their entire history.

At the 2004 WSF meeting in Mumbai, India, the global peace movement and justice globalists joined forces after making the event a transnational coordination space for the worldwide protest against the

Iraq War. At that meeting, a variety of new initiatives was discussed, including the idea of launching a World Parliamentary Forum. Most importantly, the conference participants stressed the importance of poking holes in the dominant market-globalist discourse and disseminating to people around the world a coherent "alterglobalist" vision. As Bernard Cassen, a co-organizer of the WSF meetings and president of ATTAC, put it, "We are here to show the world that a different world is possible."[16] In 2005, the WSF returned to Porto Alegre and drew a record number of participants. The year 2006 saw a series of large-scale continental social forums rather than a global forum, but the 2007 WSF meeting was once again a unified event held in Nairobi, Kenya. In 2008, a "Global Action Day" replaced the global forum, but another successful and well-attended WSF meeting was held in 2009 in Belém, Brazil.

WHAT DOES THE GLOBAL JUSTICE MOVEMENT WANT? EXAMINING THE CORE CONCEPTS AND CENTRAL CLAIMS OF JUSTICE GLOBALISM

Turning now from the political context in which the GJM operated in the 2000s to an examination of the ideological structure of justice globalism, I apply the same methodological tool I used in the previous chapter to analyze market globalism: *morphological discourse analysis* (MDA). Given the centrality of the WSF as the core site for the generation of the core concepts and central claims, it makes sense to shine our analytical spotlight on texts generated by the roughly 150 civil society organizations from around the world associated with the WSF. After all, there is virtual unanimous agreement in the authoritative literature on the significance of the WSF as the intellectual and organizational epicenter of the GJM, constituting its largest and most diverse organizational umbrella.[17] These organizations represent different interests, possess distinctive structures, pursue various projects, and are based in different geographical regions. They include labor unions (such as the Australian ACTU and the American AFL-CIO), environmental groups (such as Greenpeace), agricultural co-ops (such as the All Arab Peasants and Agricultural Cooperatives Union), think tanks and educational organizations (such as Focus on the Global South and the Transnational Institute), indigenous peoples' assemblies (such as Congreso Nacional Indigena de Mexico), financial watchdog groups (such as ATTAC and Bankwatch Network), feminist and women's networks (such as World March of Women), human-rights organizations (such as Public Citizen and Oxfam International), religiously affiliated groups (such as Caritas International), migration associations (such as the Forum des Organisations de Solidarité Internationale Issues des Migrations), peace networks (such as Peace Boat), alternative public policy organizations (such as Global Policy Network), global democracy advocacy groups (such as the Network Institute for Global Democratization), North-South networks (such as North-South Centre and Solidar), and poor people's movements (such as Poor People's Economic Human Rights Campaign).

The WSF brings together a vast diversity of social sectors, spanning North and South, crossing a range of linguistic divides. It is also politically diverse: unlike other global justice formations, it draws together a broad range of political orientations and tendencies. Although much of its membership is in Latin America, Europe, and North America, there is also significant involvement from African and Asian groups. Indeed, no other global justice coalition comes close to the geographical, ethnic, and linguistic reach and diversity existing at the WSF. Diverse as they are in many respects, these organizations nonetheless inhabit overlapping discursive spaces—framed around the resistance to corporate globalization and its social and environmental impacts—from which they address various transnational publics.

Unlike other large global justice coalitions, the WSF was consciously established as an *ideological* antithesis to the market-globalist WEF. Indeed, the fourteen clauses of its Charter of Principles constitute a particularly rich source for our search of justice-globalist *core concepts*. The charter invokes in its first clause a global "we" defined as "social forces from around the world" and "organizations and movements of civil society from all the countries in the world" that are committed to "building a planetary society directed toward fruitful relationships among humankind and between it and the Earth." These general declarations of global subjectivity are then further specified in a special 2001 WSF "Call to Mobilization" to "women and men, farmers, workers, unemployed, professionals, students, blacks, and indigenous peoples, coming from the South and from the North."[18]

Thus, the movement's affirmation of a "global we" becomes tied to its irreducible plurality and diversity. In her careful analysis of five similar documents authored by transnational networks that belong to different sectors of the GJM, Donatella della Porta also underlines the construction of a global collective self respectful of differences of views and cultural and political traditions: "[M]ultifacetedness becomes an intrinsic element of the movement's collective identity, so intrinsic that it becomes implicit."[19] Clause 8 of the charter drives home this point by declaring, "The World Social Forum is a plural, diversified, non-confessional, nongovernmental, and nonparty context that, in a decentralized fashion, interrelates organizations and movements engaged in concrete action at levels from the local to the international to build another world." Insisting that the means must be consistent with the end, the charter claims to translate its commitment to diversity and decentralization through "nonviolent social resistance" to corporate globalization. The values of justice globalism are clearly spelled out in the charter's imperative to "solve the problems of exclusion and social inequality that the process of capitalist globalization with its racist, sexist, and environmentally destructive dimensions is creating internationally and within countries." Committed to the ideal of "planetary citizenship," the WSF encourages its participant organizations and movements to introduce into the global agenda "change-inducing practices" for the "building of a new world in solidarity." In short, the charter is rooted in core ideas and values that call for a transformation of current global social structures that is fundamentally different from the "inevitable" economic integration along market-globalist lines.[20]

Indeed, the justice-globalist critique of the dominant neoliberal paradigm relies on concepts that buttress an *alternative worldview*, which sees the liberalization and global integration of markets as leading to greater social inequalities, environmental destruction, the escalation of global conflicts and violence, the weakening of participatory forms of democracy, the proliferation of self-interest and consumerism, and the further marginalization of the powerless around the world. The charter makes clear that the crucial ideological task of the GJM is to undermine the premises and ideological framework of the reigning neoliberal worldview by disseminating an alternative translation of the global imaginary based on these central ideas and values of the WSF: *transformative change, equality, social justice, diversity, democracy, nonviolence, solidarity, ecological sustainability, and planetary citizenship.* Indeed, the most comprehensive study of the ideological structure of the GJM strongly confirms these principles as the commonly shared core concepts of justice globalism.[21]

Having identified the core ideological concepts of our chosen GJM organizations, our next task is to explore how these concepts are linked in effective ideological claims that produce particular meanings. As noted in the previous chapter, we seek to determine the ability of globalisms to "lock in" meanings in the form of "decontestation chains" that assert and normalize what counts as "correct" and "real" in the global political environment.

Pertinent research shows that GJM organizations did, indeed, formulate a number of such central ideological claims.[22] They address both the alleged causes of current global problems and the meanings of core concepts by linking them in simple—and sometimes simplistic—and reiterated phrases and slogans. Most WSF-affiliated organizations managed to embed these assertions so deeply within their discursive practices that they became taken-for-granted "truths" that inspired and oriented social activists in their political struggle against market globalism. These meaning structures rooted in the core concepts can be compressed into *five central ideological claims of justice globalism*. It is important to bear in mind that these assertions represent composites of discourses that were most common and most often repeated across WSF-connected organizations. While rarely appearing verbatim in the texts, these claims nonetheless constitute realistic meaning structures derived from the linked core concepts assembled by each organization.

CLAIM NUMBER ONE:
NEOLIBERALISM PRODUCES GLOBAL CRISIS

The identification of the economic doctrine of neoliberalism as the basic cause of contemporary global crises constitutes the foundation of four claims of justice globalism. As we discussed earlier, the GJM developed originally as both a reaction against and a critique of neoliberalism. Hence, it should not be surprising that the political ideology of the GJM relied on a foundational claim that blames neoliberalism for producing global crises. But in what, precisely, lies the failure of neoliberalism? The textual samples of our chosen organizations point unmistakably to both ethical shortcomings and biased economic practices. For the GJM, neoliberalism failed ethically because it put the needs of markets and corporations ahead of the needs of individuals, families, communities, and nation-states. It came up short economically because the flawed policies of privatization, deregulation, and liberalization neither benefited ordinary people nor lifted the poorest populations of developing countries out of poverty. Instead, the GJM argument goes, poverty became more entrenched and social inequalities dramatically increased around the world. Indeed, the claim that neoliberal measures at the heart of market globalism must be held responsible for global crises emerged as the most common and consistent allegation across all forty-five organizations. The following quotations taken from the WSF-affiliated organization *Focus on the Global South* provide clear examples for the articulation of this foundational claim:

> The global financial system is unraveling at great speed. This is happening in the midst of a multiplicity of crises in relation to food, climate and energy. It severely weakens the power of the US and the EU, and the global institutions they dominate, particularly the International Monetary Fund, the World Bank and the World Trade Organization. Not only is the legitimacy of the neoliberal paradigm in question, but the very future of capitalism itself.[23]

A press statement issued by the *Congress of South African Trade Unions* (COSATU) conveys a similar message:

> COSATU regrets that the G20 meeting did not clearly acknowledge that the global economic crisis has been caused by the policies of the Washington Consensus, which propagated a "one-size-fits-all" economic model based on withdrawal of the state from the economy, emphasis on market fundamentalism, deregulation, privatization, trade liberalization, cuts in government spending, and high interest rates, implemented through lending conditions attached to IMF and World Bank loans for poor countries.

The major rationales for claim one are usually based on the forging of semantic linkages between the justice-globalist core concepts of equality, participatory democracy, universal rights, and social justice. The contextual narrative binding these building blocks often suggests that decisions made by powerful corporate elites have had a directly detrimental impact on a majority of the people on the planet. Had decision-making processes been more bottom-up and participatory, the WSF-connected organizations implied, such global crises might have never materialized. In addition, they frequently criticized the conceptual singularity ("one-size-fits-all") of neoliberalism's "free market" approach and the Eurocentric arrogance underlying its assumption of universal applicability.

Moreover, these organizations contrasted the dominant neoliberal position unfavorably with their preferred justice-globalist vision of more democratic economic approaches that empowered citizens to regulate markets in various ways in their quest for a more equitable generation and distribution of wealth. Constant repetitions of claim one in its countless mutations turned the allegation of neoliberalism's failure into a taken-for-granted "truth." This ideological foundation of justice globalism then served as the conceptual fertilizer for its other ideological claims while at the same time supporting a vigorous campaign for finding political alternatives.

CLAIM NUMBER TWO: MARKET-DRIVEN GLOBALIZATION HAS INCREASED WORLDWIDE DISPARITIES IN WEALTH AND WELL-BEING

Extending beyond the statement that neoliberalism caused global crises, claim two makes more specific assertions with regard to the social impact of market globalism. It is not difficult to see the semantic link between the condemnation of market globalism and the core concepts of equality and social justice. The latter, with its imperatives of restoration, reconciliation, and redistribution, implies a concern for individual and community well-being and the recognition of human rights. Thus containing a far broader meaning range than merely pointing out material inequalities, claim two reflects the GJM's conviction that existing disparities of wealth and well-being are fundamentally unjust because they violate universal norms of fairness. A number of organizations linked to the WSF also asserted that market-driven globalization was unsustainable because it created not only acute discrepancies in the social world but also severe imbalances in our planet's natural environment.

It is also noteworthy that this claim's emphasis on fundamental disparities implied the importance of solidarity with the disadvantaged.

For example, the America-wide social movement *Allianza Social Continental* issued the following statement:

> Neoliberal economics and its by-products, such as damage to the environment, grossly lowered production, especially of some nations' agricultural production, unemployment, and the dramatic increase in migration, have created the cultural and socio-economic conditions that through factors like poor nutrition and psychological stress cause disease in affected populations. Additionally, health care system reforms imposed by the World Bank and the International Monetary Fund with their emphasis on privatization and decentralization of health care services have destroyed the already deficient hospital care infrastructure and the existing systems of control of diseases like malaria and tuberculosis and have eliminated access to medical services for those most in need of such services.

As this passage shows, claim two carries an important emotional charge designed to confront the reader with the real-life devastation caused by the vigorous application of neoliberal doctrine during the last three decades. Like all ideologies, justice globalism generates claims designed to connect the rational and emotional aspects of human perception on the basis of concrete examples and illustrations that everyone can readily grasp. Invoking the specter of losing basic medical services, for example, creates strong anxieties for most people that easily cut across class lines or ethnic divisions.

Finally, some organizations noted a vexing paradox: while disparities in wealth and well-being produce disempowered and disenfranchised human beings, they also heighten people's awareness that alternatives must be found. As expressed in the next claim, both the formulation and application of such alternatives require broad democratic participation.

CLAIM NUMBER THREE: DEMOCRATIC PARTICIPATION IS ESSENTIAL FOR SOLVING GLOBAL PROBLEMS

Privileging justice globalism's core concept of participatory democracy, this claim implies that the rectification of the substantial disparities created by market globalism can only be achieved through bottom-up decision-making processes that consciously address the multiple global crises of our time. Most of the WSF-affiliated organizations expected social disparities and ecological imbalances to worsen in the future and thus called for collective action against the major institutions of market globalism. Once again, the core concept of participatory democracy assumes a central position in moving these GJM groups from mere rhetoric—the diagnosis of shortcomings and the blaming of market globalism—to concrete political action tackling such recalcitrant global problems as poverty, irregular migration, poor health care, and environmental degradation.

Indeed, the call for multiple models of participatory democracy on a local-global scale represents a crucial conceptual bridge that connects social activists residing in the richer countries of the Northern Hemisphere to the principal victims of distributive injustice in the global South. WSF-connected organizations recognized that democratic resistance was not guaranteed to weaken, yet nevertheless facilitated the articulation of alternatives to the dominant discourse. As the organization *Focus on the Global South* asserts,

> The false solutions to climate change—such as carbon offsetting, carbon trading for forests, agro-fuels, trade liberalization and privatization pushed by governments, financial institutions, and multinational corporations—have been exposed. Affected communities, indigenous peoples, women and peasant farmers have long called for real solutions to the climate crisis, solutions which have failed to capture the attention of political leaders.

The Brussels-based *International Trade Union Confederation* posted a similar statement on its website: "Central to [avoiding a return to the politics of greed] is restoring the role of government in regulating the private sector, and ensuring public provision to meet fundamental social needs."

In addition to embracing "participatory democracy," then, claim three also puts into operation the concept of transformative change by calling for a fundamental shift away from contemporary forms of representative democracy mired in "politics-as-usual." Indeed, the GJM's recognition of the global reach of contemporary social problems led to its explicit commitment to paradigmatic change by means of nonviolent mass action aimed at redistributing power from global corporate elites to ordinary people at the grass roots.

CLAIM NUMBER FOUR: ANOTHER WORLD
IS POSSIBLE AND URGENTLY NEEDED

A variation of the official WSF slogan, this central claim of justice globalism represents perhaps the most well-known and widely recognized demand of the GJM. At its heart lies what the German critical theorist Ernst Bloch called a *concrete utopia* of an alternative social order.[24] In particular, claim four combines the GJM's core concept of transformative change with an almost visceral sense of urgency. In the view of many WSF organizations, the world has reached a critical moment in the history of humanity. If people failed to bring about a paradigmatic shift in the basic values that drive global politics and economics within the next few decades, our species might have crossed the point of no return—especially with regard to the deteriorating natural environment. It is this sense of urgency that weaves together the core concepts of transformative change, social justice, sustainability, and equality. Claim four also builds on and extends the three previous claims: since neoliberalism has failed both economically and ethically, humanity faces the vital task of finding alternatives as soon as possible through common action in the spirit of solidarity. As the organization *Grassroots Global Justice* noted in its mission statement, "We believe by working together—Another World is Possible, a world based on the principles of international solidarity, justice, peace, dignity, equality, human rights, sustainability and democracy!" Similarly, the *World March of Women* issued a fervent call for the creation of a better world:

> The World March of Women illustrates the resolve of citizens of the world to build a peaceful world, free of exploitation and oppression—a world in which people enjoy full human rights, social justice, democracy, and gender equality. A world in which women's work, both productive and reproductive, and their contribution to society, are properly recognized. A world in which cultural diversity and pluralism are respected, and a world in which the environment is protected. We consider it is urgent to assert and defend our sexual and reproductive rights, including the right to informed choice, in particular by free access to health care and free and safe measures of contraception and abortion. In short, we believe that together we can and must build another world.

These passages point to the kind of world the GJM envisioned in the 2000s. But most of the WSF-connected organizations recognized that the establishment of "another world" had to be more than a mildly reformed version of the status quo. Thus, they expressed a strong commitment to *people power* as the chief catalyst in their effort to globalize the world of the twenty-first century in a fundamentally different way than market-globalist forces had in mind.

CLAIM NUMBER FIVE:
PEOPLE POWER, NOT CORPORATE POWER!

The justice-globalist demand for a fundamental revision of existing power relations relies heavily on the binary of people versus corporations. It was usually couched in terminology that sought to expose the undemocratic concentrations of power that dominate the supposedly "democratic" societies in the global North. However, most GJM organizations in the 2000s not only directed their critique of "power elites" toward the corporate world, but also condemned democratically elected representatives for bending all too easily to the will of moneyed interests. For many justice globalists, politics and business had formed a permanent symbiotic relationship designed to monopolize power in the name of democracy. Moreover, they accused such power elites of using crises of their own making as a pretense to keep ordinary people in line. As the Argentine Labor Union *Central de Trabajadoes Argentinos* emphasized, "Today it is clear that power groups are trying to use the economic crisis to halt the progress in the advancement in popular power that was seen in recent years in Latin America."

Once again, the nature and pace of the required social changes stand at the center of this elaborate *power debate* within the WSF. Its affiliated organizations usually started their quest for people power by calling for deep reforms in existing democratic governments and to establish democracy where there was none. Once again, the key to such reforms was seen in the encouragement of greater citizen participation in political and economic decision making. In addition, most organizations argued to reclaim people power by raising awareness of rights that might inspire ordinary citizens to confront governments that commit human rights violations.

Moreover, justice globalists consistently demanded greater corporate and government transparency and accountability. Justice-globalist core concepts such as global solidarity, participatory democracy, and universal rights were linked to specify the main features of people power. Some organizations made clear that they are not trying to usurp the power of the state. Rather, they introduced themselves as civil society partners to national governments willing to question their dependency on corporate power and expressed their desire to serve the common good.

Finally, justice globalists understood people power as extending beyond existing national borders. In this respect, the core concept of global solidarity anchors claim five and its call for profound social change. ATTAC put it well:

> What is needed, *in the interest of the large majority of the people*, are *real changes toward another paradigm*, where finance is forced to contribute to *social justice*, economic stability and *sustainable development*. . . . *The crisis* is not the result of some unfortunate circumstances, nor can it be reduced to the failure of regulation, rating agencies or misbehavior of single actors. It *has systemic roots, and hence the structure and the mechanisms of the system, in general, are at stake.* New international agreements must put other goals—like *financial stability, tax justice, or social justice and sustainability—over the free flow of capital, goods and services.*

The high levels of frequency, consistency, and clarity with which these five central claims were deployed by WSF-affiliated organizations provide ample evidence that justice globalism grew to ideational coherence and maturity during the 2000s. It not only provided an effective conceptual decontestation of its core concepts and claims but also showed a remarkable degree of responsiveness to a broad range of pressing political issues. With regard to its ideational distinctiveness, it is obvious that some of the core concepts of conventional ideologies—especially liberalism and socialism—also appear in justice globalism. Yet, these key ideas are articulated in much revised and hybridized ways and often linked to new core concepts such as "sustainability."

Moreover, although the WSF Charter identifies phenomena such as "neoliberalism," "imperialism," and the "domination of the world by capital" as the main obstacles on the path toward global democracy, it specifically rejects old Marxist or Leninist formulas derived from "reductionist views of economy" or a "totalitarian" disregard for human rights. This critique of Soviet-style communism is repeated time and again in relevant GJM texts. For example, Susan George, an

American-French progressive author and one of the driving citizen-activists behind WSF and ATTAC, rarely missed an opportunity to point to the difference between Marxism's radical antimarket rhetoric and a justice-globalist position critical of markets: "The issue as I see it is not to abolish markets. . . . Trying to ban markets would rather be like banning rain. One can, however, enforce strict limitations on what is and is not governed by market rules and make sure that everyone can participate in exchange."[25]

George also showed no hesitation to dispense with Marx's agent of social change—the international working class—as "more wishful thinking than reality." Scientific socialism's revolutionary expectation of the inevitable collapse of capitalism struck her as a "global accident" unlikely to occur. Neither is such a doomsday scenario to be cheerfully contemplated, for it would entail "massive unemployment, wiped-out savings, pensions and insurance; societal breakdown, looting, crime, misery, scapegoating and repression, most certainly followed by fascism, or at the very least, military takeovers." George's criticism of old-Left thinking culminated in a ferocious broadside against the "totalitarian systems" of "state-socialism." In her view, the gulags and killing fields of the Soviet Union, Mao's China, and other purportedly "revolutionary" Third World regimes belied their supposed humanist ideals. Thus, the justice-globalist vision of the 2000s was decidedly not about reviving a moribund Marxism-Leninism.

The programmatic core of the ideological claims of justice globalism was a "global Marshall Plan" that would create more political space for people around the world to determine what kind of social arrangements they want. To this day, millions of justice globalists believe that "another world" has to begin with a new, worldwide Keynesian-type program of taxation and redistribution, exactly as it was introduced at the national level in Western countries a century ago. As noted previously, the necessary funds for this global regulatory framework would come from the profits of TNCs and financial markets—hence the justice-globalist campaign for the introduction of the global Tobin Tax. Other proposals include the cancelation of poor countries' debts; the closing of offshore financial centers offering tax havens for wealthy individuals and corporations; the ratification and implementation of stringent global environmental agreements; the implementation of a more equitable global development agenda; the establishment of a new world development institution financed largely by the global North and administered largely by the global South; the establishment of international labor protection standards, perhaps as clauses of a profoundly reformed WTO; greater transparency and accountability provided to citizens by national governments and global economic institutions; making all governance of globalization explicitly gender sensitive; and the transformation of "free trade" into fair trade.

Justice globalism showed a remarkable ability to bring together a large number of left-wing concerns around a more pronounced orientation toward the globe as a single, interconnected arena for political action. Its unique ideological morphology was no longer bound to a largely *national* framework, but embraced concepts and claims linked to the rising *global* imaginary. Thus, justice globalism offered an alternative translation of the rising global imaginary, one that not only was critical of market-globalist claims but also rejected the jihadist-globalist visions of the political Right.

JIHADIST GLOBALISM IN THE 2000s: THE POLITICAL CONTEXT

After the al Qaeda attacks of 9/11, scores of commentators around the world pointed to radical Islamism as one of the most potent ideological challengers to market globalism. Nevertheless, except for al Qaeda's worldwide network, most of these voices saw nothing "global" in Osama bin Laden's worldview. Rather, they castigated his brand of Islamism as "backward" and "parochial"—typical of a religious fanatic who represented one of the reactionary forces undermining globalization. However, al Qaeda's potent political belief system powered by religious symbols and metaphors not only represented the second and more powerful camp of market globalism's challengers from the political Right but also reflected the complex dynamics of globalization. Just as the ideology of justice globalists clearly transcended the national framework, the same was true for jihadist globalists who incorporated into their militant version of a religiously inspired style of globalist rhetoric to create a comprehensive ideology capable of translating the rising global imaginary into concrete political terms and programs. For this reason, this ideology can best be described as *jihadist globalism*—a belief system falling under the umbrella category of religious globalism.

The origins of al Qaeda can be traced back to the *Maktab al-Khidamat* (MAK; "Office of Services"), a Pakistan-based support organization for Arab mujahideen fighting invading Soviet troops in Afghanistan. Set up in 1980 by bin Laden and his Palestinian teacher and mentor Abdullah Azzam, MAK received sizable contributions from the government of Saudi Arabia and private donors from other Islamic countries. It also enjoyed the protection of Pakistan's Inter-Service Intelligence Agency intent on replacing, with support from the Central Intelligence Agency, the communist puppet regime in Kabul with an Islamist government friendly to Pakistan. Thus, al Qaeda and other radical Islamist groups operating at the time in this region should be seen as creatures of the Cold War who eventually outlived the purpose assigned to them by their benefactors. Left without much support after the withdrawal of the Soviet troops in 1989, the multinational coalition of Arab-Afghani fighters found itself put out of business by its own success. Stranded in a country devastated by decades of continual warfare, the victorious mujahideen lacked a clear sense of purpose or mission.

Osama bin Laden was born in 1957 the seventeenth son of Muhammed bin Laden, a migrant laborer from Yemen who created a multibillion-dollar construction empire in his adopted Saudi Arabia. Bin Laden's early experiments with libertarian Western lifestyles ended abruptly when he encountered political Islam in classes taught by Abdallah Azzam and Muhammad Qutb at King Abd al-Aziz University in Jeddah. After earning a graduate degree in business administration, the ambitious young man proved his managerial talent during a short stint in his father's corporation. But his professional successes were soon trumped by his fervent religious vocation, expressed in his support of the Arab mujahideen in their struggle against the Soviet-backed Afghan regime. Acquiring extensive skill in setting up guerrilla training camps and planning military operations, bin Laden saw battle on several occasions and quickly acquired a stellar reputation for his martial valor. Euphoric at the Soviet withdrawal from Afghanistan but bitterly disappointed by the waning support of the United States and Arab countries, bin Laden returned to Riyadh in 1990 as a popular hero, his close ties to the Saudi regime still intact.

At the time, Saddam Hussein's occupation of Kuwait was threatening the balance of power in the Middle East. To counter the threat, the House of Saud invited half a million "infidels"—American and other foreign troops—into their country, ostensibly for a short period of time and solely for protective purposes. To ensure religious legitimacy for its decision, the government then pressured the Saudi *ulema* (learned interpreters of the sacred texts) to approve of the open-ended presence of foreign troops in the Land of the Holy Two Sanctuaries (Mecca and Medina). The scholars complied, ultimately even granting permission for Muslims to join the US-led "Operation Desert Storm" against Iraq in 1991.

Stung by the royal family's rejection of his proposal to organize thousands of Arab-Afghan veterans and outraged by their enlistment of foreign infidels in defense of the kingdom against a possible Iraqi attack, bin Laden severed all ties with the Saudi regime. Like tens of thousands of angry religious dissenters, bin Laden, too, denounced these acts of "religious heresy" and "moral corruption" and openly accused the rulers of selling out to the West. The Saudi government immediately responded to these accusations with political repression, arresting several opposition leaders and shutting down their organizations. Bin Laden and his closest associates fled to Sudan, where the sympathetic Islamist government of Hassan al-Turabi offered them political exile and the opportunity to create dozens of new training camps for militants. Stripped of his Saudi citizenship in 1994, bin Laden forged a lasting alliance with Ayman al-Zawahiri, the charismatic leader of the radical Egyptian group Islamic Jihad. This partnership would eventually lead to the formation of the World Islamic Front, with main branches in Pakistan and Bangladesh and an unknown number of affiliated cells around the world.

Forced to leave Sudan in 1996 as a result of mounting US pressure on the authoritarian African regime, bin Laden and his entourage returned to Afghanistan, where they entered into an uneasy relationship with the Taliban, whose forces, led by Mullah Omar, managed to capture Kabul in the same year. Imposing a strict version of *shari'a* (God-given, Islamic law) on the Afghan population, the Taliban based its rule on the "true tenets of Islam" alleged to have been realized in the world only once before by the seventh-century *salaf* (pious predecessors) who led the *umma* (community of believers) for three generations following the death of the Prophet. By the end of the 1990s, bin Laden had openly pledged his allegiance to the Taliban, most likely in exchange for the regime's willingness to shelter his organization from

US retaliation following the devastating 1998 al Qaeda bombings of the American embassies in Kenya and Tanzania. To show his gratitude to his hosts, bin Laden referred to the Taliban leader Mullah Omar as the "Commander of the Faithful"—one of the honorific titles of the caliph, the Islamic ruler of both the religious and the civil spheres. Since this designation was deprived of its last bearer in 1924 when the modernist Turkish leader Kemal Ataturk replaced the Ottoman caliphate with a secular nation-state, bin Laden's fondness for it signifies nothing less than his rejection of eight decades of Islamic modernism—in both its nationalist and its socialist garbs—as well as his affirmation of Taliban-ruled Afghanistan as the nucleus of a global caliphate destined to halt the long decline of the Islamic world and the corresponding ascendancy of the West. His anti-Western convictions notwithstanding, bin Laden never hesitated to use modern technology to communicate his message.

As Bruce Lawrence notes, the bulk of bin Laden's writings and public addresses emerged in the context of a "virtual world" moving from print to the Internet and from wired to wireless communication. Largely scriptural in mode, the sheikh's "messages to the world" were deliberately designed for the new global media. As we have seen, they appeared on video- and audiotapes, websites, and handwritten letters scanned onto computer disks and delivered to Arabic-language news outlets of global reach. Bin Laden conveyed his ideological claims in carefully crafted language that drew on the five traditional types of Muslim public discourse: the declaration, the juridical decree, the lecture, the written reminder, and the epistle. Disdainful of ghostwritten tracts of the kind supplied by professional speechwriters to many politicians, he produced eloquent pieces of Arabic prose that spoke in the "authentic, compelling voice of a visionary, with what can only be called a powerful lyricism."[26] Bin Laden's writings from the 1990s to the 2000s amounted to a coherent doctrine appealing to millions of Muslims. His post-9/11 messages, in particular, contained specific instructions to the faithful on how to resist the advances of the American Empire, the "New Rome."

The ideological edifice of the jihadist globalism of the 2000s rests on the evocation of an exceptional spiritual and material crisis: the umma has been subjected to an unprecedented wave of attacks on its territories, values, and economic resources. Although he blamed the global "Judeo-Crusader alliance," bin Laden considered its assault on

Islam to be the expression of an evil much larger than that represented by particular nation-states or imperialist alliances.[27] At the same time, however, he and his lieutenants insisted that the forces of "global unbelief" were led by specific individuals like President George W. Bush or by concrete "hegemonic organizations of universal infidelity" such as the United States and the United Nations.[28] In their view, the collapse of the Soviet Empire—attributed directly to the efforts of the Arab-Afghan mujahideen—had made America even more haughty and imperialistic:

> [I]t has started to see itself as the Master of this world and established what it calls the new world order. . . . The U.S. today, as a result of this arrogance, has set a double standard, calling whoever goes against its injustice a terrorist. It wants to occupy our countries, steal our resources, install collaborators to rule us with man-made laws, and wants us to agree on all these issues. If we refuse to do so, it will say we are terrorists.[29]

Bin Laden cited as evidence for such "Satanic acts of aggression" the open-ended presence of American troops on the Arabian peninsula, the ongoing Israeli oppression of the Palestinian people, the 1993 American operations against Muslim warlords in Somalia, the Western indifference to the slaughter of thousands of Bosnian Muslims during the 1991–1995 Yugoslav civil war, and the economic sanctions imposed by the West on Iraq after the first Gulf War that contributed to the death of countless innocent civilians. Indebted to the discursive legacy of Third World liberationism, the sheikh considered these immoral and imperialist acts inflicted by Western powers on the umma but the latest crimes in a series of humiliations that could be traced back to the Great Powers' division of the Ottoman Empire after World War I and the post–World War II establishment of the Jewish state in Palestine.

But what made contemporary "attacking enemies and corrupters of religion and the world" even more dangerous than the medieval Christian crusaders or the thirteenth-century Mongol conquerors of the mighty Abbasid Empire was their all-out "campaign against the Muslim world in its entirety, aiming to get rid of Islam itself."[30] Rather than supporting the umma at this critical point in history when the Judeo-Crusader alliance had "violated her honor, shed her blood, and occupied her sanctuaries," Saudi Arabia and other Islamic countries had colluded with the "infidel enemy." Abandoning the umma in her hour of need, these "apostate rulers" had desecrated the true religion of God's messenger and thereby lost their political legitimacy. Likewise, Islamic scholars and clerics who lent their learned voices to the defense of these "defeatist Arab tyrannies" deserved to be treated as "cowardly heretics" and "traitors to the faith."

WHAT DOES AL QAEDA WANT?
EXAMINING THE CORE CONCEPTS AND
CENTRAL CLAIMS OF JIHADIST GLOBALISM

Osama bin Laden directed his first public letter intended for a wider audience against the appointed head of Saudi Arabia's collaboration-ist *ulema*. In addition to accusing the mufti of spiritual corruption, he also objected to his alleged willingness to turn a blind eye to the moral decay of modern Islamic societies, most visibly reflected in their toleration of practices of usury expressly prohibited in the Qur'an. The letter also lamented the *ulema's* unwillingness to resort to more dras-tic measures to prevent the further intrusion of Western values at the expense of Muslim principles. In several poignant passages, bin Laden identifies as the worst feature of the present age of *jahiliyya* (ignorance; pagan idolatry) "the degree of degradation and corruption to which our Islamic *umma* has sunk."[31]

But how, precisely, did bin Laden decontest the core concept *umma*? After all, this idea, together with the other core concepts *jihad* and *tawhid*, serves as the ideational anchor of his political belief system. In the sheikh's major writings, one finds ample textual evidence for his decontestation of umma.[32] As Mohammed Bamyeh notes, the concept of the "Islamic community" has functioned historically as an equiva-lent of the Western idea of "the people," empowered to set limits to the tyrannical tendencies of governing elites.[33] Drawing on this traditional understanding of the umma, bin Laden emphasized that political au-thority can never rest on "popular sovereignty," for political rule is not the exclusive property of the people. Rather, the righteous umma exer-cises political power in the name of God only, thus building its political institutions on the foundation of Islamic sovereignty.[34] Since God's au-thority transcends all political borders and any humanly designed lines of demarcation, the umma supersedes not only ancient tribal solidari-ties and traditional kinship structures but, most importantly, modern

Western conceptions of community rooted in the national imaginary. To be sure, contemporary Muslims carry national passports, but jihadist globalists claim that their primary solidarity must lie with the umma, a community that encompasses the entire globe: "You know, we are linked to all of the Islamic world, whether that be Yemen, Pakistan, or wherever. We are part of one unified *umma*."[35]

Jihadist globalism's core concept of the umma having been commanded by God to safeguard His sovereignty and to resist the sinful influences of despots, heretics, and infidels usurping God's ultimate sovereignty received its most radical modern formulation in the writings of the Egyptian political Islamist Sayyid Qutb, the older brother of bin Laden's influential teacher at al-Aziz University. Taking as his point of departure the Islamic doctrine of *tawhid*, Qutb argued that all worldly power belongs to the one and only Lord of the Worlds whose single, unchanging will is revealed in the Qur'an. Unconditional submission to His will entails the responsibility of every member of the umma to prevent the domination of humans over humans, which violates the absolute authority of Allah. According to Qutb, the highest purpose of human existence is "to establish the Sovereignty and Authority of God on earth, to establish the true system revealed by God for addressing the human life; to exterminate all the Satanic forces and their ways of life, to abolish the lordship of man over other human beings."[36]

Having failed to repel the corrupting influences of Islam's internal and external enemies, today's umma had fallen into the equivalent of the pre-Islamic pagan age of *jahiliyya* characterized by rampant materialism and the rebellion of unbelief against the sovereignty of God on earth. Qutb even suggested that with the disappearance of proper political governance according to shari'a, the umma itself had ceased to exist in its "true" form. If only ordinary Muslims somehow could be shown the seriousness of their predicament, they might renew their faith and cleanse Islamic culture of its debasing accretions. The final goal of such an Islamic revival would be the restoration of the umma to its original moral purity under a new *salaf* (righteous leadership). As Mary Habeck notes, Qutb's seemingly premodern inclinations actually contain strong modernist influences that turn political Islam into "a sort of liberation ideology, designed to end oppression by human institutions and man-made laws and to return God to his rightful place as unconditional ruler of the world."[37]

Qutb's version of political Islam greatly influenced al Qaeda's understanding of the umma as a single global community of believers united in their belief in the one and only God. As bin Laden emphasizes, "We are the children of an Islamic Nation, with the Prophet Muhammad as its leader; our Lord is one, our prophet is one, our direction of prayer is one, we are one umma, and our Book is one."[38] Expressing a populist yearning for strong leaders who set things right by fighting corrupt elites and returning power to the "Muslim masses," al-Zawahiri shared his leader's vision of how to restore the umma to its earlier glory.[39] In their view, the process of regeneration had to start with a small but dedicated vanguard willing to sacrifice their lives as martyrs to the holy cause of awakening the people to their religious duties—not just in traditionally Islamic countries but also wherever members of the umma yearn for the establishment of God's rule on earth. With a third of the world's Muslims living as minorities in non-Islamic societies, bin Laden regarded the restoration of the umma as no longer a local, national, or even regional event. Rather, it required a concerted *global* effort spearheaded by a jihadist vanguard operating in various localities around the world. Hence, al Qaeda's desired Islamization of modernity took place in global space emancipated from the confining territoriality of "Egypt" or the "Middle East" that used to constitute the political framework of religious nationalists fighting modern secular regimes in the twentieth century. As French religion scholar Olivier Roy observes, "The Muslim *umma* (or community) no longer has anything to do with a territorial entity. It has to be thought of in abstract and imaginary terms."[40]

To further illustrate the global dynamics reflected in al Qaeda's jihadism, it is useful to consider bin Laden's personal appearance. An infamous videotape broadcast worldwide on October 7, 2001, showed the leader wearing contemporary military fatigues over traditional Arab garments. In other words, his dress reflected contemporary processes of fragmentation and cross-fertilization that globalization scholars call *hybridization*—the mixing of different cultural forms and styles facilitated by global economic and cultural exchanges. In fact, the pale colors of bin Laden's mottled combat dress betrayed its Russian origins, suggesting that he wore the jacket as a symbolic reminder of the fierce guerrilla war waged by him and other Islamic militants against the Soviet occupation forces in Afghanistan during the 1980s.

His ever-present AK-47 Kalashnikov, too, was probably made in Russia, although dozens of gun factories around the world have been building this popular assault rifle for more than forty years. By the mid-1990s, more than seventy million Kalashnikovs had been manufactured in Russia and abroad. At least fifty national armies include such rifles in their arsenals, making Kalashnikovs truly weapons of global choice. Thus, bin Laden's AK-47 could have come from anywhere in the world. However, given the astonishing globalization of organized crime during the past two decades, it is quite conceivable that bin Laden's rifle was part of an illegal arms deal hatched and executed by such powerful international criminal organizations as al Qaeda and the Russian Mafia. It is also possible that the rifle arrived in Afghanistan by means of an underground arms trade similar to the one that surfaced in May 1996, when police in San Francisco seized two thousand illegally imported AK-47s manufactured in China.

A close look at bin Laden's right wrist revealed yet another clue to the powerful dynamics of globalization. As he directed his words of contempt for the United States and its allies at his handheld microphone, his retreating sleeve exposed a stylish sports watch. Journalists who noticed this expensive accessory speculated about the origins of the timepiece in question. The emerging consensus points to a Timex product. However, given that Timex watches are as American as apple pie, it seems rather ironic that the al Qaeda leader should have chosen this particular brand. After all, Timex Corporation, originally the Waterbury Clock Company, was founded in the 1850s in Connecticut's Naugatuck Valley, known throughout the nineteenth century as the "Switzerland of America." Today, the company has gone multinational, maintaining close relations to affiliated businesses and sales offices in sixty-five countries. The corporation employs 7,500 employees located on four continents. Thousands of workers—mostly from low-wage countries in the global South—constitute the driving force behind Timex's global production process.[41]

Our brief deconstruction of some of the central images on the videotape makes it easier to detect the global within the apparently anachronistic expressions of a supposedly "antiglobalist" terrorist. The series of famous post-9/11 "Osama bin Laden videotapes" broadcast worldwide between 2001 and 2008 testified to al Qaeda's immediate access to sophisticated information and telecommunication networks that kept the leadership informed, in real time, of relevant international developments. Bin Laden and his top lieutenants may have denounced the forces of modernity with great conviction, but the smooth operation of their entire organization was entirely dependent on advanced forms of information and communcation technology developed in the context of globalization. Just as bin Laden's romantic salafist idea of a "pure Islam" is itself an articulation of the global imaginary, so has our global age, with its insatiable appetite for technology, mass-market commodities, and celebrities, indelibly shaped the ideological structure of jihadist globalism.

Although al Qaeda embraced the Manichaean dualism of a *clash of civilizations* between its imagined global umma and global *kufr* (unbelief), its religious globalism transcends clear-cut civilizational fault lines. Its desire for the restoration of a transnational umma attests to the globalization and Westernization of the Muslim world just as much as it reflects the Islamization of the West. Constructed in the ideational interregnum between the national and the global, the central claims of jihadist globalism still retain potent metaphors that resonate with people's national or even tribal solidarities. And yet, al Qaeda's focus is firmly on the global as its leaders successfully redirected militant Islamism's struggle from the traditional "Near Enemy" (secular-nationalist Middle Eastern regimes) to the "Far Enemy" (the globalizing West). This remarkable discursive and strategic shift reflects the destabilization of the national imaginary. By the early 1990s, nationally based Islamist groups were losing steam, partly as a result of their inability to mobilize their respective communities around national concerns and partly because they were subjected to more effective counterstrategies devised by secular-nationalist regimes.

If the restored, purified *umma*—imagined to exist in a global space that transcended particular national or tribal identities—was the final goal of jihadist globalism, then jihad surely served as its principal means. For our purposes, it is not necessary to engage in long scholastic debates about the many meanings and "correct" applications of *jihad*. Nor do we need to excavate its long history in the Islamic world. It suffices to note that jihadist globalists like bin Laden and al-Zawahiri endorse both "offensive" and "defensive" versions of *jihad*.[42] Their decontestation of this core concept draws heavily on interpretations offered by Azzam and Qutb, for whom *jihad* represents a divinely imposed *fard 'ayn* (individual obligation) on a par with the nonnegotiable duties of prayer and fasting. Likewise, bin Laden celebrated jihad as the "peak" or "pinnacle" of Islam, emphasizing time and again that armed struggle against global *kufr* is "obligatory today on our entire *umma*, for our *umma* will stand in sin until her sons, her money, and her energies provide what it takes to establish a *jihad* that repels the evil of the infidels from harming all the Muslims in Palestine and elsewhere."[43]

For al Qaeda, *jihad* represents the sole path toward the noble goal of returning the umma to "her religion and correct beliefs"—not just because the venerable way of *da'wa* (preaching; admonishing) has failed to reform the treacherous Muslim elites or convert the hostile crusaders but, most importantly, because Islam is "the religion of *jihad* in the way of God so that God's word and religion reign supreme." Moreover, jihadist globalists are not choosy about the means of struggle: anything that might weaken the infidels—especially imperial globalists—suffices. Such tactics include large-scale terrorist attacks, suicide bombings, and the public killing of hostages: "To kill the Americans and their allies—civilians and military—is an individual duty incumbent upon every Muslim in all countries."[44]

For bin Laden, the core concepts of *jihad* and *umma* were important manifestations of the revealed truth of *tawhid*, the oneness of God and His creation. As we have seen, it demands that Islamic sovereignty be established on earth in the form of a caliphate without national borders or internal divisions. This totalistic vision of a divinely ordained world system of governance whose timeless legal code covers all aspects of social life has prompted many commentators to condemn "jihadist Islamism" as a particularly aggressive form of "totalitarianism" or "Islamo-fascism" that poses a serious challenge to cultural pluralism and secular democracy.

Responding to this charge, the al Qaeda leadership turned the tables on its critics. Pointing to the long legacy of Western aggression against the umma, bin Laden portrayed his organization's attacks as retaliatory measures designed to respond in kind to the oppression and murder of thousands of Muslims by the "Judeo-Crusader Alliance." The leaders of al Qaeda never hesitated to include as legitimate targets of their strikes those Muslims deemed to be "apostates" and "handmaidens" of the infidel enemy. In their view, such actions of treachery put Muslim "hypocrites" outside of the umma.[45] In the end, the ideological claims of jihadist globalists fell back on a Manichaean dualism that divides the world into two antagonistic camps: "One side is the global Crusader alliance with the Zionist Jews, led by America, Britain, and Israel, and the other side is the Islamic world." For bin Laden and al-Zawahiri, any possible reconciliation violated the Islamic imperatives of unconditional loyalty to the umma and absolute enmity to the non-Muslim world: "The Lord Almighty has commanded us to hate the infidels and reject their love. For they hate us and begrudge us our religion, wishing that we abandon it."

Consequently, the jihadist-globalist message to Muslims all over the world was to nurture "this doctrine in their hearts" and release their hatred on Americans, Jews, and Christians: "This [hatred] is a part of our belief and our religion."[46] In an impassioned post-9/11 letter, bin Laden offered a detailed refutation of the notion that Islam should be a religion of "moderation" or "balance." In his view, "[I]t is, in fact, part of our religion to impose our particular beliefs on others. . . . And the West's notions that Islam is a religion of *jihad* and enmity toward the religions of the infidels and the infidels themselves is an accurate and true depiction." He also considered UN-sponsored calls for a "dialogue among civilizations" nothing but an "infidel notion" rooted in the "loathsome principles" of a secular West advocating an "un-Islamic" separation of religion and the state.[47]

His central ideological claims notwithstanding, bin Laden never lost sight of the fact that jihadist globalists were fighting a steep uphill battle against the forces of the recently hard-powered market globalism. For example, he discussed in much detail the ability of "American media imperialism" to "seduce the Muslim world" with its consumerist messages. He also made frequent references to a "continuing and biased campaign" waged against jihadist globalism by the corporate media—"especially Hollywood"—for the purpose of misrepresenting Islam and hiding the "failures of the Western democratic system."[48] The al Qaeda leader left little doubt that what he considered to be the "worst civilization witnessed in the history of mankind" had to be fought for its "debased materialism" and "immoral culture" as much as for its blatant "imperialism." He repeatedly accused the United States of trying to "change the region's ideology" through the imposition of Western-style democracy and the "Americanization of our culture."[49]

And yet, even against seemingly overwhelming odds, bin Laden and al-Zawahiri expressed their confidence in the ultimate triumph of jihad over the "American Empire." The destruction of New York's "immense materialistic towers by nineteen young men" served as an especially powerful symbol for the alleged "waning global appeal" of "Western civilization backed by America."[50] September 11 and other terrorist attacks that followed in its wake in the 2000s assumed great significance in al Qaeda's jihad insofar as such large-scale operations offered the faithful clear proof that "this destructive, usurious global economy that America uses, together with its military force, to impose unbelief and humiliation on poor people, can easily collapse. Those blessed strikes in New York and other places forced it [America] to acknowledge the loss of more than a trillion dollars, by the grace of God Almighty."[51] Gloating over the staggering financial toll of the terrorist attacks on the global economy, bin Laden presented a chilling cost-benefit analysis of jihadist strategy:

> [A]l-Qaeda spent $500,000 on the September 11 attacks, while America lost more than $500 billion, at the lowest estimate, in the event and its aftermath. That makes a million American dollars for every al-Qaeda dollar, by the grace of God Almighty. This is in addition to the fact that it lost an enormous number of jobs—and as for the federal deficit, it made record losses, estimated over a trillion dollars. Still more serious for America was the fact that the *mujahideen* forced Bush to resort to an emergency budget in order to continue fighting in Afghanistan and Iraq. This shows the success of our plan to bleed America to the point of bankruptcy, with God's will.[52]

This passage is part of a videotaped address aired around the world only a few days before American voters went to the national polls on November 3, 2004. Bin Laden ended his speech with a warning to the American people that their security was their own responsibility, not that of corrupt Democrat or Republican political elites. Thus, the sheikh managed to inject himself into a national electoral contest as the self-appointed leader of the global umma. Articulating the rising global imaginary as a set of interrelated political and religious claims, jihadist globalism appeared on the TV screens of a global audience as the world's chief critic of American democracy. As Faisal Devji notes, bin Laden's brand of jihadism projected no national ambitions, for it was as global as the West itself, both being intertwined and even internal to each other: "This is why Bin Laden's calls for the United

States to leave the Muslim world do not entail the return to a cold-war geopolitics of detente, but are conceived rather in terms of a global reciprocity on equal terms."[53]

Another videotaped message delivered by the al Qaeda leader in September 2007 unleashed further verbal broadsides against market globalism and the "corrupt American political system." He linked the Bush administration's involvement in Iraq to transnational corporate interests that held "the American people" hostage to their all-out scramble for war-related profits. Bin Laden's critique showed some resemblance to right-wing populist tirades against corporate elites. Indeed, the sheikh charged "the capitalist system" with seeking "to turn the entire world into a fiefdom of the major corporations under the label of 'globalization.'"[54] However, unlike the defensive attempts of contemporary national populists such as Marine Le Pen or Donald Trump to hold on to the weakening national imaginary, jihadist globalists projected an ideological alternative that, despite its chilling content, imagines community in unambiguously global terms. Like justice-globalist groups, al Qaeda or ISIS are not "antiglobalization" but "alterglobalization."

A product of the ongoing deterritorialization of Islam, jihadist globalism constituted the most significant ideological attempt in the 2000s to articulate the rising global imaginary around religious ideas—in this case, the core concepts of *umma*, *jihad*, and *tawhid*. Al Qaeda's central ideological claims—all of which converged in the assertion that the rebuilding of a unified global *umma* involved global *jihad* against global *kufr*—resonated with the dynamics of a globalizing world. In particular, jihadist globalism holds a special appeal for Muslim youths between the ages of fifteen and twenty-five who have lived for sustained periods in the individualized and often decultured environments of Westernized Islam or an Islamized West.[55]

As Olivier Roy reminds us, this "second wave" of al Qaeda and, later, ISIS recruits, was responsible for the most spectacular terrorist operations in the first two decades of the twenty-first century. Products of a Westernized Islam, most of these jihadists resided in Europe or North America and had few or no links to traditional Middle Eastern political parties. Their affinity for al Qaeda's idea of a transnational umma and its rigid religious code divorced from traditional cultural contexts made them prime candidates for recruitment. Thus, these young men and women followed in the footsteps of al Qaeda's "first-wavers" in Afghanistan in the 1980s who developed their ideological outlook among a multinational band of idealistic mujahideen.[56]

MARKET GLOBALISM REACTS TO ITS CHALLENGERS: TOWARD IMPERIAL GLOBALISM

If market globalists sought to conceal their imperial ambitions in the 1990s behind the largely soft-power operations of a free-trade empire anchored in the myth of the market's "invisible hand," then the gloves definitely came off after 9/11. The US government led by President George W. Bush resembled an irate giant ready to resort to hard-power tactics for the defense of "liberty, democracy, and free markets" against "terrorist evil-doers." The ideological implications of this post-9/11 turn toward neoconservatism became evident soon after the terrorist attacks. If it were to continue as the dominant ideology in our new era of global warfare, market globalism had to accommodate to the realities of a newly declared "global war on terror." Reflecting growing security concerns following the 9/11 attacks, market globalism's neoliberal program of economic deregulation, privatization, free trade, unfettered capital movements, low taxation, and fiscal austerity was merged with this so-called global war on terror and other neoconservative attempts to shape the entire globe according to American interests. As militarism and the market merged in a Hummerized discursive landscape, *neoconservatives* joined *neoliberals* in the intensifying public debate about the "backlash against globalization."

In this context, it is crucial to bear in mind that *neoconservativism* and *neoliberalism* in the United States are not ideological opposites. In fact, they represent variations on the same liberal theme, and their similarities often outweigh their differences. American neoconservatives are far removed from classical British traditionalists who expressed a fondness for aristocratic virtues and bemoaned radical social change, disliked egalitarian principles, and distrusted progress and reason. Rather, American neoconservatives in the 2000s subscribed to a variant of liberalism they relate to the worldviews espoused by Ronald Reagan, Theodore Roosevelt, Abraham Lincoln, and James Madison.

In the harsh political climate following the attacks of September 11, many market globalists struggled to maintain the viability of their project. One obvious solution was to toughen up their ideological claims to fit the neoconservative vision of a benign US empire relying on overwhelming military power. As a result, market globalism morphed into *imperial globalism*.[57] The market-globalist claims one (globalization is about the liberalization and integration of markets) and four (globalization benefits everyone) remained remarkably stable throughout the 2000s. As the prominent economist Jagdish Bhagwati noted in his best-selling book *In Defense of Globalization*, "economic globalization is on balance socially benign."[58] September 11 and the Global War on Terror did not have much impact on market-globalist claim four; in fact, it seems that the terrorist attacks actually added to the fervor with which market globalists spoke of the supposed benefits accruing from the rapid liberalization and global integration of markets. Indeed, throughout their respective terms in office, both Bill Clinton and George W. Bush consistently argued that "[f]ree trade and free markets have proven their ability to lift whole societies out of poverty—so the United States will work with individual nations, entire regions, and the entire global trading community to build a world that trades in freedom and therefore grows in prosperity."[59]

After September 11, however, it became increasingly difficult to maintain claim three—that "nobody is in charge of globalization." While a number of corporate leaders still reflexively talked about the "leaderless market," imperial globalists close to the Bush administration openly proclaimed that global security and a global liberal order "depend on the United States—that 'indispensable nation'—wielding its power."[60] After all, if America spearheaded the cause of universal principles, then it had a responsibility to make sure that the spread of these values was not hampered by ideological dissenters. Indeed, President Bush ended his preface to the *National Security Strategy of the United States of America* by glorifying US global leadership: "Today, humanity holds in its hands the opportunity to further freedom's triumph over all these [terrorist] foes. The United States welcomes our [*sic*] responsibility to lead in this great mission."[61] In other words, on the issue of expanding American influence around the world, the ideology of American Empire found common ground with market discourse. Armed US world hegemony was not only good for business—particularly the American military-industrial complex—it also made sense for a variety of political reasons. September 11 changed the terms of the discourse in that it enabled neoconservatives to put their global ambitions explicitly before a public traumatized by the terrorist attacks and thus vulnerable to what Claes Ryn, chairman of the National Humanities Institute, calls the "neo-Jacobin spirit" of the Bush administration. Many market globalists were willing to adapt to this new militancy—after all, the French Jacobins also wanted greater economic freedom.[62]

The resulting move toward imperial globalism meant that the claim "nobody is in charge of globalization" had to be abandoned and replaced by Bush's aggressive pronouncement of global leadership. However, the replacement of claim three with a more aggressive pronouncement of global Anglo-American leadership should not be read as a sign of market globalism's ideological weakness. Rather, it reflected its ideational flexibility and growing ability to respond to a new set of political issues. Indeed, like all full-fledged political belief systems, market globalism increasingly bore the marks of an "ideational family" broad enough to contain the more economistic variant of the 1990s as well as its more militaristic post-9/11 manifestation.

After September 11, claim five (globalization furthers the spread of democracy in the world) became firmly linked to the Bush administration's controversial security agenda culminating in the famous "Bush doctrine" that legitimated the use of "preemptive strikes" against potential enemies. To be sure, the president did not mince words in "Securing Freedom's Triumph," his *New York Times* op-ed piece a year after the attacks: "As we preserve the peace, America also has an opportunity to extend the benefits of freedom and progress to nations that lack them. We seek a peace where repression, resentment and poverty are replaced with the hope of democracy, development, free markets and free trade."[63] Several months later, Bush reaffirmed this "forward strategy for freedom" by referring to his country's unwavering "commitment to the global expansion of democracy" as the "third pillar" of America's "peace and security vision for the world." The same assertion took center stage in Bush's 2005 inaugural address: "The best hope for peace in our world is the expansion of freedom in all the world. . . . So it is the policy of the United States to seek and support the growth of democratic movements and institutions in every nation and culture, with the ultimate goal of ending tyranny in our world."[64] Indeed, Bush's definition of globalization as "the triumph of human liberty stretching across national borders" remained the same before and after 9/11, yet the emphasis shifted from freedom's "promise of delivering billions of the world's citizens from disease and want" to a militarized security narrative.[65] The idea of securing "freedom" through an American-led drive for political and economic "democratization" around the globe—thus connecting the military objectives of the War on Terror to the neoliberal agenda—emerged as the conceptual hallmark of what could be called *imperial globalism*.

As Richard Falk notes, such a design

> combines ideas of American dominance associated with economic globalization, that were prevalent before September 11, with more militarist ideas associated with the anti-terrorist climate of the early 21st century. . . . While not abandoning the ideological precepts of neoliberal globalization, the Bush administration places its intense free market advocacy beneath the security blanket that includes suspect advice to other governments to devote their resources to non-military activities.[66]

Cultural theorist William Thornton concurs: "Empire keeps all the major features of globalization, plus one: it stands ready to enforce market privileges the old-fashioned way. . . . Emphatically, however, power economics did not surrender the field to resurgent power politics. Rather the two joined forces in the common cause of Empire."[67]

Thus, the market-globalist claim of spreading freedom and democracy became a convenient narrative for the Bush administration and its supporters in Congress to secure and expand their country's influence and power globally by combining military interventions and market liberalization. Indeed, "expansion" was the logic that held these two dimensions together. These operations amounted to what Claes Ryn calls American "armed world hegemony" exercised by imperialist ideologues in Washington who have convinced themselves and who seek to convince others that their country's turbo-capitalism and military might are the greatest forces for freedom in human history.[68] In combating the evil forces of terrorism, the United States and its allies spearheaded the cause of universal principles—of course, democracy and free markets being first and foremost among them.

At this point, it is not difficult to grasp why, in the post-9/11 context, it became necessary for market-globalist forces to add another claim to their existing discursive arsenal: *globalization requires a war on terror*. If globalization, understood as the liberalization and global integration of markets, was to remain a viable project (as demanded by neoliberals), then the full coercive powers of the state had to be employed against those who threatened it—both GJM dissenters and jihadist globalists. To be sure, massive state intervention on behalf of corporate interests constituted a glaring contradiction of a central tenet of classical liberalism, but many market globalists were willing to strike a compromise on this point as long as such political interventions not only maintained their access to established markets but also opened up new markets in populous and resource-rich regions of the world.

As noted previously, the "necessary elimination" of "terrorists" and other "radical forces" hostile to the spread of democracy and the free market made untenable claim three that nobody is in charge of globalization. Putting the public on notice that the War on Terror would be a long-term commitment for the United States, the Bush administration left no doubt that it had taken it upon itself to protect the free market against the new barbarian forces bent on destroying Western civilization. The necessary military infrastructure to engage in an open-ended, global conflict was already in place. As political scientist Chalmers Johnson points out in his sobering analysis of American Empire, the United States currently operates at least 725 military bases worldwide and maintains some form of military presence in 153 of 189 member countries of the United Nations.[69]

Indeed, power elites around the world put forward the new claim six—globalization requires a global war on terror—on countless occasions and in numerous contexts. Let us consider three versions of presenting American-led perpetual warfare as the necessary bodyguard of corporate-led globalization. The first came from neoconservative veteran Robert McFarlane, President Reagan's former national security advisor. Shortly after the US military's opening "shock and awe" Iraq campaign in March 2003, McFarlane teamed with Michael Bleyzer, CEO of an international equity fund management company, to write a revealing op-ed piece for the *Wall Street Journal*. Bearing the suggestive title "Taking Iraq Private," the article praised the military operations in Iraq as an "indispensable tool" for establishing security and stability in the region. According to the imperial-globalist duo, the Global War on Terror prepared the ground for the profitable enterprise of "building the basic institutions that make democracy possible."[70]

Representing the second version of claim six, Robert Kaplan pondered how a "Global American Empire" should "manage an unruly world" after 9/11. The award-winning journalist and influential Pentagon insider quickly settled on the claim that globalization required a global war on terror. Arguing that free markets cannot spread without military power, Kaplan advised the Bush administration to adopt the "pagan warrior ethos" of second-century Rome, which he distilled into "ten rules" for the expansion of American Empire. These included fast-track naturalization for foreign-born soldiers fighting for the empire; training special forces to be "lethal killers one moment and humanitarians the next"; using the military to promote democracy; preventing military missions from being compromised by diplomacy; establishing the resolve to "fight on every front," including the willingness to strike potential enemies preemptively on limited evidence; dealing with the media "more strictly"; and cracking down on internal dissent, targeting justice globalists and antiwar demonstrators in particular.[71]

Similarly, Norman Podhoretz, foreign policy adviser to the 2008 Republican presidential candidate Rudy Giuliani, called for the escalation of the US-led Global War on Terror into a full-blown "World War IV" (apparently, "World War III" ended in the defeat of the Soviet Union). Podhoretz surveyed a post-9/11 landscape teeming with "enemies" of all kinds, the two principal ones being "Islamofascism" and misguided Western leftist intellectuals critical of US operations in Iraq. For Podhoretz, only a "tough" and "unforgiving" approach of the kind adopted by the Bush administration might eventually succeed in "draining the swamps" of terrorism and political treachery, thus assuring the full globalization of liberal democracy and free markets.[72]

The third and perhaps most original version of the new imperial-globalist claim that globalization requires a global war on terror flowed from the pen of Thomas P. M. Barnett, managing director of a global security firm and former professor of military strategy at the US Naval War College. A former assistant for strategic futures in the Pentagon's Office of Force Transformations, the Harvard-educated strategist provided regular briefings to Secretary of Defense Donald Rumsfeld and the inner circle of the US intelligence community. He also interacted regularly with thousands of high-ranking officers from all branches of the US armed forces. *The Pentagon's New Map*, Barnett's best-selling reexamination of

American national security, linked the author's military expertise to his long-standing interests in economic globalization.[73] The book presented a straightforward thesis: in the global age, America's national security was inextricably bound with the continued global integration of markets and increasing flows of trade, capital, ideas, and people across national borders. Since 9/11, it had become "abundantly clear" to the author that the one-sided identification of globalization with an "economic rule set" had to be complemented by an understanding of globalization as a "security rule set" mandating the destruction of transnational terrorist networks and all states harboring them.

For Barnett, both of these "rule sets" were normatively anchored in the universal values of individual freedom, democracy, multicultural-ism, and free markets. At the same time, however, these norms were also uniquely "American," for they found their political expression for the first time in human history in the eighteenth-century Ameri-can experiment of an expanding democratic union of *united states.*[74] In a daring conflation of national interest with global interest that ran counter to the nation-centered mind-set of the US defense estab-lishment, Barnett presented America as "globalization's ideological wellspring" destined to bring to the world nothing less than what its citizens already enjoyed today: "the individual pursuit of happiness within free markets protected from destabilizing strife by the rule of law." For the strategist, American interests were by definition global interests precisely because the country was built on universal ide-als of freedom and democracy and not restricted to narrow ethnic or national identities. As the world's first truly multinational union, the United States *was* globalization incarnate. Moreover, the universal values at the heart of its Constitution allowed the American govern-ment to judge the rest of the world in universal terms of right and wrong, good and evil: "What gives America the right [to render these judgments] is the fact that we are globalization's godfather, its source code, its original model." And so it appeared that by human design and historical destiny, the United States served as the evolutionary engine of a multicultural "world-system" that ascended toward ever-higher levels of connectivity, rule-bound behavior, wealth, security, and hap-piness. Although Barnett considered this course likely, he disavowed historical determinism by conceding that there were no guarantees. In his mind, al Qaeda and other "antiglobalization forces" committed to "a sort of permanent civilizational apartheid" were capable of derailing the globalization of individualism, democracy, and free markets. Thus, 9/11 marked a critical juncture in human history where America—"globalization's source code"—was called upon to guide the rest of the world toward the noble goals of "universal inclusiveness" and "global peace." Its Herculean task was to "make globalization truly global"—by any means necessary.[75]

This is, of course, where the new claim six of globalization requiring a global war on terror came in. In order to defeat the enemies of global interdependence, the Pentagon had to devise a new strategy that, once and for all, abandoned antiquated *international* thinking. National security in the twenty-first century had to be reimagined in *global* terms as the ruthless destruction of all forces of disconnectedness and the nurturing of the "networks of political and security connectivity commensurate with the mutually assured dependence that now existed among all states that were deeply integrated with the growing global economy." In short, the Pentagon's new global strategy required a new map—in both a cognitive and a geographical sense—that divided the globe into three distinct regions. This meant that, unlike the three-world order of the Cold War, the entire world was now fair game for US military operations.

Barnett called the first region on the Pentagon's new map the "Functioning Core," defined as "globalization thick with network connectivity, financial transactions, liberal media flows, and collective security." Featuring stable democratic governments, transparency, rising standards of living, and more deaths by suicide than by murder, the core was made up of North America, most of Europe, Australia, New Zealand, a small part of Latin America, and, with significant reservations, possible "new core" countries such as India and China. Conversely, he referred to areas where "globalization was thinning or just plain absent" as the "Non-Integrating Gap." This region was plagued by repressive political regimes, handcuffed markets, mass murder, and widespread poverty and disease. For Barnett, the Gap provided a dangerous breeding ground for "global terrorists" and other "forces of disconnectedness" opposed to the "economic and security rule sets we call globalization." This region included the Caribbean Rim, virtually all of Africa, the Balkans, the Caucasus, parts of Central Asia, the Middle East, and parts of Southeast Asia. Along the Gap's "bloody boundaries," the military strategist located "Seam States" such as Mexico, Brazil, South Africa, Morocco, Algeria, Greece, Turkey, Pakistan, Thailand, Malaysia, the Philippines, and Indonesia. Lacking the Core's high levels of connectivity and security, these countries were the logical entry point for terrorists plotting their attacks.[76]

Despite its horrific toll, Barnett considered 9/11 a necessary "wake-up call" that forced the United States to make a long-term military commitment to "export security" to the Gap. The Core had no choice but to treat the entire Gap region as a "strategic threat environment." Inaction or a premature retreat from Iraq and Afghanistan would jeopardize the fledgling world order based on America's universal values. Hence, Barnett proposed a "global transaction strategy" built on three basic principles. First, the United States had to increase the Core's "immune system capabilities" by responding quickly and efficiently to 9/11-like "system perturbations." Second, it had to pressure the Seam States to "firewall the Core from the Gap's worst exports," namely, terror, drugs, and pandemics. Finally, America had to remain firmly committed to a global war on terror and its overriding objective of "shrinking the Gap." There could be no compromise or vacillation. Globalization's enemies had to be eliminated, and the Gap region must be integrated into the Core. As Barnett emphasized, "I believe it is absolutely essential that this country lead the global war on terrorism, because I fear what will happen to our world if the forces of disconnectedness are allowed to prevail—to perturb the system at will."[77]

Barnett's portrayal of globalization as market connectivity inextricably intermingled with collective security in military terms explained why globalization required a war on terror. After September 11, Barnett insisted, the project of expanding the Core could no longer be achieved by soft US hegemony anchored in a benign Clintonian multilateralism that utilized international economic institutions to enforce its market paradigm but that kept the iron fist of military power firmly in the velvet glove of globalism. What was required in our new age of terrorism, Barnett argued, was a conscious switch to "hard-power" tactics rooted in unilateralism and preemptive warfare, regardless of what the rest of the world thinks. If other countries bestowed on the United States the pejorative label "empire," so be it. Americans should accept it as a badge of honor.

CONCLUSION

While acknowledging the shift toward imperial globalism after 9/11, both market globalists and their ideological challengers on the Left emphasized the continued viability of the project of market liberalization and global integration. For example, the Indian writer and social activist Arundhati Roy, one of the most eloquent critics of corporate globalization, argued that the neoliberal project of "breaking open different markets" was merely receiving more open US military backing in the ongoing Global War on Terror. Claiming that "there isn't a country on God's earth that is not caught in the cross-hairs of the American cruise missile and the IMF checkbook," Roy insisted that those nations with the greatest reserves of natural wealth are most at risk: "Unless they surrender their resources willingly to the corporate machine, civil unrest will be fomented or war will be waged."[78]

Approaching the subject from the opposing ideological perspective in his updated account of globalization in "the age of terrorism," Thomas Friedman nonetheless agreed with Roy's assessment that the neoliberal "globalization system" defined as the liberalization and global integration of markets was still "alive and well" in the post-9/11 era: "Not only will September 11 not be remembered for ending the process of global financial, trade, and technological integration, but it may well be remembered for bringing some sobriety to the anti-globalization movement." But perhaps the most important reason that globalization was alive and well, Friedman continued, was that the two most populous countries in the world—India and China—had long moved beyond the question of "*whether* countries should globalize [emphasis added]." Citing India's leading globalist voices, like Sanjay Baru, the editor of India's *Financial Express*, and Jairam Ramesh, the Congress Party's top economic adviser, Friedman concluded that most countries in the world were still fond of globalization, given their "great desire for participation in the economic expansion process."[79]

However, like many optimistic market globalists, Friedman was caught off guard by the 2008–2009 Global Financial Crisis (GFC). As discussed in the next chapter, the GFC marked a watershed in the ideological landscape of the dominant world order. Ushering in our current period of economic stagnation, political instability, and social fragmentation, it also reinvigorated old political belief systems linked to the national imaginary of the previous century.

CHAPTER 5

SECOND-WAVE CHALLENGERS IN THE 2010S

ANTIGLOBALIST POPULISM

As we noted in the previous chapter, the relentless jihadist terrorist attacks around the world that ramped up in the 2000s and continued throughout the 2010s fanned the flames of a growing global climate of fear and insecurity. Transnational terrorism exposed what many public commentators had begun to call "the dark side of globalization." These new anxieties raised the specter of a return to a deglobalized world of fortified borders and protectionist barriers stemming the global flow of goods, services, ideas, and people. Proliferating news stories of the coming end of the globalization paradigm dovetailed with equally pessimistic academic accounts touting the impending "collapse of globalism." For example, globalization expert John Ralston Saul asserted that "At the most basic level of societal knowledge, we do know that globalization—as announced, promised, and asserted to be inevitable in the 1970s, '80s and much of the '90s—has now petered out."[1]

However, as Western liberal democracies appeared to recover from their terror-induced shock and pursued their so-called Global War on Terror under American leadership, market globalism returned slowly to its dominance by adopting a more "imperialist" posture. By the mid-2000s, it seemed that the obituaries for neoliberal globalization had been written far too hastily. Enter the *2008 Global Financial Crisis* (GFC) that morphed into the *Eurozone Debt Crisis*. This unexpected economic meltdown of global proportions shattered the market globalists' newly found confidence in the inexorable integration of finance, trade, and political structures. The GFC caused a profound shift in the ideological landscape away from the neoliberal vision of a globally integrated world. To add insult to injury, mainstream governments around the world put together gigantic bailout packages for the corporate financial sector at the expense of ordinary taxpayers. Even market globalists with a pronounced social conscience like US President Barack Obama bowed to the dictates of global capitalism and signed off on hundreds of billions of dollars to rescue Wall Street. While such efforts to prop up neoliberal globalization may have saved the global financial infrastructure, they also strengthened both the progressive vision of justice globalism and the reactionary rhetoric of nationalists. New transnational social justice movements on the Left such as *Los Indignados* and Occupy Wall Street emerged together with right-wing populist groups and antiglobalist forces such as the American Tea Party renegades or France's refurbished *Front National* under the charismatic leadership of Marine Le Pen.

Thus, with the benefit of hindsight, the GFC and the ensuing Eurozone crisis—together with growing migration flows into the global North in the 2010s—marked a watershed not only in the development of disintegrative tendencies in the global system but also in the ideological landscape of the new century.[2] Caught in the throes of this three-pronged challenge, journalists and academics alike proclaimed the "end of the globalization era" once more. They speculated that the Great Recession and accelerated migration streams might turn into a chronic condition, ushering in a long period of economic stagnation, political instability, cultural backlash, and social fragmentation. Even some avowed market globalists no longer disparaged the possibility of retreating into more regulated forms of capitalism and fortified borders as the unrealistic knee-jerk reaction of "globalization losers." The respected mainstream economist Dani Rodrik, for example, sought to impress upon his readers the enduring importance of a national regulation of the global economy. He argued forcefully that when the social arrangements of democracy clashed with the demands of market globalism, there was only one rational solution: national priorities should take precedence over global concerns.[3]

This chapter will explore how market globalism became increasingly battered by the gales of growing social inequalities and rising cultural tensions around migration, identity, and security issues.

THE THREEFOLD SYSTEMIC GLOBAL CRISIS

The negative consequences of a deregulated global financial infrastructure advocated by market globalists had already been visible in the *1997–1998 Southeast Asia Crisis*. In the early 1990s, the governments of Thailand, Indonesia, Malaysia, South Korea, and the Philippines had gradually abandoned control over the domestic movement of capital in order to attract foreign direct investment. The ensuing influx of global investment translated into soaring stock and real estate markets all over Southeast Asia.

But when those investors realized that prices had become inflated much beyond their actual value, they withdrew a total of $105 billion from these countries. As a result, economic output fell, unemployment increased, and wages plummeted. By late 1997, the entire region found itself in the throes of a financial crisis that threatened to push the global economy into recession. This disastrous result was only narrowly averted by a combination of international bailout packages and the immediate sale of Southeast Asian commercial assets to foreign corporate investors at rock-bottom prices.[4]

A decade later, the world was not as lucky. The 2008 GFC has its roots in the 1980s and 1990s, when three successive US governments under Presidents Reagan, George H. W. Bush, and Clinton pushed for the significant deregulation of the domestic financial services industry. Perhaps the most important initiative in this regard was the 1999 repeal of the Glass-Steagall Act, which was signed into law by President Roosevelt in 1933 to prohibit commercial banks from engaging in investment activities on Wall Street.

After all, the 1929 crash and ensuing Great Depression had exposed the dangers of the savings and loan industry partaking in the speculative frenzy on Wall Street, which had ultimately led to the bankruptcy of many commercial banks and the loss of their customers' assets. Similarly, the 2008 GFC was the product of financial deregulation, unrestrained competition, and marketization of large corporations, which invited the increasingly speculative, high-risk activities of the financial sector during the 1990s and 2000s.[5] The neoliberal deregulation of US finance capital resulted in a frenzy of mergers that gave birth to huge financial-services conglomerates eager to plunge into securities ventures in areas that were not necessarily part of their underlying business. *Derivatives, financial futures, credit default swaps,* and other esoteric financial instruments became extremely popular when new computer-based mathematical models suggested more secure ways of managing the risk involved in buying an asset in the future at a price agreed to in the present. Relying far less on savings deposits, financial institutions borrowed from each other and sold these loans as securities, thus passing the risk on to investors in these securities. Other "innovative" financial instruments such as *hedge funds* leveraged with borrowed funds fueled a variety of speculative activities. Billions of investment dollars flowed into complex "residential mortgage-backed securities" that promised investors up to a 25 percent return on equity.[6]

Assured by monetarist policies aimed at keeping interest rates low and credit flowing, investment banks eventually expanded their search for capital by buying risky "subprime" loans from mortgage brokers who, lured by the promise of big commissions, were accepting applications for housing mortgages with little or no down payment and without credit checks. Increasingly popular in the United States, most of these loans were adjustable-rate mortgages tied to fluctuations of short-term interest rates. Investment banks snapped up these high-risk loans knowing that they could resell these assets—and thus the risk involved—by bundling them into composite securities no longer subject to government regulation. Indeed, one of the most complex of these "innovative" instruments of *securitization*—so-called collateralized debt obligations—often hid the problematic loans by bundling them with lower-risk assets and reselling them to unsuspecting investors.

But why, given the poor quality of collateral, did individual and institutional investors continue to buy these mortgage-backed securities?

One can think of three principal reasons. First, as noted above, esoteric forms of securities often concealed the degree of risk involved, and investors failed to grasp the complexity of these new investment funds. Second, investors relied on the excellent reputation of such financial giants as Bank of America or Citicorp. Third, they trusted the positive credit ratings reports issued by Standard and Poor's or Moody's, failing to see how these firms were themselves implicated in the expanding speculative bubble. Seeking to maximize their profits, these credit ratings giants had a vested interest in the growth of securities markets and thus took an extremely rosy view of the inherent risks.[7]

The high yields flowing from these new securities funds attracted more and more investors around the world, thus rapidly globalizing more than a trillion US dollars' worth of what came to be known as "toxic assets." In mid-2007, however, the financial steamroller finally ran out of fuel when seriously overvalued American real estate began to drop, and foreclosures shot up dramatically. Investors finally realized the serious risks attached to the securities market and lost confidence. Consequently, the value of securitized mortgage funds fell, and banks desperately tried in vain to somehow eliminate the debts showing on their balance sheets.

Some of the largest and most venerable financial institutions, insurance companies, and government-sponsored underwriters of mortgages such as Lehman Brothers, Bear Stearns, Merrill Lynch, Goldman Sachs, AIG, Citicorp, JPMorgan Chase, IndyMac Bank, Morgan Stanley, Fannie Mae, and Freddie Mac—to name but a few—either declared bankruptcy or had to be bailed out by the US taxpayer. Both the conservative Bush II and the liberal Obama administrations championed spending hundreds of billions of dollars on a rescue package for distressed mortgage securities in return for a government share in the businesses involved. Britain and most other industrialized countries followed suit with their own bailout packages worth billions of dollars, hoping that such massive injections of capital into ailing financial markets would help prop up financial institutions deemed "too large to be allowed to fail." But these generous rescue packages allowed large financial conglomerates to lose even more money without having to declare bankruptcy. The cost passed on to the world's taxpayers was truly staggering and committed future generations to repay trillions of dollars used for financing these bailout packages.

However, one of the major consequences of the failing financial system was that banks trying to rebuild their capital base could hardly afford to keep lending large amounts of money. The flow of global credit slowed to a trickle and businesses and individuals who relied on credit found it much more difficult to obtain. This credit shortage, in turn, impacted the profitability of many businesses, forcing them to cut back production and lay off workers. Industrial output declined; unemployment shot up as the world's stock markets dropped dramatically. By 2009, $14.3 trillion, or 33 percent of the value of the world's companies, was wiped out by the GFC. The developing world was especially hard hit with a financial shortfall of $700 billion by the end of 2010.[8]

As the Global *Financial* Crisis solidified into a global *economic* crisis known as the *Great Recession*, the leaders of the world's twenty largest economies—the so-called G-20—met repeatedly to devise a common strategy to combat a global depression. Although these efforts prevented the wholesale collapse of the world's financial infrastructure, economic growth in the early 2010s in many parts of the world remained anemic and unemployment numbers came down only very slowly. Soon, it also became clear that the Great Recession had spawned a second related crisis in the form of severe sovereign debt and banking problems, especially in the European Union. This rapidly escalating financial turmoil in the Eurozone affected first Greece and then rapidly spilled over into Spain, Portugal, Ireland, and other EU countries.

Indeed, the structural crisis of the global economy almost bankrupted the birthplace of Western civilization—Greece. What came to be known as the *Greek debt crisis* began in 2009 and 2010—in the wake of the GFC—when the Greek government announced that it had understated its national budget deficits for years and was running out of funds. As Greece was shut out from borrowing in global financial markets, the International Monetary Fund (IMF) and European Central Bank were forced to put together two gigantic bailout packages totaling $275 billion in order to avoid the country's financial collapse. But the EU lenders imposed harsh austerity terms in exchange for the loan, which caused further economic hardship and failed to restore economic stability. Greece's economy shrank by a quarter and the national unemployment rate shot up to 25 percent. This disastrous economic development exacerbated people's resentment of the neoliberal policies of austerity and sharpened the country's political polarization.

In 2015, the left-leaning populist Syriza Party scored a surprising election victory, which made its forty-one-year-old charismatic leader Alexis Tsipras Greece's new prime minister. Assisted by his flamboyant finance minister, Yanis Varoufakis, Tsipras negotiated a short extension of the loan packages only to face an ultimatum from the Germany-led EU lenders to implement even further austerity measures. Tsipras refused and called for a national referendum on the acceptance of these draconic conditions. The defeat of the so-called bailout referendum by 61 percent of the popular vote was followed by weeks of frantic negotiations between Tsipras and the EU under German leadership. Finally, the creditors offered an even larger multibillion-dollar loan over three years with similar austerity conditions attached. Taking advantage of the defiant popular mood, Tsipras resigned and called for new elections. His gamble paid off when Syriza won a resounding election victory in September 2015.

Less than two months later, however, Tsipras was forced to bow to growing popular fears that the dire economic situation in the country would become even worse without the EU bailout package. After a heated debate, the Greek parliament approved of the debt relief measure and promised to implement its highly contentious conditions, which included tax increases for farmers and major cuts in the public pension system. In the years that have followed, it is not clear if the EU's third bailout package has finally put Greece on a path toward economic recovery. Judging from the mixed signs of improvement, and the fact that living standards for most Greek citizens remain far below the levels before the crisis hit, a full economic recovery has yet to emerge.

This new era of global economic volatility that started with the GFC soon encountered a third crisis in the 2010s in the form of increasing migration flows. Let us consider what came to be seen as an especially challenging example: the *Syrian refugee crisis*. It started in March 2011 when, as part of the wider Arab Uprisings that swept across the Middle East region from Tunisia to the Gulf States, pro-democracy protests erupted in Syria that challenged the authoritarian rule of President Bashar al-Assad and his Baath Party. At first, Assad seemed to bow to mounting domestic foreign pressure to hold free elections and respect basic human rights. But once Russian President Vladimir Putin offered his support, the Syrian dictator embarked on a confrontational course with pro-democracy demonstrators, whom he vilified as "rebel forces." The country quickly descended into an all-out civil war that would ultimately kill more than 400,000 people by 2019, when Assad declared victory.[9]

The relentless fighting triggered a humanitarian crisis of truly epic proportions. By 2016, nearly six million Syrians—out of a total population of twenty-three million—had been internally displaced. Close to five million people had fled the country in search of both personal safety and economic opportunity. The majority of Syrian refugees ended up in camps in the neighboring countries of Jordan, Lebanon, Iraq, and Turkey, where they received some humanitarian assistance from local governments, international NGOs such as Mercy Corps and World Vision, and global institutions like the United Nations. Still, in most cases, the massive refugee flows pouring out of Syria strained the available material resources of host communities and also created significant cultural tensions with domestic populations who saw these "outsiders" as a drain on their country's economic resources.

In recent years, hundreds of thousands of Syrian refugees have attempted the dangerous trip across the Mediterranean from Turkey to Greece, hoping to find a better future in the prosperous states of the European Union. Germany, in particular, emerged as their preferred place of refuge. But in order to reach their destination, Syrian migrants had to embark on a long route that led them from Greece across Macedonia, Serbia or Croatia, Hungary or Slovenia, and Austria, until they finally arrived in Bavaria hoping for a swift approval of their residence applications. Even though some EU countries like Hungary resorted to inhumane policies and drastic measures to keep refugees out of their territory, their hastily erected border fences stretching over many miles ultimately proved to be ineffective in stopping such massive population movements.

In fact, the Syrian refugee crisis revealed the inadequacy of the EU's current institutional immigration arrangements based on national preferences. The so-called Schengen Agreement that had for years provided for open borders among EU core countries lacked the robustness and comprehensiveness necessary for coping with this crisis. As policy differences among various national governments became more pronounced, some member countries temporarily withdrew from the agreement and reinstituted systematic border controls. Others placed arbitrary limits on the number of refugees they were willing to process and refused to consider a more coordinated approach. Unable to deal with the huge influx of migrants, the EU faced a predicament that laid bare deep political divisions over migration policy among member states.

Moreover, the Syrian refugee crisis also made visible existing cultural biases and strengthened deep-seated "us" versus "them" binaries that fueled right-wing populist messages about the impending "replacement" of Western civilization by "Muslim invaders." For example, a number of right-wing populist government ministers in member states such as Poland, Slovakia, and Hungary openly expressed their opposition to the "Islamization of Europe" and stated their preference for a limited number of Christian refugees. Countries like Germany and Austria, on the other hand, experienced a polarization of public sentiments with roughly even numbers of citizens supporting or opposing more liberal immigration measures. In the face of such politically explosive divisions, the conservative German government under Chancellor Angela Merkel showed tremendous courage and compassion by welcoming more than one million refugees in 2015 alone—half of whom hailed from Syria. To put this remarkable number into perspective, this means that Germany accepted more Syrian refugees than the US refugee total for all asylum seekers in 2015.

With additional social and political crises mounting in the global South throughout the 2010s—especially some serious political and ecological troubles in Africa, Southeast Asia, and Central America—large transnational migration streams seemed likely to continue for many years, perhaps even decades. Fearful of this trend, governments of rich, democratic countries increased their efforts to limit the number and ethnicity of those seeking to approach their borders, which often led to refugees breaking immigration laws. Drawing on official government documents and interviews with asylum seekers, sociologist David Scott FitzGerald traced how Western democracies deliberately and systematically shut down many legal paths for numerous migrants. In fact, his recent research findings demonstrated that for 99 percent of political refugees, the only way to safety in one of the prosperous countries of the global North was to try to reach its territory and then ask for asylum.[10] This is precisely what happened in 2018 and 2019 at the US-Mexican border when hundreds of thousands of Central American refugees fleeing violence and persecution in their home countries tried to reach US territory only to be subjected to draconian treatment by the Trump administration's hardline anti-immigration methods, which included separating small children from their parents and relatives.

THE IDEOLOGICAL CONSEQUENCES OF THE THREEFOLD SYSTEMIC GLOBAL CRISIS

A good number of political commentators likened the threefold systemic global crisis as a "gathering storm" that threatened the dominance of market globalism—an ideological vision that had ruled the world for nearly three decades.[11] But little did these pundits know that the full force of the cyclone was about to bear down on the global North, reflected most spectacularly in the unexpected victory of the pro-Brexit forces in the United Kingdom and the stunning 2016 election of Donald J. Trump in the United States. Indeed, the growing power of *right-wing national populism*—and the crucial role played by the new digital media in its meteoric rise—prompted influential commentators to coin popular catchphrases such as "new populist wave," "populist explosion," "populist moment," or "populist temptation."[12]

The French philosopher Pierre-André Taguieff coined the term *national populism* in 1984 in reference to the political discourse of Jean-Marie Le Pen and his newly founded French political party, *Front National* (FN), renamed in 2018 under the leadership of his daughter Marine Le Pen as *Rassemblement National* (RN).[13] Soon after the FN party's founding in the 1980s, some of its key politicians openly embraced Taguieff's initially critical term "with much pride."[14] These national populists imagined a mythical national unity based on an essentialized identity through permutations of the ethnic and the cultural. They claimed to defend and protect the pure "common people" against the treachery of "corrupt elites" and "parasitical" social institutions. Privileging a direct relationship between the leader and "the people," French national populists sometimes combined social values of the Left with the political values of the Right.[15] Over the years, a growing number of populism scholars adopted *national populism* as an umbrella term for a range of right-wing variants linked to different geographic regions in the world.[16]

It is important to note that more pluralistic and culturally inclusive forms of *left-wing populism* were on the march as well. This development was accompanied by new academic publications recommending "populism" as an effective strategy to revitalize a Left enervated by the apparent petering out of the Occupy Movement.[17] For example, the appeal of nationalist discourses for left-wing populist leaders was reflected in the strong performance of Senator Bernie Sanders in the 2016 and 2020 US presidential campaign or the landslide victory of Andrés Manuel López Obrador in the 2018 Mexican presidential election. Still, antiglobalist populisms like those espoused by President Trump constitute a far greater threat to a market globalism struggling to maintain its discursive dominance in the increasingly nationalist global political climate.

As some observers were quick to point out, the latest surge of right-wing national populism was intricately connected to shifting perceptions of the role of globalization in the world.[18] In a widely cited research paper, Dani Rodrik argued that the populist backlash was directly "related to the forms in which globalization shocks made themselves felt in society."[19] Neoliberal globalization had shifted the balance of power between big business and labor decisively in favor of the former, and middle- and working-class people in the global North paid the price as their wages stagnated and "good jobs"—especially in manufacturing—disappeared or turned into precarious and casual work arrangements. Moreover, wealthy liberal democracies like the United States failed to implement adequate social protections, like new labor-market programs and redistributive tax policies. The resulting polarization of class structure into "globalization winners" at the top 10 percent of income earners and the rest of "globalization losers" prompted social thinkers like Guy Standing to advance the thesis of the birth of a new class: the *Precariat*.[20]

The growing public perception of the link between globalization and the hollowing out of the long-standing social contract rooted in the postwar "class compromise" that lasted until the 1980s was demonstrated, for example, by the fact that the tone of news stories containing the word *globalization* in leading US and UK newspapers were taking a sharply negative swing by the 2010s.[21] This shifting mood also reflected the growing impact of populist posturing against globalization in the public discourse of those countries. Thus, a growing number of scholars explained the rise of right-wing populism in terms of a "globalization backlash"—fueled, in large part, by the economic and cultural dynamics associated with the threefold systemic crisis that had unfolded over the last decade. Sociologist Colin Crouch puts it aptly:

> Various kinds of upheaval—economic, cultural and political—accompany globalization, producing a backlash among those who feel negatively affected. From being a process that seemed simply to be bringing us both cheaper products from abroad and new export opportunities, globalization has come for many to mean the loss, not just of individual jobs, but of entire long-established industries and the communities and ways of life associated with it, spiraling into further disorientation as foreign customs and large numbers of persons from other cultures invade and obscure life's familiar landmarks.[22]

However, as Pippa Norris and Ronald Inglehart point out, the globalization backlash was a relatively short-term reaction rooted in long-term social structural changes in the living conditions and security of citizens in liberal democracies, and the profound transformation of cultural values that was part of these developments. In short, the *antiglobalist* "populist explosion" of the 2010s had been in the making since the turn toward socially liberal and postmaterialist values in postindustrial societies of the 1960s. Over time, Norris and Inglehart argue, it fueled a conservative reaction, which, in turn, stimulated an "authoritarian reflex."[23] Right-wing populism shifted into hyperdrive in the aftermath of the Great Recession when increasing levels of economic inequality and the shift of income and wealth toward the "1 percent" became palpable for large segments of the middle and working classes in the global North.

At the beginning of the 2010s, it appeared that justice globalists affiliated with "Occupy Wall Street"—a transnational movement whose founders had coined the immensely popular slogan "The 99 percent versus the 1 percent"—would succeed in attracting to their worldview millions of people passed over by the promise of market globalism. Ultimately, however, it was media-savvy *antiglobalist national populists* such as Trump, Nigel Farage, and Marine Le Pen, who managed to convince large segments of the middle and working classes that globalism's great experiment of transcending the nation-state had spiraled out of control and needed to be curbed. Feeding the growing public perception that the integration of markets and societies has failed to deliver on its promises, they supplied scapegoating narratives that responded to the growing "demand-side": people's fear, alienation, anger, and resentment against market-globalist practices of "outsourcing of good jobs" and "opening borders" to transnational flows of capital, commodities, ideas, and people. Thus exploiting and exacerbating existing cultural and economic cleavages, they denounced "globalism" as a "vicious, violent, and murdering ideology" hatched by "cosmopolitan elites." By 2016, their emotional promises of a return to national greatness and ethnocultural nativism were finding more resonance among "the forgotten people" than the rational assurances of market globalists that, in the long run, trade liberalization and the worldwide integration of markets was bound to benefit everyone.

By the closing of the 2010s, antiglobalist right-wing populism seems to be everywhere and anywhere, proving its tremendous adaptability to sociopolitical, cultural, and geographic contexts as different as Viktor Órban's Hungary, Norbert Hofer's Austria, Marine Le Pen's France, Matteo Salvini's Italy, Jarosław Kaczyński's Poland, Nigel Farage's United Kingdom, Pauline Hanson's Australia, Iván Duque's Colombia, Rodrigo Duterte's Philippines, Jair Bolsonaro's Brazil, and, of course, Donald Trump's America. But its ubiquity is not only a sign of its global geographical reach and growing political potency; national populism also contains a glaring paradox by having become part of a multidimensional process that cuts across national borders and cultural divisions.

But what, exactly, is "populism," and how did it come to target "globalization" and "globalism"?

WHAT IS POPULISM?

Deriving from the Latin *populus*—"the people"—populism is one of social science's *essentially contested concepts*.[24] Its notorious slipperiness—reflected in sprouting adjectives such as "chameleonic," "mercurial," "episodic," "culture-bound," or "context-dependent"—has been blamed for the many failed attempts to construct a dominant meaning.[25] Cas Mudde and Cristobal Rovira Kaltwasser define populism as a "thin-centered ideology that considers society separated into two homogenous and antagonistic camps, 'the pure people' versus the 'corrupt elite', and which argues that politics should be an expression of the *volonté générale* (general will) of the people."[26] Others, however, like political theorist Chantal Mouffe, insist that populism "is not an ideology and cannot be attributed to a specific programmatic content."[27] Still others define it as "a social movement," "a strategy of political mobilization," "a political outlook," "a mentality," "a political syndrome," or "an emotional appeal."[28]

But none of these characterizations has achieved universal acceptance in the academy. Margaret Canovan, one the world's foremost authorities on the subject, has pointed out that the meaning of populism varies from context to context, thus demanding different kinds of analysis.[29] The lack of academic consensus on the "true nature" of populism, however, has not put an end to continuous academic quarrels arising from these clashing theoretical perspectives, typologies, and methodological approaches.

It is possible to simplify matters of classification by consolidating these competing perspectives into two distinct intellectual positions differentiated by their focus on either the *content* or *form* of populism. Content-centered approaches emphasize the significance of populism as an *ideology*, whereas form-oriented approaches underscore populism's functional role as an instrumental *style* or *strategy* lacking substantive ideas and values. Thus, form-oriented critics have called for the replacement of the focus on the "what" of ideological approaches to populism with an emphasis on the "how" as reflected in its political logic and performance.[30]

Such calls for the displacement of content with form typically go hand in hand with the assertion that populisms lack "ideological coherence" and "conceptual substance."[31] These critics often utilize the findings of quantitative case studies to bolster their assertion that, "populism quite obviously falls short of the status of ideology."[32] From their perspective, its conceptual "thinness" forces populism to fatten its ideational substance by cannibalizing conventional "thick ideologies" such as conservatism or fascism. Without the ingestion of conceptual chunks taken from other thought-systems, critics argue, populism's status would remain that of an "empty signifier" that "can be filled and made meaningful by whatever is poured into it."[33]

The problem with this assertion of populism's *conceptual thinness* is twofold. First, by presenting this condition as populism's defining conceptual condition—said to apply to all of its subtypes, and across time and space—populism is rendered a static entity consisting of a limited number of core concepts. But rather than reducing populism to an unchanging phenomenon characterized by a "thin" ideational essence, systematic ideological mappings such as the morphological discourse analysis (MDA) utilized in this study project a more dynamic understanding of ideologies as variable and unstable belief systems whose content can wax and wane as a result of ideational flows and changing social contexts.

This is exactly what happened with antiglobalist populism in the 2000s and 2010s: the flow of new ideas—especially "globalization" and "globalism"—into its conceptual core as well as the crisis-ridden social context led to the "fattening" of populism from a "thin" into a "thick" ideology. Given its obvious spatial limitations, this chapter cannot examine the ideological makeup of various antiglobalist populisms in their full global context and in all of their ideational permutations. Rather, my investigation focuses on one significant case—"Trumpism" in the United States. The flow of antiglobalist ideas from the periphery to the ideational core of Trumpist populism was a gradual process that occurred over two decades. Indeed, this current antiglobalist strain can be linked to an earlier populist wave that started to target market globalism at the turn of the twenty-first century.[34]

THE ROOTS OF ANTIGLOBALIST POPULISM

At the 1999 Battle of Seattle, justice globalists made up the vast majority of those millions who protested worldwide against market globalism, but they were not the only political camp opposed to it. There also marched a number of people who championed the nationalist perspective of the radical right. Hard-edged soldiers of neofascism such as Illinois-based World Church of the Creator founder Matt Hale, who was convicted in Illinois in 2004 for instigating the killing of a judge, encouraged their followers to come to Seattle and "throw a monkey wrench into the gears of the enemy's machine." The dangerous neo-Nazi group National Alliance was represented as well. White supremacist leader Louis Beam praised the demonstrators, emphasizing that the "police state goons" in Seattle were paid by international capital to protect "the slimy corporate interests of 'free trade' at the expense of free people." In the sea of signs bearing leftist slogans, there were occasional posters bitterly denouncing the "Jewish Media Plus Big Capital" and the "New World Order."[35] These national-populist dynamics represented the first stirrings of what would become full-blown "alt-right" demonstrations such as the violent 2017 Charlottesville "Unite the Right Rally," which President Trump refused to denounce in explicit terms.

At the dawning of the twenty-first century, market globalism became a target not only for these marginal right-wing radicals, members of the American militia movement, and white supremacists but also for a growing number of more moderate national populists in the Republican Party like Patrick J. Buchanan.[36] Indeed, there are striking ideational continuities between what eventually became Trumpism and earlier discourses of national populism articulated by the likes of Ross Perot, Lou Dobbs, and John Bolton, and European national populists in the 1990s and 2000s. Indeed, Buchanan's ideas proved to be especially influential for the formation of the full-blown antiglobalist populism of Donald Trump and Steve Bannon, cofounder and editor in chief of the "alt-right" platform *Breitbart News Network*. Bannon ultimately became the chief executive officer of Trump's 2016 presidential bid and, after Trump's election victory, his chief strategist for eight months until he left this position to lead the transnational effort to assemble "the infrastructure, globally, of the global populist movement."[37]

Associated with the nationalist wing of the Republican Party since the early 1960s, Buchanan served as an aide and speechwriter for President Richard Nixon from 1966 to 1974. After Nixon's resignation, he became a successful newspaper columnist and popular TV talk-show host. In the mid-1980s, he briefly interrupted his media career to serve as President Ronald Reagan's director of communications. Buchanan has been credited with scripting Reagan's controversial remarks that German SS soldiers buried in Bitburg Veterans' Cemetery in Germany were victims, "just as surely as the victims in the concentration camps." In 1992, Buchanan mounted an impressive challenge to President George H. W. Bush for the presidential nomination of the Republican Party. Four years later, he defeated Senator Robert Dole in the important New Hampshire Republican presidential primary. Although Buchanan ultimately lost the primary contest, he received almost a quarter of the national Republican primary vote. By the late 1990s, Buchanan had emerged as the most prominent leader of right-wing populism in the United States.

After serious disagreements with leading Republicans on issues of free trade and immigration, Buchanan left the Republican Party to pursue the presidential nomination of the Reform Party, the brainchild of Texas billionaire H. Ross Perot, who had captured an astonishing 19 percent of the national vote as an independent presidential candidate in 1992. Perot had built the Reform Party on an ideological platform that combined familiar populist themes with strong nationalist-protectionist appeals to safeguard the economic national interest and reduce the exploding trade deficit. Most famously, he opposed the expansion of the regional free-trade agreement between the United States and Canada. Convinced that the North American Free Trade Agreement (NAFTA) carried the "virus of globalism," he argued that the inclusion of Mexico would lead to a massive flight of manufacturing capital to the south in search of cheap labor. Emerging as one of the principal spokespersons of the anti-NAFTA campaign, Perot forged tactical alliances with organized labor, environmentalists, and import-competing agricultural and industrial interests. His public utterances on the subject often conveyed thinly veiled anti-immigration sentiments.

Although Buchanan eventually beat out a well-financed challenge by Donald Trump to win the Reform Party nomination, the former would come to adopt many of Buchanan's populist ideas, which he developed after ending his political career in the wake of his disappointing showing in the 2000 presidential elections. Trumpism integrated and further developed three central features of Buchanan's worldview.

The first was Buchanan's fierce opposition to domestic and transnational "elites" whom he accused of engineering a "Darwinian world of the borderless economy, where sentiment is folly and the fittest alone survive. In the eyes of this rootless transnational elite, men and women are not family, friends, neighbors, fellow citizens, but 'consumers' and 'factors of production.'" Buchanan's populist focus on the "treacherous" activities of the neoliberal "Washington establishment" served as the foundation for his rejection of the market-globalist claim that nobody was in charge of globalization. He pointed his finger at "greedy global mandarins who have severed the sacred ties of national allegiance" to be found among the members of the US Council on Foreign Relations and the Business Roundtable. Their elitist conspiracy, he insisted, had eroded the power of the nation-state and replaced it with a neoliberal new world order. As a result, most mainstream American politicians were becoming beholden to transnational corporate interests that are undermining the sovereignty of the nation by supporting the World

Trade Organization (WTO) and other international institutions. He accused the "Washington establishment" of channeling billions of dollars to the IMF and the World Bank for the purpose of bailing out undeserving developing countries in Africa, Latin America, and Asia. Evoking the wrath of "the little man"—in this case the "American taxpayer" who was saddled with the costs of these bailouts—Buchanan demanded severe punishment for the market globalists at the helm of the American government and international economic institutions such as the IMF, WTO, and World Bank. And even earlier than Trump, Buchanan had touted global climate change as an invention of scheming elites: "This, it seems to me, is what the global-warming scare and scam are all about—frightening Americans into transferring sovereignty, power and wealth to a global political elite that claims it alone understands the crisis and it alone can save us from impending disaster."[38]

The second feature adopted and further developed by Trump in his 2016 presidential campaign was Buchanan's vehement attack on free trade, which he combined with his "America First" slogan. Turning the ideological table on free-trade Republicans who were dismissing his arguments as "antiquated protectionism," Buchanan reminded his former comrades of the Republican Party's traditional perspective on trade policy. "For not only was the party of Lincoln, McKinley, Theodore Roosevelt, Taft, and Coolidge born and bred in protectionism, it was defiantly and proudly protectionist." For Buchanan, "Protectionism is the structuring of trade policy to protect the national sovereignty, ensure economic self-reliance and 'prosper America first.'"[39] Chiding his former party friends, he wondered, "How long before the GOP wakes up to the reality that globalism is not conservatism, never was, but is the pillar of Wilsonian liberalism, in whose vineyards our faux conservatives now daily labor."[40]

Buchanan referred to his position as "economic nationalism." Popularized by Stephen Bannon in the 2016 election cycle, this perspective holds that the economy should be designed in ways that serve, first and foremost, the nation. Buchanan defined economic nationalism as "America first" policies that put the nation before the global economy and the well-being of its own people before what was best for humankind. "Our trade and tax policies should be designed to strengthen US sovereignty and independence and should manifest a bias toward domestic, rather than foreign, commerce."[41] Buchanan claimed that his economic nationalism reflected the "noble ideas" that "Washington, Hamilton, and Madison had taken to Philadelphia and written into the American Constitution, and that Henry Clay had refined to create 'The American System' that was the marvel of mankind."[42]

Indeed, Buchanan's writings and speeches conveyed his Manichaean conviction that there existed at the core of contemporary American society an "irrepressible conflict between the claims of a New American nationalism and the commands of the Global Economy." Assuring his audience that he considered himself a strong proponent of a free-market system operating within a national context, he insisted that global markets must be harnessed in order to work for the good of the American people. This meant that the leaders of the United States have to be prepared to make economic decisions for the benefit of the nation, not in the interests of "shameless cosmopolitan transnational elites" who are sacrificing "the interests of their own country on the altar of that golden calf, the Global Economy."[43]

Mirroring the strategy of his market-globalist opponents, Buchanan relied on an endless stream of "hard data" to make his protectionist case to the public, hurling it at his readers as evidence against the market-globalist claim that globalization benefits everyone.[44] Arguing that globalization benefited only the wealthy transnational elites, he noted that since its onset in the late 1970s, real wages of working Americans had fallen by as much as 20 percent. By the mid-1990s, top CEO salaries skyrocketed to 212 times more than an average worker's pay, and corporate profits more than doubled between 1992 and 1997. In 2007, the US trade deficit with Mexico and China soared to a record $73 billion and $256 billion, respectively. Under the "globalist presidency" of George W. Bush, he continued, three million American manufacturing jobs were lost, inflation shot up, foreclosures mounted, credit card debt exploded, oil surged to nearly $150 a barrel, and the dollar fell by 50 percent against the euro. As Buchanan put it, "The chickens of globalism are coming home to roost."[45] As we shall see, Buchanan's claims of the loss of economic independence and national sovereignty as a result of "globalism" were greatly intensified in Trump's antiglobalist populism and skillfully deployed against the "globalist presidency" of Barack Obama and his "globalist" political opponent, Hillary Clinton.

The third prominent feature of Buchanan's populism appropriated and developed further by Trump was the familiar nationalist-populist move of scapegoating outsiders. In particular, Buchanan accused the nation's "liberal advocates of multiculturalism" of tolerating and even encouraging the influx of "12 to 20 million illegal immigrants roosting here." His fundamentally inegalitarian and nativist message was especially obvious in his derogatory language toward irregular migrants from the global South. Making them responsible for the economic and moral decline of the United States, he evoked the specter of the cultural dissolution of the United States: "With the 45 million Hispanics here to rise to 102 million by 2050, the Southwest is likely to look and sound more like Mexico than America. Indeed, culturally, linguistically and ethnically, it will be part of Mexico."[46] In fact, during the acrimonious public debate over the 2006–2007 immigration reforms in the United States, Buchanan accused Latinos of Mexican extraction of promoting the cultural and political *Reconquista* of the US Southwest. He insisted that most of "them" lacked a passionate attachment to the core of America—its land, its people, its past, its heroes, literature, language, traditions, culture, and customs.[47]

Foreshadowing Trump's xenophobic promise to "build a wall" on the Mexican border to keep "rapists and murderers" out, Buchanan declared himself in favor of drastic anti-immigration policies designed to "strengthen the Border Control, lengthen the 'Buchanan Fence' on the southern frontier, repatriate illegals, and repair the great American melting pot."[48]

National populists like Buchanan habitually combine their xenophobic attacks on immigrants with a retroactive construction of a homogeneous "heartland" based on an idealized picture of the past. Moreover, their implied moralism lends itself to the easy incorporation of religious and mystical themes that resonate particularly well with conservative or anti-intellectual audiences.

Yet, current proponents of Buchanan's national populism like Stephen Bannon use their speeches and writings to show that the evocation of faith and tradition does not necessarily result in an endorsement of the religious establishment. Apocalyptic narratives and millennial visions, generally downplayed in mainstream religions, loom large in Bannon's political vision of a crisis-ridden "fourth turning."[49] He often expressed this hope for a "new beginning" in terms of combating the demographic "catastrophe" resulting from the immigration of Muslims and other "undesirables" who are changing the face of "Western civilization." As Bannon laid out in his 2014 Skype presentation for a conservative conference held inside the Vatican:

> And we're at the very beginning stages of a very brutal and bloody con-
> flict, of which if the people in this room, the people in the church, do not
> bind together and really from what I feel is an aspect of church militant,
> to really be able to not just stand with our beliefs, but to fight for our be-
> liefs against this new barbarity that is starting, that will completely eradi-
> cate everything that we've been bequeathed over the last 2,000, 2,500
> years. . . . They have a Twitter account today, ISIS does, about turning the
> United States into a "river of blood" if it comes in and tries to defend the
> city of Baghdad. And trust me, that is going to come to Europe. That is
> going to come to Central Europe, it's going to come to Western Europe,
> it's going to come to the United Kingdom. And so I think we are in a
> crisis of the underpinnings of capitalism, and on top of that we're now, I
> believe, at the beginning stages of a global war against Islamic fascism.[50]

Here Bannon followed a trope frequently used by national populists: the evocation of an extreme crisis that requires an immediate and
forceful response. Usually directed to segments of the population most
threatened by the forces of modernization, such appeals thrive on the
alleged discrepancy between the idealized values of the "heartland" and
existing political practices.[51] Finally, national populists imagine "the
people" as a homogeneous national unit welded together by a common will, a single interest, an ancestral heartland, shared cultural and
religious traditions, and a national language. However, the common
"we" applies only to those persons deemed to belong to the nation. The
presumed identity of "our" people-nation—often conveyed in racial
terminology—allows populists to fuel and exploit existing hostilities
against those whose very existence threatens their essentialist myth of
homogeneity and unity.

Bannon's apocalyptic narrative can also be linked to associations such
as the John Birch Society, the Christian Coalition, the Liberty Lobby,
so-called patriot and militia movements, and the alt-right. All these
groups are convinced that globalization lies at the root of an incipient
anti-American new world order. Regarding neoliberal internationalism as
an alien and godless ideology engulfing the United States, they fear that
globalism is relentlessly eroding individual liberties and the "traditional
American way of life."

John Bolton, who served in the Bush II administration as US ambassador to the United Nations and became President Trump's national security advisor in 2018, aptly summarized this right-wing populist view in 2010 in a short book that accused the Obama administration of "endangering our national sovereignty": "We have been locked in a struggle between sovereignty and 'global governance' that most Americans didn't even know was happening. Not surprisingly, therefore, 'Americanists' have been losing to the 'globalists,' and the general public does not yet appreciate the chasm between these two worldviews."[52]

As demonstrated by the following MDA of key speeches delivered by Trump during his 2016 presidential campaign, the Trumpist strain of right-wing, *antiglobalist populism* seized upon Bolton's binary of "us" ("Americanists") and "them" ("globalists") and elevated it to its ideological "credo."[53]

WHAT DO ANTIGLOBALIST POPULISTS WANT? EXAMINING THE CORE CONCEPTS AND CENTRAL CLAIMS OF TRUMPISM

Unsurprisingly, the MDA of Trump's 2016 campaign speeches clearly revealed two concepts at the heart of his populist discourse: "the people" and "the elites." This confirms the rare agreement among populism scholars that these keywords sit at the core of all explanatory schemes of the phenomenon. Appearing prominently in all of Trump's public remarks, the concept of "the people" is, first and foremost, decontested in *national* terms by means of the adjacent concept "American."[54] Accordingly, the presidential candidate addressed "the American people" whom he also imagined as a homogenous community "united in common purposes and dreams" and enjoying the privilege of living in the "greatest nation on earth."[55]

Second, "the people" are identified as "*common* people"—especially as "workers," "working people," and "middle-class people." Indeed, these crucial terms appear very frequently in Trump's speeches and are often embedded in nationalist narratives: "The legacy of Pennsylvania steelworkers lives in the bridges, railways, and skyscrapers that make up our great American landscape."[56]

Third, Trump imbues "the people" with meanings that are sharpened by additional terms such as "sovereignty" and "independence."[57]

The concepts, too, are consistently linked to nationalistic themes such as his celebration of America's unique political system manifested in "a government of the people, by the people, and for the people."[58]

Thus, MDA confirms the presence of three major populist meanings of "the people" as identified by Mudde and Rovira Kaltwasser: the people as sovereign, as common people, and as the nation.[59] We also found ample evidence for Müller's contention that the populist core concept of "the people" is imbued with a deeply moralistic hue.[60] Trump's campaign speeches are rife with essentialist depictions of the "pure" character of the "American people" in such moralistic superlatives as "great," "patriotic," "loyal," "hardworking," "daring," "brave," "strong," "energetic," "decent," "selfless," "devoted," and "honest." Consider, for example, this striking, yet factually incorrect, passage highlighting some of the essential qualities of the American people: "Americans are the people that tamed the West, that dug out the Panama Canal, that sent satellites across the solar system, that build great dams, and so much more."[61]

Trump continues his decontestation of the core concept "American people" by making the familiar populist turn to its "other." Accordingly, he asserts that the people's proven loyalty to, and hard work for, the nation has been "repaid with total betrayal."[62] Slandered as "deplorables" and demeaned by the coercive discourse of "political correctness," "American patriots who love our country and want a better future for all of our people" have been robbed of their dignity and respect. However, thanks to their "common sense"—expressed in their "clear understanding of how democracy really works"—the American people will debunk this deception and refuse to sit idly by as they are "being ripped off by everybody in the world."[63]

At this point in his decontestation of "the American people," Trump begins to draw on the notion of their unmediated and incorruptible "general will," which, though thwarted and ignored, is bound to reassert itself and "smash the establishment."[64] Roused by true tribunes of the people such as Donald Trump, ordinary Americans are encouraged to "create a new American future" in which the people will be "first" again.[65] In a joint campaign appearance with Trump, Nigel Farage, the British politician who spearheaded the successful pro-Brexit campaign, offered the following powerful affirmation of this activist construction of "the people" and their "true aspirations":

> I come to you from the United Kingdom with a message of hope and
> a message of optimism. It's a message that says if little people, the real
> people, if ordinary decent people are prepared to stand up and fight for
> what they believe in, we can overcome the big banks, we can overcome
> the multinationals. . . . We reached those people. We reached those
> people who have never voted in their lives, but believe by going out and
> voting for Brexit they can take back control of their country, take back
> control of their borders, and get back their pride and self-respect.[66]

This antagonistic turn in the construction of "the people" leads us
to the second core concept that emerged from our MDA: the "guilty"
party identified as "elites," "the establishment," "politicians," and
"leadership class."[67] Undermining the will of the people with the help
of the "corporate media," these economic, political, and cultural insid-
ers are accused of "rigging" the system of representative democracy—
most clearly manifested in the "Washington swamp"—to the end of advancing their morally corrupt practices of "selling out the wealth of our
nation generated by working people" and filling their own pockets.[68]
In short, "the elites" or "the establishment" are always decontested in
terms of a denigrated "other" that contrasts sharply with the valoriza-
tion of "the people."

Most importantly, Trump links the meaning of "the elites" to the notion of "globalist enemies" working against the interests of the country.
While some of them are explicitly identified as domestic actors such
as "Wall Street bankers" or "Washington politicians," many are characterized as "foreign agents," which includes both individuals such as
George Soros and other members of the "international financial elite"
or entire countries like China, Mexico, and Japan, which are denounced
for the alleged misdeeds of "subsidizing their goods," "devaluing their
currencies," "violating their agreements," and "sending rapists, drug
dealers, and other criminals into America."[69]

Trump consistently showcases "Hillary" and "the Clintons" as the
"un-American" epitome of the corrupt globalist elites—a politically
effective and rhetorically skilled move that allows him to collapse the
distinction between domestic and global foes by creating a unified
enemy image under the sign of "globalization." An abbreviated list of
Hillary Clinton's alleged "crimes against the American people" includes
proposing mass amnesty for illegal immigrants; advocating for open
borders; spreading terrorism; pursuing an aggressive, interventionist

foreign policy; making America less secure; robbing workers of their future by sending their jobs abroad; ending American sovereignty by handing power over to the United Nations and other "globalist" institutions; abandoning Israel in its national struggle for survival; supporting free-trade agreements inimical to American interests; tilting the economic playing field toward other countries at America's expense; and advancing global special interests.

Most importantly, Trump persistently employs the terms *global* or *globalist* to flesh out the precise meaning of the elites' betrayal as reflected in the crimes of "crooked Hillary" and the "global establishment" she represents. His decontestation of "the elites" allows us to identify the first central ideological claim that associates the decontested meanings of the core concepts of "the people" and "the elites" with the adjacent term *global*.

CLAIM NUMBER ONE: CORRUPT ELITES BETRAY THE HARDWORKING AMERICAN PEOPLE BY SHORING UP A GLOBAL ORDER THAT MAKES THEM RICH AND POWERFUL WHILE COMPROMISING THE SOVEREIGNTY AND SECURITY OF THE HOMELAND AND SQUANDERING THE WEALTH OF THE NATION

This claim helps Trump to present his electoral campaign against Hillary Clinton, the treacherous "globalist" *par excellence*, as something much bigger than just a familiar political contest that repeats itself every four years. Rather, he frames the presidential election as a Manichean struggle that pits America against two "globalist" enemies: a hostile "world order" and "a leadership class that worships globalism over Americanism."[70] During his many stump appearances of the 2016 campaigning season, this assertion of an irreconcilable opposition between "Americanism" and "globalism" that first appeared in the national-populist discourse of Pat Buchanan, John Bolton, Stephen K. Bannon, and others grew into Trumpism's second central ideological claim—his "credo" appearing in almost every speech.

CLAIM NUMBER TWO: AMERICANISM, NOT GLOBALISM, WILL BE OUR CREDO

In this context, it is important to remember that the meaning of "credo" carries deeply religious connotations that signify the very essence of a belief system. The constant repetition of this "Americanist credo"—and its numerous permutations such as "Hillary defends globalism, not Americanism" or "Hillary wants America to surrender to globalism"— indicates the enormous significance of globalization-related concepts in Trump's political discourse.[71] For this reason, I refer to this strain of national populism as "antiglobalist populism." Warning his audience not to surrender to "the false song of globalism," Trump emphasized that "[t]he nation-state remains the true foundation for happiness and harmony."[72] Thus, he decontests "globalism" as both a set of misguided public policies and a "hateful foreign ideology" devised by members of "the global power structure" who plot "in secret to destroy America."[73] Indeed, globalists serve the larger material process of "globalization," defined by Trump as an elite-engineered project of "abolishing the nation-state" and creating an international system that functions "to the detriment of the American worker and the American economy."[74] In short, he denounces both the economic and political dimensions of "globalization" by arranging suitable core and adjacent concepts such as "jobs," "free trade," "financial elites," "open borders" and "immigration" into potent narratives.

With respect to its economic dimension, Trump accuses globalization of "wiping out the American middle class and jobs" while making the "financial elites who donate to politicians, very, very, wealthy. I used to be one of them."[75] Indeed, almost all of the speeches analyzed in this chapter contain substantial discussions of the dire economic impacts of globalization as reflected in disadvantageous international trade deals, outsourced American jobs, stagnant wages and salaries, the crumbling of America's manufacturing base, hostile foreign corporate takeovers, and unfair, corrupt economic practices devised by the likes of China and Mexico aided by treacherous domestic politicians who have "sold America to the highest bidder."[76] But such lengthy tirades against the nation's "globalist enemies" are always followed by passionate assurances that America's dire situation could be reversed under the antiglobalist leadership of Donald J. Trump. At times, he delivers this message with surprising policy detail, thus providing clear evidence of Trumpism's responsiveness to concrete political issues and problems.[77]

With regard to its political dynamics, Trump associates "globalization" with what he calls the "complete and total disasters" of immigration, crime, and terrorism that are "destroying our nation."[78] Immigration, in particular, receives ample treatment in the form of vigorous denunciations of the establishment's "globalist policies of open borders" that endanger the "safety" and "security" of the American people. Once again, "Hillary" becomes a convenient signifier in Trump's decontestation of globalization as a nefarious process of border erasure: "National security is also immigration security—and Hillary wants neither. Hillary Clinton has put forward the most radical immigration platform in the history of the United States. She has pledged to grant mass amnesty and, in her first 100 days, end virtually all immigration enforcement, and thus create totally open borders in the United States."[79]

Trump's semantic linkage of "globalization" and (lack of) "security" confirms populism's affinity for a charismatic, authoritarian leader who can protect "the people" from a hostile world. Such patriarchal sentiments are reflected in the candidate's occasional direct appeals to the women's vote: "Women also value security. They want a Commander-in-Chief that will defeat Islamic terrorism, stop the massive inflow of refugees, protect our borders, and who will reduce the rising crime and violence in our cities."[80] For Trump, the realization of his campaign slogan "make America great again" requires the systematic separation of the "national" from the "global" in all aspects of social life in the United States. Politically, this severance requires "the American people" to support a nationalistic leader who is "not running to be President of the World," but "to be President of the United States": "I am for America—and America first."[81]

In other words, the inherent greatness and goodness of the American people must be reactivated in the patriotic struggle against the essential evil of globalization and its domestic handmaidens. As Trump puts it, "The central base of world power is here in America, and it is our corrupt political establishment that is the greatest power behind the efforts at radical globalization and the disenfranchisement of working people."[82] Yet, as is the case with Trump's economic narrative, the decontestation of the negative political consequences of globalization is always combined with assurances of the impending glorious rebirth of the nation. Trump's antiglobalist optimism can be articulated in a third central ideological claim.

CLAIM NUMBER THREE: THE DEFEAT OF GLOBALISM AND ITS TREACHEROUS IDEOLOGUES WILL USHER IN A BRIGHT FUTURE THROUGH THE GLORIOUS REBIRTH OF THE NATION

It is important to note that Donald Trump did not abandon his anti-globalist populist oratory after his 2016 electoral victory. Quite to the contrary, his ultra-nationalist attacks on "globalism" became enshrined in most of his major public speeches. Two years into his presidency, Trump delivered a high-profile address at the seventy-third session of the UN General Assembly that contained the following ideological centerpiece:

> We will never surrender America's sovereignty to an unelected, unaccountable, global bureaucracy. America is governed by Americans. We reject the ideology of globalism, and we embrace the doctrine of patriotism. . . . To unleash this incredible potential in our people, we must defend the foundations that make it all possible. Sovereign and independent nations are the only vehicle where freedom has ever survived, democracy has ever endured, or peace has ever prospered. And so, we must protect our sovereignty and our cherished independence above all.[83]

At a pre-midterm election rally in Texas a month later, Trump unabashedly referred to himself as a "nationalist" and urged his audience not to be ashamed to use the word. As he explained, the term *nationalist* signified the opposite of *globalist*: "You know what a globalist is, right? You know what a globalist is? A globalist is a person that wants the globe to do well, frankly, not caring about our country so much. And you know what? We can't have that."[84]

Indeed, there seems to be little evidence that the American president embraces antiglobalist populism for *purely* instrumental reasons. Rather than representing a mere "strategy" or "style," Trump's speeches reveal not only his deep commitment to specific antiglobalist ideas and values but also the richness of the ideational environment in which they are rooted.[85]

CONCLUSION

This chapter traced the tremendous ideological impact of the threefold systemic crises that unfolded in the wake of the devastating 2008–2009

GFC. The widespread excitement over the promises of market globalists has given way to rising fears that their great experiment of transcending the nation-state has spiraled out of control and needs to be
curbed. Numerous commentators have been feeding the growing public
perception that the integration of markets and societies has failed to deliver on its promises. As market globalism failed to live up to its central
claims, ordinary people turned against it.

This was true especially in the global North where working- and
middle-class people found themselves at the receiving end of profound social changes triggered by such transnational dynamics as the
outsourcing of manufacturing jobs and enhanced levels of migration.
The once hegemonic market-globalist discourse struggled to contain
a rising antiglobalist populist narrative that unleashed its fury on
the grand liberal vision of the good life in open and interconnected
societies. Right-wing populists blamed "globalization" and "globalism" for most of the social, economic, and political ills afflicting their
home countries. Threatened by the slow erosion of old social patterns
and traditional ways of life, they denounce free trade, the increasing
power of global investors, and the neoliberal "internationalism" of
transnational corporations as unpatriotic practices that have contributed to falling living standards and moral decline. Fearing the loss of
national self-determination and the destruction of a circumscribed
national culture, they pledge to protect the integrity of their nation
from those "foreign elements" that they identify as responsible for
unleashing the forces of globalization.

Media-savvy national populists like Donald J. Trump in the United
States or Marine Le Pen in France focused on the challenges and dislocations brought about by globalization dynamics to appeal to those
segments of the population most in danger of losing their status in the
conventional social hierarchies of the nation-state. They responded to
people's growing sense of fragmentation, anxiety, and alienation by presenting themselves as strong leaders capable of halting the erosion of
conventional social bonds and familiar cultural environments. Lending
an authoritarian voice to their audiences' longing for the receding world
of cultural uniformity, moral certainty, and national parochialism, populists refuse to rethink old notions of "national community" in light of
the social changes wrought by globalization. Rather, they unapologeti-
cally put the well-being of their own citizens above the construction of a

more equitable international order based on global solidarity. Frustrated voters across different national and cultural environments responded in droves by venting their anger at "elitist globalists" at the ballot box. Capitalizing on this backlash against globalization, right-wing populists celebrated their spectacular success at the polls, which demonstrated the remarkable resilience of the national imaginary.

Focusing on the investigation of Trumpism in the United States as an especially potent example of the contemporary strain of *antiglobalist populism*, this chapter demonstrated the growing significance of the concepts of "globalization" and "globalism" for this right-wing ideology. Our morphological discourse analysis confirmed the flow of "antiglobalist" ideas from its periphery to the ideational core—a gradual process starting with Patrick Buchanan's national-populist discourse in the 1990s and 2000s. Linking with conventional national-populist core concepts such as "the people," "the elites," and "the general will," globalization-related ideas have produced strong ideological claims that have challenged the dominant globalization meanings of neoliberal market globalism. By the mid-2010s, this process of fattening national populism's conceptual core had proceeded sufficiently to make Trumpism a full-fledged ideology.

As a result of these ideational reconfigurations, national populism's conceptually sturdier and more coherent *antiglobalist strain* was born. Far from being locked in static, frozen ideas, its distinct narratives convey authoritative meanings and messages capable of responding quickly and effectively to pressing political problems and policy challenges such as migration, taxation, trade, military, and others. While the findings offered in this chapter need to be confirmed and further developed in future qualitative and quantitative analyses of contemporary national populisms, corroborating empirical evidence of the increasing salience of antipopulist ideas has already been confirmed in recently published studies.[86]

As the world wavers between globalist expansion and nationalist retrenchment, market globalism and antiglobalist populism remain locked in a fierce ideational struggle over the meaning of globalization. The latter attempts to break the ideological hegemony of the former's core concepts by attacking the five central claims of its neoliberal adversary identified in chapter 3: globalization is about the liberalization and global integration of markets; globalization is inevitable and irreversible; nobody is in charge of globalization; globalization benefits everyone; and globalization furthers the spread of democracy. The objective of antiglobalist populists like Trump, Farage, and Le Pen is to decontest "globalization" and "globalism" in very specific ways that contrast sharply with the dominant neoliberal meanings.

To some extent, then, antiglobalist national populism mimics the strategy of justice globalism, which amasses ideational gravity by contesting market globalism's central claims and filling them with contrary contents. This strategy requires these ideological challengers to move "globalization" and "globalism" to their conceptual core. Yet, unlike the chief codifiers of justice globalism who attempted to formulate an ideological alternative to market globalism that drew on the rising *global imaginary*, populists like Trump or Farage seek to reinvigorate a *national imaginary* that has come under significant strain by the destabilizing dynamics of globalization. As Nigel Farage proclaimed in his post-2016 celebration of a "global political revolution" ushered in by Brexit and Trump's victory: "2016 was the year the nation-state democracy made a comeback against the globalism of those who wish to destroy everything we have ever been."[87]

The changeability and adaptability of antiglobalist populism underscores the importance of contextual factors such as increasing inequality, growing migration flows, erosion of traditional collective identities, decreasing legitimacy of conventional political institutions, and the segmentation of the digital media environment—all of which are likely to increase the resonance of antiglobalist populism's ideological claims across a wide range of economic, cultural, and sociopolitical change associated with globalization.[88] The attention to context that should be paid by students of the ideological dimension of globalization demands the rejection of the false dichotomy between ideas and material forces as rival causal agencies in favor of linking conceptual maps to what happens on the ground, and vice versa. As nationalism scholar Rogers Brubaker emphasizes, explaining the current populist moment requires a layered explanatory strategy capable of discussing structural trends of global social change—often appearing in the form of "crises"—that have gradually expanded opportunities for populism and thus serve as superconductors of national populism's ideological claims to protect the people against threats to their security.[89]

The political significance of antiglobalist populism's growing ideological stature seems obvious. By adding new ideas to its arsenal, the surging political belief system enhances its ability to respond to a wide array of political questions and thus broadens their appeal to ever-larger segments of the population. Their growing ideational power means that antiglobalist strains of national populism have transcended the proximate context in which they emerged. Thus, its denunciation of globalization notwithstanding, national populism has itself become part of a global process.

CHAPTER 6

GLOBALISMS IN THE 2020S

THREE FUTURE SCENARIOS

As I have discussed in this book, the ongoing ideological confrontation between market globalism and its three main challengers constantly produces competing claims, slogans, metaphors, and mental frames designed to win over the hearts and minds of a global audience. Will this epic contest of ideas contribute to more extensive forms of inter-connectivity, or will it slow down the powerful momentum of neoliberal globalization? The sheer magnitude of the antiglobalist populist challenge mounted in the late 2010s has raised the possibility that the three ideological articulators of the global imaginary—market globalism, justice globalism, and religious globalism—might find themselves eclipsed by the resurgent translators of the national imaginary. While the prospects of globalisms remain uncertain, one thing seems clear: the political stakes in the current ideological contest between antiglobalist populism and the major globalisms—especially the once-dominant market globalism—are enormously high. The goal of these conflicting visions is nothing less than to achieve the successful decontestation of the meaning of "globalization." As I noted in chapter 1, control over "globalization talk" would translate directly into political power and, in turn, contribute to the realization of concrete public policies.

Will the national-populist surge of the 2010s turn out to be a short-lived protest against the dislocations wrought by neoliberal globalization, or might it actually develop into an enduring ideological tradition? After all, the originally thin ideational clusters of fascism and communism bulked up in the early twentieth century through fierce competition with more mature ideologies such as conservatism and socialism. Will market globalism face extinction or might it stage a successful comeback in the coming decade? Could the sagging fortunes of justice globalism experience a reversal in light of intensifying global problems such as climate change and widening disparities in wealth and well-being? Or will religious globalism be the main beneficiary of an increasingly chaotic world teetering at the brink of environmental or nuclear apocalypse?

Responding to these questions, this concluding chapter offers a brief speculation on possible trajectories of the ideological confrontation over the direction and meaning of globalization in the coming decade. The ensuing discussion offers *three competing future scenarios* in response to the current populist challenge: the *backlash scenario*, the *rebound scenario*, and the *stalemate scenario*.

THE BACKLASH SCENARIO: THE POPULIST CHALLENGE SUCCEEDS

In the previous edition of this book—completed just weeks before the 2008 Global Financial Crisis (GFC) hit with full force—I introduced what I considered to be the very real possibility of a severe social backlash caused by the negative consequences of the unbridled economic and cultural dynamics of neoliberal globalization. This explosive reaction against market globalism, I argued, could unleash nationalist political forces similar to those responsible for the deaths and suffering of millions during the dark decades of the 1930s and 1940s. If the current antiglobalist populist challenge succeeds in dominating its ideological competitors, then the 2020s fall victim to similar extremist right-wing formations of the national imaginary.

But let us first consider the theoretical arguments underpinning such a *backlash scenario*. These are often associated with the work of the late political economist Karl Polanyi, who located the origins of the social crises that gripped the world during the first half of the twentieth century in excessive efforts to liberalize markets. In his celebrated book, *The Great Transformation* (1944), the author chronicled how commercial interests came to dominate European societies by means of a ruthless market logic that effectively disconnected people's economic activities from their social relations. The unbridled principles of the free market destroyed complex social relations of mutual obligation and undermined communal values such as civic engagement, reciprocity, mutual aid, and redistribution. As large segments of the population found themselves without an adequate system of social security and communal support, they rallied behind hypernationalist political leaders promising to curb the dynamics of marketization.

Extending his analysis to the workings of advanced capitalism in general, Polanyi extrapolated that all modern societies contained two organizing principles that were fundamentally opposed to each other. The first was the *principle of economic liberalism*, aiming at the establishment of a self-regulating market. It relied on the support of the trading classes and used largely laissez-faire and free trade as its method. The second was the *principle of social protection* aiming at the conservation of humans and nature as well as productive organizations. It garnered the support of those most immediately affected by the deleterious actions of the market—primarily but not exclusively the working and the landed classes—and used protective legislation, restrictive associations, and instruments of intervention as its method.[1]

Referring to these dialectical principles as a *double movement*, Polanyi suggested that the stronger the liberal impulse became, the more it would be able to dominate society by means of a market logic that effectively "disembedded" people's economic activity from their social relations. Hence, in the name of advancing human freedom in general, the principles of economic liberalism provided a powerful justification for leaving large segments of the population to "fend for themselves." In a capitalist world organized around the notion of individual liberty—

understood primarily as unrestrained economic entrepreneurship—the market ideals of competition and self-interest trumped old social conceptions of cooperation and solidarity.[2]

But it is important to remember the other half of Polanyi's *theory of double movement*: the rapid advance of free-market principles also strengthened the resolve of working people to oppose what they saw as "liberal elites" and denounce the negative social effects of their policies. Polanyi noted that labor movements in Europe eventually gave birth to illiberal political parties that forced the passage of protective social legislation on the national level. After a prolonged period of severe economic dislocations following the end of World War I, the nationalist impulse experienced its most extreme manifestations in Italian fascism and German Nazism. In the end, the grand liberal dream of subordinating the nation to the requirements of the free market had generated an equally extreme countermovement that turned markets into mere appendices of totalitarian nation-states.[3]

Back in 2008, I neither envisioned that the backlash scenario would materialize so quickly in the second half of the 2010s, nor did I foresee the exact form it would take. However, the applicability of Polanyi's analysis to our current situation seems obvious. Like its nineteenth-century predecessor, the market globalism of the 1990s represented an excessive experiment in unleashing the utopia of the self-regulating market on society. In fact, the acolytes of neoliberalism were prepared to turn the entire world into their laboratory. From the political Left, justice globalists challenged this project vigorously in the streets of the world's major cities. From the political Right, the religious-globalist forces of radical Islamism launched a massive attack against what they considered to be a morally corrupt ideology of secular materialism that had allegedly engulfed the entire world. By the mid-2010s, however, it was neither of these two challengers of market globalism that won out. Rather, the antiglobalist populist message of providing nationalist protection against the extraordinary speed and severity of social change brought on by globalization triumphed. Indeed, it appealed to millions of people around the world who favored a retreat to the familiar nationalist imaginary.

What could be the ideological consequences of a further strengthening of antiglobalist populism over the next decade? The backlash scenario suggests that the three forms of globalisms would suffer. To

explain this outcome, let us briefly consider three social dynamics connected to the possible growing stature of antiglobalist populism: the
multiplication of restrictions on major forms of mobility; the decline
of representative democracy and the surge of illiberal authoritarianism;
and the failure to build new institutional forms of international coordination capable of tackling our mounting global problems.

With regard to the growth of restrictions of major forms of mobility such as the movement of goods, services, and money, the current
populist surge has already provided us with some early warning signs.
More intense border controls and national security measures at the
world's major airports and seaports have made international trade
more cumbersome. Most importantly, however, populist leaders like
President Trump see global trade as a zero-sum game between self-
interested nations. Thus, they are prepared to impose steep tariffs on
goods and services in order to reduce their countries' trade deficit.
One could easily imagine that what started in 2019 as a trade skirmish
between the United States and China could grow over the next decade
into a full-blown trade war that might draw other countries and regions into its orbit. As a result, consumers—especially those located
in the more prosperous global North—would not only have to put up
with higher prices for many commodities and services, but also face
the likelihood of the intensifying trade war adversely affecting the
health of the entire world economy.

After all, for all of the inequalities created by unbridled free-market
capitalism, the history of the twentieth century teaches us that trade
protectionism often fuels a logic of nationalist competition that rarely
remains confined to the economic sphere. This applies even more so in
our present era of multiple national powers that, once again, compete
for honor and influence. With the world's largest war-making arsenal
at the command of an unpredictable populist president promising to
make his nation "great again," any real or perceived threats to America's economic dominance by publicly identified "adversaries" such
as China or Iran might turn into a military confrontation that could
engulf the whole planet.

The same troubling outlook also holds for enhanced restrictions
on transnational movements of people, whether in the form of business travelers, tourists, economic migrants, or political refugees. As
demonstrated by drastic populist measures against the 2015 Syrian

refugees fleeing their war-torn country, the 2018–2019 Latin American "migrants caravans" at the US-Mexican border, and the throngs of African migrants crossing the Mediterranean in pursuit of their dream for a better life, the backlash scenario favors a future characterized by the widespread curtailment of the movement of human bodies in ways that have already compromised the civil liberties of tens of millions of migrants and violated their basic human rights. National populists are especially skillful in exploiting people's legitimate fears of the social and cultural consequences of large numbers of newcomers by branding them as undesirable "others," unworthy of sustained aid or systematic measures of integration. Open hostility directed at these "undeserving foreigners," in turn, would further exacerbate the exploitation of existing political divisions and cultural cleavages.

But even if the backlash scenario were to materialize in the 2020s, it might be premature to speak of a coming decade of *deglobalization*. To be sure, some empirical data seem to confirm the widespread impression that globalization is in decline. The KOF Globalization Index, a sophisticated social index measuring material globalization flows, recorded a downward movement in 2017—the first since 1975—and is expected to flatline or further decrease over the next ten years. World trade in goods and services has leveled off in the late 2010s, buttressing the notion that we might have reached "peak trade" and could be approaching the limits of global economic integration. Often associated with globalization, automation and robotization is estimated to result in anything from a 20 percent to a 30 percent decline in global merchandise trade over the next decade. Cross-border financial flows have dipped from 22 percent of world gross domestic product (GDP) in 2007 to merely 6 percent in 2016—about the same level as in 1996. Similarly, transnational bank flows and foreign direct investment have stagnated at lower levels. While the costs of communication have been falling quickly and consistently over the past three decades, global transportation costs have been extremely jittery and sluggish, plagued by uncertainty around highly volatile oil prices and shifting consumption patterns.[4]

Still, there is one dimension of mobility that seems highly unlikely to slow down even under a pronounced populist backlash scenario: the flow of data and information across national borders. Though everpresent and critically important, *embodied globalization—the move-*

ment of peoples across the world, characterized by the movements of refugees, emigrants, travelers, and tourists—is no longer the defining form of contemporary globalization. Similarly, *object-extended globalization*—the global movement of objects, particularly traded commodities and material objects of exchange and communication such as coins and banknotes—should not be seen as its most important manifestation.

Rather, the dominant form of contemporary globalization is *disembodied globalization*—the movement of abstracted capital and culture, including words, images, electronic texts, or encoded capital, including crypto-currencies, through processes of disembodied exchange. The latest available data on digital global flows show that disembodied globalization has neither stalled nor declined. To the contrary, the amount of cross-border bandwidth, in 2014, has grown by a factor of 45 compared to 2005! This suggests that the world has become more digitally connected than ever. As discussed in the second future scenario, commentators attuned to these disembodied dynamics of space-time compression speak of a "new era of digital globalization."[5] Although authoritarian governments in China and Russia have attempted to control the flow of digital data and information by seeking to carve out separate Internet systems, it is highly unlikely that their digital delinking efforts will ever fully succeed.

Ironically, one of the major dynamics behind the current success of populists is their adroit use of the social media as well as cutting-edge psychometric computer techniques employed by worldwide political consulting firms such as Cambridge Analytica. In other words, antiglobalist populists have greatly benefited from the very process of interconnectivity they denounce so passionately. Yet, it seems that the explosive growth of disembodied globalization in its many manifestations will hamper their nostalgic efforts to turn back the clock to a time of self-contained nation-states with impermeable borders.

The unfolding of the Brexit process and the first term of the Trump presidency are instructive examples of the second major social dynamic fueling the backlash scenario: the weakening of representative democracy and the strengthening of political authoritarianism. As the promises of market globalists—especially the central ideological claim that it will benefit everyone—have turned into the reality of runaway inequality and the perceived loss of national traditions and cultural identity, people blame governing elites usually affiliated with established mainstream parties, for the dire consequences of what appears to them as "globalization run amok." The result is a loss of legitimacy of national governments that seem to be unwilling to protect their citizens from the dizzying speed and tremendous force of social change brought on by globalization.

Moreover, the dynamics of regionalization that have accompanied globalizing movements in Europe and other parts of the world strike many ordinary citizens as the illegitimate transfer of political power to remote elites outside their homeland. The related lack of accountability and transparency provides antiglobalist populists with a welcome opportunity to demand a return of power to the national community while disparaging the proponents of transnational integration as "treacherous" and "corrupt." Drastic times require drastic actions, they argue, and thus support the expansion of executive power in the hands of "patriotic leaders" determined to save the homeland from the alleged machinations of "international financial elites" and the "invasion of immigrants" that threaten to replace established cultural practices and identities.

For example, the national-populist Hungarian prime minister, Viktor Orbán, has openly embraced what he calls "illiberal democracy." He adopted this model of political authoritarianism from Russian President Vladimir Putin, who has routinely expressed his distaste for "the decadence of Western democracy." Indeed, under the backlash scenario, even extreme measures—such as the suspension or major revision of established democratic constitutions—adopted by determined populist leaders who claim to act in the face of a "national emergency"—should not be dismissed as unrealistic.

Recent empirical data drawn from major democratic countries around the world confirms the steep loss of people's trust in government and the related rise of their pro-authoritarian sentiments.[6] A strengthening of these tendencies in the next decade would reverse the unprecedented post–World War II expansion of liberal democracy, in the process shifting the balance of power from democratically elected legislatives to authoritarian executives prepared to curtail hard-won political liberties such as freedom of assembly, freedom of expression, and freedom of the press. For example, Donald Trump's incessant and blunt attacks on journalists and media outlets he accuses of spreading "fake news" represent an ominous sign of what the new decade might hold in store for public critics of populist governments.

A third dynamic fueling the backlash scenario is the loss of momentum in building new global governance structures and transnational institutional networks capable of coordinated action to solve the global problems of our time. Climate change tops the list of these pressing issues. As recent reports have shown, the climatic changes affecting our planet are both real and profound. Debates actively resound through the halls of academe and the seminar rooms of international and nongovernmental organizations—though less urgently in the world's parliaments and corporate boardrooms—suggesting that climate change is on a runaway course.

According to a 2018 report by the United Nations Intergovernmental Panel on Climate Change (IPCC), the world reached 1°C global warming above preindustrial levels in 2017 and is heading toward 1.5°C within a decade or so—the *high confidence* range predicted for this threshold is between 2030 and 2052. At more than 2°C global warming, it has been suggested that the world will head toward global chaos, albeit with more severe impacts in the equatorial regions. To give some sense of the difference between these two crucial thresholds, at 1.5°C, the IPCC estimates that around 80 percent of coral reefs will be gone; at 2°C, they will be 99 percent destroyed.[7]

Obviously, these catastrophic outlooks demonstrate that the negative consequences of human impact on the planet can only be ignored at our own peril. Yet, the backlash scenario favors knee-jerk deniers like Trump and other antiglobalist populists who refuse to shoulder the necessary task of building new transitional networks and institutional frameworks to combat climate change. Quite to the contrary, within months of his inauguration, President Trump employed his trademark populist rhetoric to announce his country's withdrawal from the Paris Agreement on climate change: "The Paris Agreement handicaps the United States economy in order to win praise from the very foreign capitals and global activists that have long sought to gain wealth at our country's expense. They don't put America first. I do, and I always will."[8]

The persistence, and even worsening, of other global problems such as new epidemics like Ebola or SARS, chronic financial instability and volatility, and the international failure to denuclearize—combined with the refusal of populists to tackle these issues in a systematic way—suggests that the backlash scenario may not have much staying power beyond the 2020s. As problems worsen, the current populist surge might falter and reveal itself as the last gasp of a national imaginary that no longer meets the transnational demands of the twenty-first century. Still, the populists' hold on political power for some years to come would retard the creation of new institutional networks of global cooperation. By the 2030s, it could be too late to reverse course; we might have reached a point of no return—especially with regard to the rapid environmental degradation of our planet.

THE REBOUND SCENARIO: THE POPULIST CHALLENGE FAILS

This future scenario is built on the possibility of massive and persistent losses of antiglobalist populists at the ballot box, thus indicating the failure of the populist challenge and the return of a more globally oriented outlook. Such a *rebound scenario* might start with the electoral defeat of President Trump in 2020 and a new Brexit referendum that reverses the 2016 outcome. The question is, what sort of political ideology would take the place of antiglobalist populism?

There seem to be two possibilities. The first is propagated by leading left-wing populists such as Bernie Sanders in the United States or Jeremy Corbyn in the United Kingdom, who strongly oppose the xenophobic and anti-pluralist message of national populists yet embrace the twentieth-century Keynesian ideal of a strong nation-state committed to regulating capitalism for the benefit of working people. The second possibility would be the return of centrist political leaders committed to the restoration of a *reformed* version of market globalism. The first option would indicate the staying power of the national imaginary, whereas the second would demonstrate the strength of the global imaginary. Given that this rebound scenario is built upon the sagging fortunes of right-wing *nationalists*—and thus the waning appeal of the national imaginary—it appears unlikely that left-wing *nationalists* would be returned to power. For this reason, let us briefly play out the more likely second option, which could be called *market globalism with a human face.*

Having been confronted with the populist backlash to the negative consequences of unbridled global market integration, newly empowered market globalists in the 2020s might exert more caution and make some moderate adjustments to their ultimate goal, the creation of a single global free market. Most likely, they would pledge to restore the liberal postwar international order of the past and propose more "socially responsible" forms of neoliberal globalization to the public. There is ample evidence for such a course of action. For example, market globalists like Nobel Prize–winning economist Joseph Stiglitz have long conceded that globalization has been badly "mismanaged" and requires a serious overhaul.[9] These reformist market globalists nonetheless insist that their original project of liberalizing trade and integrating markets is still valid. As James Mittelman has pointed out, Stiglitz and Co. tend to reduce structural problems in the world's economic architecture to mere "management issues": "Having criticized the market fundamentalists, Stiglitz then expresses his unshaken faith in the redeeming value of competition. At the end of the day, the agenda is to stabilize globalizing capitalism. It is to modify neoliberal globalization without tugging at the roots of its underlying structures."[10]

The programmatic outline of such reformed market globalism for the 2020s is already in the making at important ideological sites of global capitalism such as the World Economic Forum (WEF). Built upon claims of the touted benefits of digital globalization, the new vision has been called "Globalization 4.0" and has been heavily promoted by Klaus Schwab, the German founder and executive chairman of the WEF. Indeed, the official theme of the 2019 WEF Annual Meeting in Davos, Switzerland, was *Globalization 4.0: Shaping a New Global Architecture in the Age of the Fourth Industrial Revolution*. In a major article published in the influential American policy periodical *Foreign Affairs*, Schwab presents the gist of the reformed market-globalist vision for the new decade and beyond.

The article begins with arguments in favor of constructing a new global architecture of cooperation that would be more attuned to the needs of ordinary people around the world. The author then asserts that the world finds itself today in the throes of the *fourth industrial revolution*—the "complete digitization of the social, political, and economic." This revolution is said to transform existing social structures in profound ways that would blur the lines between physical, digital, and biological spheres. Admitting that the free-market consensus of the 1990s and 2000s had been smashed by the populist challenge and was beyond repair, Schwab further concedes that, although neoliberal globalization has "lifted millions out of poverty" in the global South, it has also produced "eroding incomes" and "precarious working conditions" for many people in the global North. Populists and protectionists had fed on these ills, but their solutions were misguided attempts to return to a less globalized world that had vanished for good. The solution is to reform globalization by means of the new leading technologies of the twenty-first century such as artificial intelligence, autonomous vehicles, quantum computing, 3D printing, and the Internet of Things. As Schwab puts it, "The real issue . . . is that the production and exchange of physical goods matters less and less each year. From here on out, decisive competitive advantages in the global economy will stem less from low-cost production and more from the ability to innovate, robotize, and digitalize."[11]

The WEF boss understands that there remain serious issues with Globalization 4.0, such as the "widening gap between winners and losers of the Fourth Industrial Revolution," "the digitized spread of misinformation" through social media, and the increasing reliance on robots and algorithms in decision making. The solution to these problems is to create a global framework of government-society relations that "can leverage the opportunities of the Fourth Industrial Revolution, designing and governing inclusive platforms and systems that are fit to deal with the complexity of the new wave of global integration." What, then, should this "new global operating system" look like? Unsurprisingly, Schwab's reformist vision relies heavily on the core concepts of the "old" market globalism dressed up in new high-tech clothing:

> It [Globalization 4.0] should begin by accepting the reality that the Fourth Industrial Revolution is even more borderless, interconnected, and independent than the global economy of integrated supply chains. Second, global cooperation should focus on the governance issues at the heart of the current transformation: cybersecurity, the uses of AI and the gene-editing technology CRISPR, and the intellectual property and data protection agreements. Security, above all, has always been a precondition for globalization. That remains true in cyberspace: when the Internet is not safe, economies suffer. We must ensure the safety of Globalization 4.0's digital sea-lanes and havens.

Schwab insists, however, that such digital turbocharged resuscitations of the market-globalist paradigm can only succeed if *three crucial principles* are put in place. It is worth quoting these in full:

> First, the dialogues that take place to shape Globalization 4.0 must involve all the relevant global players. Governments, of course, have a key leadership role to play, but business is the driver of innovation and civil society serves a critical role in making sure this innovation is applied with the public's interest in mind. Second, the preservation of social and national cohesion should be placed front and center. Safeguarding and strengthening the pillars of social justice and equity will be necessary to sustain national social contracts and preserve an open world. This cannot happen without bottom-up decision making, which enables the substantive engagement of citizens around the world. Third, coordination—achieving shared objectives—will yield more successes than cooperation—acting out common strategy. The Paris Agreement on climate change and the United Nations Sustainable Development Goals are examples of a coordinated approach that leaves room for actors to devise their own strategies.[12]

Note how Schwab's reformed Globalization 4.0 ideology shrewdly incorporates significant portions of the justice-globalist agenda such as "social justice" and "equity" as well as offering an olive branch to populism in its explicit acknowledgment of the importance of "national cohesion" and "national social contracts." Most importantly, the market rhetoric of Globalization 4.0 seeks to strike a pronounced pragmatic tone in emphasizing the crucial role of innovative digital technology to solve pressing global problems—"threats from the nondigital world," as Schwab puts it—especially the deteriorating environmental conditions of our planet.

Over the last few years, Schwab and his fellow market globalists have produced a respectable output of articles and policy papers on how to organize global action to combat climate change, "arguably humanity's most existential challenge," as they note perceptively. True to their neoliberal sympathies, these figures emphasize that the necessary leadership to combat climate change should be provided by business, primarily by "building new forms of alliances within and between the private and public sectors" and "forging new clubs of like-minded governments, cities, states, and provinces." For these reformist market globalists, meeting the ecological challenge in the new decade and beyond requires a corporate-led institutional framework consisting of "global public-private 'platforms' for action" that are designed to handle the social transformations wrought by the fourth industrial revolution.[13]

To draw this rebound scenario to a close, it is important to note that the return of a reformist version of market globalism would, most likely, help to address some of the looming global problems that are likely to worsen in the coming decade. However, if implemented at all, Globalization 4.0 would leave the underlying economic base of global capitalism largely intact. Still, without the implementation of far-reaching systemic reforms on a global level offered primarily by justice globalists, national and transnational disparities in wealth and well-being would continue to widen while top earners around the world would continue to benefit from neoliberal measures.

Still, in this rebound scenario, neither justice globalism nor religious globalism would make much headway. The latter would simply tread water as a mostly reactive ideology fiercely opposing the secularism accompanying the digitalized version of market globalism, while the former would continue to suffer from neoliberal attempts to steal and reinterpret some of its best ideas to make the resulting ideological stew more palatable to global audiences. *Sustainability* and *global citizenship* are two such core concepts torn from the ideological flanks of justice globalism only to be endowed with altered market-globalist meanings. Moreover, efforts by the political Left to subject the global marketplace to greater democratic accountability by means of more effective global regulatory institutions have not gained much political traction. In short, the prospect for a "global new deal" through the building of global networks of solidarity would be rather dim, to say the least. The only realistic change for both justice globalism and religious globalism to gain in popularity in this scenario would be the rather unpleasant prospect of a major global crisis emerging in the 2020s that would unsettle the technology-heavy agenda of Globalization 4.0. Let us contemplate this possibility in the discussion below.

THE STALEMATE SCENARIO: THE POPULIST CHALLENGE NEITHER FAILS NOR SUCCEEDS

The final future scenario for the coming decade to be discussed—perhaps the most likely of the three—requires little elaboration. It would simply amount to a prolonged stalemate between the somewhat weakening national-populist forces and slightly waxing phalanx of reformist market globalists. Some recent political developments such as the results of the 2018 US midterm elections and the 2019 European parliamentary elections seem to point to a roughly equal balance of power between centrist parties and the right-wing populists. Also notable was a clear upswing of Green parties and the broadening appeal of their environmentalist issues, which would indicate good news for the currently stagnant fortunes of justice globalism.

However, if such an ideological stalemate between nationalist and globalists were to last throughout the 2020s, it would mean that little meaningful progress could be made toward addressing brewing global problems. The resulting political gridlock would increase the chances of systemic crises rearing their heads in the financial world, cyberspace, the environment, the workplace, and so on—or perhaps a noxious combination of several of these maladies. It is difficult to predict what would happen if another global calamity of the magnitude of the 2008 GFC would hit the world. The political history of the last two centuries suggests that the reactionary forces of the Right might find themselves at an advantage, because they have proven to be more adroit in using people's fears for their purposes than the Left. The resulting shift to authoritarianism—or, even worse, dictatorship—would spell the end of the era of liberal democracy as we know it. And yet, in the face of such a deep and persistent crisis, it is obvious that the world would need, more than ever, a fundamentally different vision of what our planet could look like. Perhaps the ultimate outcome of such a prolonged stalemate scenario of the 2020s would be the narrowing of the contest between the national and global imaginary to a struggle between two ideologies: antiglobalist populism and justice globalism.

CONCLUDING REFLECTIONS ON A GLOBAL ETHIC OF RESPONSIBILITY

Writing at the end of the second decade of the twenty-first century, it strikes this author that we have perhaps already reached the most critical juncture in the history of our species. Lest we are willing to jeopardize our collective future and that of countless other forms of plant and animal life, we ought to link the future course of globalization to a global ethic that demands the global distribution of wealth and privilege and the restoration of a sustainable planet. As emphasized throughout this book, there is nothing wrong with greater manifestations of social interdependence that emerge as a result of globalization as long as these transformative social processes address our global problems before it is too late. And we may have less time to act than we think.

The United States of America and rising powers such as China, India, Russia, and Brazil carry a special responsibility to put their collective weight behind a form of globalization that is not defined by economic self-interest alone but rather is deeply infused with ethical concerns for humanity and our natural environment. In order to tackle our global problems, it is incumbent on all of us to reconsider the crucial role of ethics in global politics and economics that has been echoed by many prominent spiritual and religious leaders. In fact, some of them, such as the Dalai Lama and Pope Francis, have explicitly called for a *global ethic* that would serve as the normative framework for a democratic global society.[14] The Swiss theologian Hans Küng suggests that such a global ethic contains *four commitments*: to a culture of nonviolence and respect of life; to a culture of solidarity and a just economic order; to a culture of tolerance and a life of truthfulness; and to a culture of equal rights, particularly racial and gender equality.[15]

The Dalai Lama concurs, adding that imparting a critical mind and a sense of universal responsibility to the young is especially important. Ideals constitute the engine of progress; hence, it is imperative to introduce new generations to an ethical vision for a global society.[16] The positive role to be played by the younger generations is vividly apparent in the social engagement of individuals like the American high school students working to curb gun violence or the ecological imperative so beautifully expressed by Greta Thunberg, the teenaged Swedish schoolgirl who, at the age of fifteen, raised her voice in support of immediate action to combat climate change, and has since become an outspoken global climate activist inspiring millions of young people around the world to follow in her footsteps.

For scholars, the most obvious step in spreading a global ethic consists of developing a critical theory of globalization that contests both the script of market globalism, antiglobalist populism, and violent forms of religious globalism, while subjecting the claims of justice globalism to sustained scrutiny. Education and the media—especially the new social media—are key dimensions in any progressive strategy built around the idea that *another world is possible*. Once harmful articulations of the global and national imaginaries and their corresponding power bases in society begin to lose their grip on the construction of meaning, alternative interpretations of globalization can circulate more freely in public discourse. As a result, more and more people will realize that they have an active stake in shaping the world they want to live in.

Ultimately, the three future scenarios laid out in this concluding chapter remain inextricably intertwined with matters of ideology: the kinds of ideas, values, and beliefs about globalization and its social practices that shape our communities. It would be foolish to expect that the populist challenge will fade without ideational contestation. Ideas matter because they provide the motivation for social action. It seems certain that the great ideological struggle of the twenty-first century will not end anytime soon. Ultimately, it could bring disaster or, conversely, open up constructive ways of dealing with the immensity of the *global system shift* that is already upon us.[17] The coming decade could be a turning point. While the severity of our current global problems should never be downplayed, it would be equally imprudent to bank on humanity's inability to arrive at general principles that govern the world in a more peaceful, sustainable, and just manner.

NOTES

CHAPTER 1: IDEOLOGY AND THE MEANING OF GLOBALIZATION

1. Daniel Bell, *The End of Ideology: On the Exhaustion of Political Ideas in the Fifties* (Glencoe, IL: Free Press, 1960). See esp. 13–18, 369–75.

2. Francis Fukuyama, "The End of History?" *National Interest* 16 (Summer 1989): 4. See also Francis Fukuyama, *The End of History and the Last Man* (New York: Free Press, 1992).

3. Fukuyama, "The End of History?" 18.

4. "Transcript of President Bush's Address to Nation on U.S. Policy in Iraq," *New York Times*, January 11, 2007.

5. "Donald J. Trump addresses the 73rd Session of the United Nations—September 25, 2018," accessed January 13, 2019, https://factba.se/transcript/donald-trump-speech-un-general-assembly-september-25-2018.

6. Michael Freeden, *Ideologies and Political Theory: A Conceptual Approach* (Oxford: Clarendon Press, 1996), 77. My own thinking on ideology is greatly indebted to Freeden's pioneering efforts.

7. Michael Freeden, *Ideology: A Very Short Introduction* (Oxford: Oxford University Press, 2003), 54–55.

8. Harold D. Lasswell, *Politics: Who Gets What, When and How* (New York: Meridian Books, 1958).

9. Terrell Carver, "Ideology: The Career of a Concept," in *Ideals and Ideologies: A Reader*, 10th ed., ed. Terrence Ball and Richard Dagger (New York and London: Routledge, 2016), 11.

10. Paul Ricoeur, *Lectures on Ideology and Utopia* (New York: Columbia University Press, 1986). My summary of Ricoeur's discussion of ideology draws on George Taylor's "Editor's Introduction," ix–xxxvi.

11. Ricoeur, *Lectures*, 266.

12. Antonio Gramsci, *Selections from Prison Notebooks* (New York: International Publishers, 1971).

13. William I. Robinson, *Promoting Polyarchy: Globalization, U.S. Intervention, and Hegemony* (Cambridge: Cambridge University Press, 1996), 30.

14. Robert J. Samuelson, "Why We're All Married to the Market," *Newsweek*, April 27, 1998, 47–50.

CHAPTER 2: THE ACADEMIC
DEBATE OVER GLOBALIZATION

1. The parable of the "Blind Scholars and the Elephant" originated most likely in the Pali Buddhist *Udana*, which was apparently compiled in the second century BCE. Its many versions spread to other religions as well, most significantly Hinduism and Islam. For example, in his *Theology Revived*, Muhammad al-Ghazzali (1058–1128) refers to the tale in a discussion on the problem of human action in which the inadequacy of natural reason becomes evident. I am grateful to Ramdas Lamb in the Department of Religion at the University of Hawai'i at Mānoa for explaining to me the origins of the parable.

2. Nayan Chanda, *Bound Together: How Traders, Preachers, Adventurers, and Warriors Shaped Globalization* (New Haven, CT: Yale University Press, 2007), 246.

3. See Paul James and Manfred B. Steger, "A Genealogy of 'Globalization': The Career of a Concept," *Globalizations* 11, no. 4 (2014): 417–34.

4. James N. Rosenau, *Distant Proximities: Dynamics beyond Globalization* (Princeton, NJ: Princeton University Press, 2003), 12.

5. Stephen J. Rosow, "Globalisation as Democratic Theory," *Millennium: Journal of International Studies* 29, no. 1 (2000): 31.

6. For various definitions of globalization, see, for example, Manfred B. Steger, *Globalization: A Very Short Introduction*, 4th ed. (Oxford: Oxford University Press, 2017); Frank J. Lechner and John Boli, eds., *The Globalization Reader*, 5th ed. (Oxford: Blackwell, 2015); David Held and Anthony McGrew, *Globalization/Antiglobalization*, 2nd ed. (Cambridge: Polity, 2007); Malcolm Waters, *Globalization*, 2nd ed. (London: Routledge, 2001); Roland Robertson, *Globalization: Social Theory and Global Culture* (London: Sage, 1992); Anthony Giddens, *The Consequences of Modernity* (Stanford, CA: Stanford University Press, 1990); and David Harvey, *The Condition of Postmodernity* (Oxford: Blackwell, 1989).

7. For a book-length treatment of the global imaginary, see Manfred B. Steger, *The Rise of the Global Imaginary: Political Ideologies from the French Revo-*

lution to the Global War on Terror (Oxford and New York: Oxford University Press, 2008). For an updated discussion, see Manfred B. Steger and Paul James, "Levels of Subjective Globalization: Ideologies, Imaginaries, Ontologies," *Perspectives on Global Development and Technology* 12, nos. 1–2 (2013): 17–40.

8. See, for example, Held and McGrew, *Globalization/Anti-Globalization*; James H. Mittelman, *The Globalization Syndrome* (Princeton, NJ: Princeton University Press, 2000); and Jan Aart Scholte, *Globalization: A Critical Introduction*, 2nd ed. (Houndmills, UK: Palgrave Macmillan, 2005).

9. See, for example, John Keane, *Global Civil Society?* (Cambridge: Cambridge University Press, 2003); and Mary Kaldor, Henrietta Moore, and Sabine Selchow, eds., *Global Civil Society 2012: Ten Years of Critical Reflection* (Houndmills, UK: Palgrave Macmillan, 2012).

10. See, for example, Alison Brysk, ed., *Globalization and Human Rights* (Berkeley: University of California Press, 2002); and Alison Brysk, *The Future of Human Rights* (Cambridge: Polity, 2018).

11. Martin Shaw, *Theory of the Global State: Globality as an Unfinished Revolution* (Cambridge: Cambridge University Press, 2000), 16.

12. David Held, *Democracy and the Global Order: From the Modern State to Cosmopolitan Governance* (Stanford, CA: Stanford University Press, 1995); and David Held, *Models of Democracy*, 3rd ed. (Stanford, CA: Stanford University Press, 2006).

13. See, for example, Rodney Bruce Hall and Thomas J. Biersteker, eds., *The Emergence of Private Authority in Global Governance* (Cambridge: Cambridge University Press, 2002); and Daniele Archibugi, *The Global Commonwealth of Citizens: Toward Cosmopolitan Democracy* (Princeton, NJ: Princeton University Press, 2015).

14. See Robert Holton, *Globalization and the Nation-State*, 2nd ed. (Houndmills, UK: Palgrave Macmillan, 2011).

15. Kenichi Ohmae, *The Borderless World: Power and Strategy in the Interlinked World Economy* (New York: Harper Business, 1990), and *The End of the Nation-State: The Rise of Regional Economies* (New York: Free Press, 1995).

16. Colin Hay and David Marsh, eds., *Demystifying Globalization* (Basingstoke, UK: Palgrave, 2000); and Barrie Axford, *Theories of Globalization* (Cambridge: Polity, 2013).

17. Robert Wade, "Globalization and Its Limits: Reports on the Death of the National Economy Are Greatly Exaggerated," in *National Diversity and Global Capitalism*, ed. Suzanne Berger and Ronald Dore (Ithaca, NY: Cornell University Press, 1996), 60–88; and Paul Hirst and Grahame Thompson, *Globalization in Question: The International Economy and the Possibilities of Governance*, 3rd ed. (Cambridge: Polity, 2009).

18. Hirst and Thompson, *Globalization in Question*, 2.

19. See, for example, David Held, Anthony McGrew, David Goldblatt, and Jonathan Perraton, *Global Transformations: Politics, Economics, and Culture* (Stanford, CA: Stanford University Press, 1999).

20. William I. Robinson, *Global Capitalism and the Crisis of Humanity* (New York: Cambridge University Press, 2014), 2.

21. Susan Strange, *The Retreat of the State: The Diffusion of Power in the World Economy* (Cambridge: Cambridge University Press, 1996), xii–xiii; and Linda Weiss, *The Myth of the Powerless State: Governing the Economy in a Global Era* (Ithaca, NY: Cornell University Press, 1998), 212.

22. For an illuminating discussion of the notion of "globaloney," see Michael Veseth, *Globaloney 2.0: The Crash of 2008 and the Future of Globalization* (Lanham, MD: Rowman & Littlefield, 2010).

23. Robert Gilpin, *The Challenge of Global Capitalism: The World Economy in the 21st Century* (Princeton, NJ: Princeton University Press, 2000), 294–95. For a similar assessment, see Dani Rodrik, *Has Globalization Gone Too Far?* (Washington, DC: Institute for International Economics, 1997), 7–8; and Dani Rodrik, *The Globalziation Paradox: Democracy and the Future of the World Economy* (New York: Norton, 2012).

24. Immanuel Wallerstein, *The Capitalist World Economy* (Cambridge: Cambridge University Press, 1979), and *The Politics of the World Economy* (Cambridge: Cambridge University Press, 1984); and Andre Gunder Frank, *ReORIENT: Global Economy in the Asian Age* (Berkeley: University of California Press, 1998); Giovanni Arrighi, *The Long Twentieth Century* (London: Verso, 1994); and Christopher Chase-Dunn, *Global Formation: Structures of the World Economy* (Lanham, MD: Rowman & Littlefield, 1998).

25. Immanuel Wallerstein, *World-Systems Analysis: An Introduction* (Durham, NC: Duke University Press, 2004), x.

26. Immanuel Wallerstein, "Culture as the Ideological Battleground of the Modern World System," in *Global Culture*, ed. Mike Featherstone (London: Sage, 1990), 38.

27. Ash Amin, "Placing Globalization," *Theory, Culture and Society* 14, no. 2 (1997): 123–38.

28. Barry Gills, *Globalization and the Politics of Resistance* (New York: St. Martin's, 2000).

29. Leslie Sklair, *Globalization: Capitalism and Its Alternatives*, 3rd ed. (Oxford: Oxford University Press, 2002).

30. Held et al., *Global Transformations*, 23.

31. The most comprehensive treatment of this nature is Robert O. Keohane, *After Hegemony* (Princeton, NJ: Princeton University Press, 1984). For a more recent update of his position on globalization, see Robert O. Keohane,

"Governance in a Partially Globalized World," *American Political Science Review* 95, no. 1 (March 2001): 1–13.

32. Gilpin, *Challenge of Global Capitalism*, 299.

33. Beth A. Simmons and Zachary Elkins, "Globalization of Liberalization: Policy Diffusion in the International Political Economy," *American Political Science Review* 98, no. 1 (February 2004): 171–89.

34. Bill Gates, *Business @ the Speed of Thought: Succeeding in the Digital Economy* (New York: Warner Books, 2000).

35. Gilpin, *Challenge of Global Capitalism*, 20.

36. Ameet Sachdev, "Law Firms Slow to Outsource," *Chicago Tribune*, January 19, 2004, sec. 4, 1.

37. See Gary Gereffi, "The Elusive Last Lap in the Quest for Developed-Country Status," in *Globalization: Critical Reflections*, ed. James H. Mittelman (Boulder, CO: Lynne Rienner, 1996), 64–69; and Gary Gereffi and Miguel Korzeniewicz, eds., *Commodity Chains and Global Capitalism* (Westport, CT: Greenwood, 1993).

38. See, for example, Lowell Bryan and Diana Farrell, *Market Unbound: Unleashing Global Capitalism* (New York: Wiley, 1996); and Richard Baldwin, *The Great Convergence: Information Technology and the New Globalization* (Cambridge, MA: Belknap, 2018).

39. Richard Langhorne, *The Coming of Globalization: Its Evolution and Contemporary Consequences* (New York: Palgrave, 2001), 2.

40. Bryan and Farrell, *Market Unbound*, 187.

41. Ohmae, *The End of the Nation-State*; *The Borderless World*; and *Next Global Stage: Challenges and Opportunities in Our Borderless World* (Philadelphia: Wharton School, 2005).

42. Caroline Thomas, "Globalization and the South," in *Globalization and the South*, ed. Caroline Thomas and Peter Wilkin (New York: St. Martin's, 1997), 6.

43. See, for example, Peter Gowan, *The Global Gamble: Washington's Faustian Bid for World Dominance* (London: Verso, 1999); and Sam Gindin and Leo Panich, *The Making of Global Capitalism: The Political Economy of American Empire* (London: Verso, 2013).

44. Daniel Singer, *Whose Millennium? Theirs or Ours?* (New York: Monthly Review Press, 1999), 186–87.

45. Saskia Sassen's work emphasizes the key role played by global cities in the organization and control of globally oriented economic and social processes. See Saskia Sassen, *The Global City: New York, London, Tokyo*, 2nd ed. (Princeton, NJ: Princeton University Press, 2001). See also Neil Brenner, ed., *The Global Cities Reader* (London: Routledge, 2006); and Mark Amen, Kevin

Archer, and Martin Bosman, eds., *Relocating Global Cities: From the Center to the Margins* (Lanham, MD: Rowman & Littlefield, 2006).

46. Scholte, *Globalization*.

47. For an excellent exposition of this argument, see Edward S. Cohen, *The Politics of Globalization in the United States* (Washington, DC: Georgetown University Press, 2001); and Eric Helleiner, *States and the Reemergence of Global Finance* (Ithaca, NY: Cornell University Press, 1994).

48. John Tomlinson, *Globalization and Culture* (Chicago: University of Chicago Press, 1999), 1.

49. Tomlinson, *Globalization and Culture*, 28.

50. George Ritzer, *The McDonaldization of Society: An Investigation into the Changing Character of Contemporary Social Life* (Thousand Oaks, CA: Pine Forge Press, 1993).

51. Benjamin R. Barber, *Jihad vs. McWorld* (New York: Ballantine Books, 1996), 17. For a more skeptical assessment of the supposed "Americanness" of globalization, see William H. Marling, *How "American" Is Globalization?* (Baltimore: Johns Hopkins University Press, 2006).

52. Barber, *Jihad vs. McWorld*, 19. For a neo-Marxist perspective on the rise of a global capitalist monoculture, see Herbert Schiller, "The Global Information Highway: Project for an Ungovernable World," in *Resisting the Virtual Life*, ed. James Brook and Iain A. Boal (San Francisco: City Lights, 1995), 17–33.

53. Samuel P. Huntington, *The Clash of Civilizations and the Remaking of World Order* (New York: Touchstone, 1997), 26–27, 45–48.

54. Amy Chua, *World on Fire: How Exporting Free Market Democracy Breeds Ethnic Hatred and Global Instability* (New York: Doubleday, 2003), 9; Roger Scruton, *The West and the Rest: Globalization and the Terrorist Threat* (Wilmington, DE: ISI Books, 2002), 157–58.

55. Scruton, *The West and the Rest*, 159.

56. Serge Latouche, *The Westernization of the World* (Cambridge: Polity, 1996), 3.

57. Selma K. Sonntag, *The Local Politics of Global English: Case Studies in Linguistic Globalization* (Lanham, MD: Lexington, 2003), 123.

58. See Robert McCrum, *Globish: How English Became the World's Language* (New York: Norton, 2011).

59. See, for example, Arjun Appadurai, *Modernity at Large: Cultural Dimensions of Globalization* (Minneapolis: University of Minnesota Press, 1996); and Ulf Hannerz, *Cultural Complexity: Studies in the Social Organization of Meaning* (New York: Columbia University Press, 1992); and *Transnational Connections: Cultures, People, Places* (London: Routledge, 1996). Peter Berger and Samuel Huntington offer a highly unusual version of this "pluralism thesis." Emphasizing that cultural globalization is "American in origin and

content," they nonetheless allow for "many variations and sub-globalizations" on the dominant US cultural theme in various parts of the world. See Peter L. Berger and Samuel P. Huntington, eds., *Many Globalizations: Cultural Diversity in the Contemporary World* (Oxford: Oxford University Press, 2002).

60. Roland Robertson, *Globalization*, and "Glocalization: Time-Space and Homogeneity-Heterogeneity," in *Global Modernities*, ed. Mike Featherstone, Scott Lash, and Roland Robertson (London: Sage, 1995), 25–44.

61. Jan Nederveen Pieterse, *Globalization and Culture: Global Mélange*, 3rd ed. (Lanham, MD: Rowman & Littlefield, 2015), 175.

62. Ulf Hannerz, *Cultural Complexity* (New York: Columbia University Press, 1993), 96. See also Eduardo Mendieta, *Global Fragments: Latinamericanisms, Globalizations, and Critical Theory* (Albany: State University of New York Press, 2007).

63. Appadurai, *Modernity at Large*, 33.

64. Martin Albrow, *The Global Age: State and Society beyond Modernity* (Cambridge: Polity, 1996), 192.

65. See Anthony Giddens, *The Consequences of Modernity* (Stanford, CA: Stanford University Press, 1990).

66. UN IPCC Special Report: "Global Warming of 1.5°C," December 2018, accessed January 27, 2019, https://www.ipcc.ch/sr15.

67. Franz J. Broswimmer, *Ecocide: A History of Mass Extinction of Species* (London: Pluto Press, 2002).

68. Robyn Eckersley and Peter Christoff, *Globalization and the Environment* (Lanham, MD: Rowman & Littlefield, 2013), chapter 5.

69. Fredric Jameson, "Preface," in *The Cultures of Globalization*, ed. Fredric Jameson and Masao Miyoshi (Durham, NC: Duke University Press, 1998), xvi.

70. For a discussion of emerging points of agreement among globalization scholars, see Manfred B. Steger and Paul James, *Globalization Matters: Engaging the Global in Unsettled Times* (Cambridge: Cambridge University Press, 2019), chapter 3.

71. Ian Clark, *Globalization and International Relations Theory* (Oxford: Oxford University Press, 1999), 39.

72. See Claus Offe, *Modernity and the State: East, West* (Cambridge: Polity, 1996), 5.

73. See Mauro F. Guillen, "Is Globalization Civilizing, Destructive or Feeble? A Critique of Five Key Debates in the Social Science Literature," *Annual Review of Sociology* 27, no. 1 (2001): 237.

74. Hans-Georg Gadamer, *Truth and Method* (New York: Seabury Press, 1975).

75. Robert W. Cox, "A Perspective on Globalization," in *Globalization: Critical Reflections*, ed. James H. Mittelman (Boulder, CO: Lynne Rienner,

1996), 21–30; and Stephen Gill, "Globalization, Democratization, and the Politics of Indifference," in Mittelman, *Globalization*, 205–28.

76. Alan Scott, "Introduction—Globalization: Social Process or Political Rhetoric?" in *The Limits of Globalization: Cases and Arguments*, ed. Alan Scott (London: Routledge, 1997), 2.

CHAPTER 3: THE DOMINANCE OF
MARKET GLOBALISM IN THE 1990s

1. David Ricardo, *The Principles of Political Economy and Taxation* (Mineola, NY: Dover, 2004).

2. Herbert Spencer, *On Social Evolution*, edited by J. D. Y. Peel (Chicago: University of Chicago Press, 1972).

3. John Maynard Keynes, *The General Theory of Employment, Interest and Money: With the Economic Consequences of the Peace* (London: Wordsworth Editions, 2017).

4. Edward Luttwak, *Turbo-Capitalism: Winners and Losers in the Global Economy* (New York: HarperCollins, 1999).

5. Joseph E. Stiglitz, *The Roaring Nineties: A New History of the World's Most Prosperous Decade* (New York: Norton, 2003).

6. For a detailed description of this "transnational historic bloc of internationally oriented capitalists," see Mark Rupert, *Ideologies of Globalization: Contending Visions of a New World Order* (London: Routledge, 2000); William I. Robinson, *Global Capitalism and the Crisis of Humanity* (Cambridge: Cambridge University Press, 2014); and Peter Phillips, *Giants: The Global Power Elite* (New York: Seven Stories Press, 2018).

7. See Harvey Cox, "The Market as God: Living in the New Dispensation," *Atlantic Monthly*, March 1999, 18–23.

8. Theodore Levitt, "The Globalization of Markets," *Harvard Business Review* 61, no. 3 (1983): 92–102.

9. David M. Kotz, *The Rise and Fall of Neoliberal Capitalism* (Cambridge, MA: Harvard University Press, 2015).

10. Daniel Yergin and Joseph Stanislaw, *The Commanding Heights: The Battle between Government and the Marketplace That Is Remaking the Modern World* (New York: Simon & Schuster, 1998).

11. Thomas Frank, *One Market under God* (New York: Anchor, 2000).

12. See Michel Foucault, *The Birth of Biopolitics: Lectures at the College de France, 1978–1979* (New York: Picador, 2010); and Wendy Brown, *Undoing the Demos: Neoliberalism's Stealth Revolution* (New York: Zone Books, 2017).

13. Timothy Erik Ström, "Expand and Centralize: Twenty Years of Google," *Arena Magazine* 153 (2018): 23–32; and Nick Srnicek, *Platform Capitalism* (Cambridge: Polity, 2017).

14. All citations are taken from Aaron Bernstein, "Backlash: Behind the Anxiety over Globalization," *BusinessWeek*, April 24, 2000, 44.

15. Bernstein, "Backlash," 38–40.

16. See Zygmunt Bauman, *In Search of Politics* (Stanford, CA: Stanford University Press, 1999), 28–29; 127–28; and Pierre Bourdieu, *Acts of Resistance: Against the Tyranny of the Market* (New York: New Press, 1999), 95.

17. Judith Butler, "Gender as Performance," in *A Critical Sense: Interviews with Intellectuals*, ed. Peter Osborne (London: Routledge, 1996), 112.

18. Michel Foucault, *The Archeology of Knowledge* (New York: Pantheon, 1972), 59–68.

19. See Michael Freeden, *Ideologies and Political Theory* (Oxford: Oxford University Press, 1996); Michael Freeden, *Ideology: A Very Short Introduction* (Oxford: Oxford University Press, 2003); Manfred B. Steger, *The Rise of the Global Imaginary: Political Ideologies from the French Revolution to the Global War on Terror* (Oxford and New York: Oxford University Press, 2008); and Manfred B. Steger, James Goodman, and Erin Wilson, *Justice Globalism: Ideology, Crises, Policy* (London: Sage, 2013).

20. Michael Freeden's morphological approach to political ideologies introduces a nexus linking (a) ineliminable concepts located at the core of thought-systems; (b) fewer central adjacent concepts allowing for necessary meaning permutations; and (c) peripheral concepts that add a vital gloss to the core concepts.

21. Andrew Chadwick, "Studying Political Ideas: A Public Political Discourse Approach," *Political Studies* 48 (2000): 283–301.

22. Freeden, *Ideology*, 103.

23. See Chadwick, "Studying Political Ideas," 290–92.

24. Michael Veseth, *Selling Globalization: The Myth of the Global Economy* (Boulder, CO: Lynne Rienner, 1998), 16–18.

25. Friedrich Hayek, *Law, Legislation, and Liberty*, 3 vols. (London: Routledge & Kegan Paul, 1979), 1:55.

26. Isaiah Berlin, "Two Concepts of Liberty," in *Four Essays on Liberty* (Oxford: Oxford University Press, 1969), 121–22.

27. Milton Friedman, *Capitalism and Freedom* (Chicago: University of Chicago Press, 1962), 9.

28. Editorial, *BusinessWeek*, December 13, 1999, 212.

29. Martin Wolf, "Why This Hatred of the Market?" 9–11, and Peter Martin, "The Moral Case for Globalization," 12–13, both in *The Globalization Reader*, 3rd ed., ed. Frank J. Lechner and John Boli (Oxford: Blackwell, 2007).

30. Charlene Barshefsky, cited in Mark Levinson, "Who's in Charge Here?" *Dissent* (Fall 1999): 22.

31. Michael Camdessus, cited in Levinson, "Who's in Charge Here?"; Michael Camdessus, "Globalization and Asia: The Challenges for Regional

Cooperation and Implications for Hong Kong" (address to Hong Kong Monetary Authority, Hong Kong, March 7, 1997), http://www.imf.org/external/np/speeches/1997/MDS9703.html.

32. See, for example, William Bole, "Tales of Globalization," *America* 181, no. 18 (December 4, 1999): 14–16.

33. Thomas L. Friedman, *The Lexus and the Olive Tree: Understanding Globalization* (New York: Farrar, Straus & Giroux, 1999), xii, 23–24.

34. Friedman, *Lexus and the Olive Tree*, 9.

35. Friedman, *Lexus and the Olive Tree*, 104, 152.

36. Friedman, *Lexus and the Olive Tree*, 105.

37. Friedman, *Lexus and the Olive Tree*, 109–10.

38. For a detailed discussion of these neoliberal policy initiatives, see John Micklethwait and Adrian Woolridge, *A Future Perfect: The Challenge and Hidden Promise of Globalization* (New York: Crown, 2000), 22–54; and John Ralston Saul, *The Collapse of Globalism and the Reinvention of the World* (London: Penguin, 2005).

39. Edward Luttwak, *Turbo-Capitalism: Winners and Losers in the Global Economy* (New York: HarperCollins, 1999), 152.

40. Ulrich Beck, *What Is Globalization?* (Cambridge: Polity, 2000), 122.

41. See Robert W. McChesney, "Global Media, Neoliberalism, and Imperialism," *Monthly Review* (March 2001), http://www.monthlyreview.org/301rwm.html.

42. For a critical assessment of Thatcher's experiment, see John Gray, *False Dawn: The Delusions of Global Capitalism* (New York: New Press, 1998), 24–34.

43. Bill Clinton, "Remarks by the President on Foreign Policy" (San Francisco, February 26, 1999), https://www.mtholyoke.edu/acad/intrel/clintfps.htm.

44. President Clinton, cited in Sonya Ross, "Clinton Talks of Better Living," Associated Press, October 15, 1997, http://more.abcnews.go.com/sections/world/brazil1014/index.html.

45. Stuart Eizenstat, "Remarks to Democratic Leadership Council" (January 19, 1999), http://www.usinfo.org/wf/990120/epf305.html.

46. Economic Strategy Institute Editorial, "International Finance Experts Preview Upcoming Global Economic Forum," April 1, 1999, http://www.econstrat.org/pctranscript.html.

47. Friedman, *Lexus and the Olive Tree*, 407.

48. Rahul Bajaj, "The Rediff Business Interview," February 2, 1999, https://www.rediff.com/money/1999/feb/02bajaj.htm.

49. Manuel Villar Jr., "High-Level Dialogue on the Theme of the Social and Economic Impact of Globalization and Interdependence and Their Policy Implications" (speech delivered at the United Nations, New York, September 17, 1998), http://www.un.int/philippines/villar.html.

50. Masaru Hayami, "Globalization and Regional Cooperation in Asia" (speech delivered at the Asian Pacific Bankers Club, Tokyo, March 17, 2000), https://www.bis.org/review/r000324b.pdf.

51. John R. Malott, "Globalization, Competitiveness, and Asia's Economic Future" (speech delivered in Kuala Lumpur, Malaysia, March 13, 1998), http://www.csis.org/pacfor/pac1198.html.

52. Alain Lipietz, *Towards a New Economic Order* (Oxford: Oxford University Press, 1993), x.

53. David Smith, "Putting a Human Face on the Global Economy: Seeking Common Ground on Trade" (1999 DLC Annual Conference, Washington, DC, October 14, 1999), http://www.connectlive.com/events/dlc/dlc-101499.html.

54. Lorenzo Zambrano, "Putting the Global Market in Order," http://www.globalprogress.org/ingles/Mexico/Zambrano.html.

55. Merrill Lynch Forum, "Economic Globalization and Culture: A Discussion with Dr. Francis Fukuyama," http://www.ml.com/woml/forum/global2.html.

56. Friedman, *Lexus and the Olive Tree*, 474–75. See also Friedman's remark on page 294: "Today, for better or worse, globalization is a means for spreading the fantasy of America around the world. . . . Globalization is Americanization."

57. Gray, *False Dawn*, 131.

58. Steven Kline, "The Play of the Market: On the Internationalization of Children's Culture," *Theory, Culture and Society* 12 (1995): 110.

59. See Benjamin R. Barber, *Jihad vs. McWorld* (New York: Ballantine Books, 1996), 119–51. For Barber's more recent analysis of consumerism, see his *Consumed: How Markets Corrupt Children, Infantilize Adults, and Swallow Citizens Whole* (New York: Norton, 2008). See also Lane Crothers, *Globalization and American Popular Culture*, 4th ed. (Lanham, MD: Rowman & Littlefield, 2018).

60. Robert Hormats, "PBS Interview with Danny Schechter," February 1998, http://pbs.org/globalization/hormats1.html.

61. Friedman, *Lexus and the Olive Tree*, 112–13.

62. Steward Brand, "Financial Markets," Global Business Network Book Club, December 1998, http://www.gbn.org/public/services/bookclub/reviews/ex_8812.html.

63. Michael Hardt and Antonio Negri, *Empire* (Cambridge, MA: Harvard University Press, 2000), 3.

64. Cited in Richard Gott, *In the Shadow of the Liberator: Hugo Chávez and the Transformation of Venezuela* (London: Verso, 2000), 52–53.

65. Will Hutton, "Anthony Giddens and Will Hutton in Conversation," in *Global Capitalism*, ed. Will Hutton and Anthony Giddens (New York: Free Press, 2000), 41.

66. Friedman, *Lexus and the Olive Tree*, 381.

67. Friedman, *Lexus and the Olive Tree*, 464.

68. Statement of Joseph Gorman before the Subcommittee on Trade of the Committee on Ways and Means, March 18, 1997, https://www.congress.gov/congressional-record/1997/3/18/daily-digest.

69. Economic Communiqué, Lyon G7 Summit, June 28, 1996, http://www.g8.utoronto.ca/summit/1996lyon/index.htm.

70. Robert Rubin, "Reform of the International Financial Architecture," *Vital Speeches* 65, no. 15 (1999): 455.

71. Denise Froning, "Why Spurn Free Trade?" *Washington Times*, September 15, 2000.

72. Alan Greenspan, "The Globalization of Finance," *Cato Journal* 17, no. 3 (1998).

73. See Laura Secor, "Mind the Gap," *Boston Globe*, January 5, 2003.

74. Jay Mazur, "Labor's New Internationalism," *Foreign Affairs* (January/February 2000): 80–81.

75. "Tropical Disease Drugs Withdrawn," *BBC News*, October 31, 2000.

76. John J. Meehan, "Globalization and Technology at Work in the Bond Markets" (speech given in Phoenix, AZ, March 1, 1997), http://www/bond markets.com/news/Meehanspeech final.shtml.

77. Newt Gingrich, interview with Danny Schechter at the 1998 World Economic Forum in Davos, Switzerland, http://www.pbs.org/globalization/newt.html.

78. See Barber, *Jihad vs. McWorld*, 77–87.

79. Friedman, *Lexus and the Olive Tree*, 364.

80. Merrill Lynch Forum, "Economic Globalization and Culture."

81. William I. Robinson, *Promoting Polyarchy: Globalization, U.S. Intervention, and Hegemony* (Cambridge: Cambridge University Press, 1996), 56–62.

82. Friedman, *Lexus and the Olive Tree*, 187.

83. Friedman, *Lexus and the Olive Tree*; and Thomas Friedman, *The World Is Flat 3.0: A Brief History of the Twenty-First Century* (New York, Picador, 2007).

84. Micklethwait and Woolridge, *Future Perfect*.

CHAPTER 4: FIRST-WAVE
CHALLENGERS IN THE 2000s

1. Anthony Giddens, *Beyond Left and Right: The Future of Radical Politics* (Stanford, CA: Stanford University Press, 1994).

2. Giddens, *Beyond Left and Right*, 251.

3. Norberto Bobbio, *Left and Right: The Significance of a Political Distinction* (Chicago: University of Chicago Press, 1996), 60–71.

4. Bobbio, *Left and Right*, 90.

5. Alain Noël and Jean-Philippe Therien, *Left and Right in Global Politics* (Cambridge: Cambridge University Press, 2008), esp. chapter 2.

6. Sidney Tarrow, *The New Transnational Activism* (Cambridge: Cambridge University Press, 2005), 40–60.

7. Subcomandante Marcos, "First Declaration of La Realidad," August 3, 1996, http://www.struggle.ws/mexico/ezln/ccri_1st_dec_real.html.

8. See Alexander Cockburn, Jeffrey St. Clair, and Allan Sekula, *Five Days That Shook the World: Seattle and Beyond* (London: Verso, 2000).

9. Charlene Barshefsky, cited in Martin Khor, "Seattle Debacle: Revolt of the Developing Nations," in *Globalize This! The Battle against the World Trade Organization*, ed. Kevin Danaher and Roger Burbach (Monroe, ME: Common Courage Press, 2002), 51.

10. See Jay Mazur, "Labor's New Internationalism," *Foreign Affairs* (January/February 2000): 79–93. See also Dimitris Stevis and Terry Boswell, *Globalization and Labor: Democratizing Global Governance* (Lanham, MD: Rowman & Littlefield, 2007).

11. Mary Kaldor, *Global Civil Society: An Answer to War* (Cambridge: Polity, 2003), 78.

12. "Police Quell Davos Protests," BBC News, January 28, 2001, http://www.bbc.co.uk; Onna Coray, "Swiss Police Catch Heat for Anti-Global Melee," *Chicago Tribune*, January 30, 2001.

13. Associated Press, "Police and Protesters Clash as Economic Summit Opens," *New York Times*, July 20, 2001; David E. Sanger and Alessandra Stanley, "Skirmishes Mark Big Protest March at Talks in Italy," *New York Times*, July 22, 2001.

14. Melinda Henneberger, "Italians Hold Large Protest Rally after Parliament Clears Police," *New York Times*, September 23, 2001.

15. Naomi Klein, "Signs of the Times," *The Nation*, October 22, 2001, 15–20.

16. Bernard Cassen, cited in Tony Smith, "Anti-Globalization Summit Opens," *AP International News*, January 25, 2001, http://www.news.excite.com/news/ap/010125/20/int-world-social-forum.html.

17. See, for example, Jackie Smith, *Social Movements for Global Democracy* (Baltimore: Johns Hopkins University Press, 2007).

18. "World Social Forum 2001 Charter of Principles" and "World Social Forum 2001 Call for Mobilization," in *The World Social Forum: Strategies of Resistance*, ed. José Corrêa Leite (Chicago: Haymarket Books, 2005), 9–13, 181–86.

19. Donatella della Porta, Massimiliano Andretta, Lorenzo Mosca, and Herbert Reiter, *Globalization from Below: Transnational Activists and Protest Networks* (Minneapolis: University of Minnesota Press, 2006), 68.

20. "World Social Forum 2001 Charter of Principles" in Leite, *World Social Forum*, 11–13.

21. Manfred B. Steger, James Goodman, and Erin Wilson, *Justice Globalism: Ideology, Crises, Policy* (London: Sage, 2013).

22. Steger, Goodman, and Wilson, *Justice Globalism*.

23. The chapter's citations related to the five claims of justice globalism are taken from Steger, Goodman, and Wilson, *Justice Globalism*, 46–52.

24. Ernst Bloch, *The Principle of Hope*, 2 vols. (Cambridge, MA: MIT Press, 1995).

25. Susan George, *Another World Is Possible If . . .* (London: Verso, 2004), 90–96.

26. Bruce Lawrence, "Introduction," in Osama bin Laden, *Messages to the World: The Statements of Osama Bin Laden*, ed. Bruce Lawrence and trans. James Howarth (London: Verso, 2005), xvii; xi. See also Bernard Lewis, "License to Kill," *Foreign Affairs* (November–December 1998).

27. Osama bin Laden, "Under Mullah Omar" (April 9, 2001), in *Messages to the World*, 96, and "The Winds of Faith" (October 7, 2001), 104–105.

28. Ayman al-Zawahiri, "Loyalty and Enmity" (n.d.), in *The Al Qaeda Reader*, ed. and trans. Raymond Ibrahim (New York: Broadway Books, 2007), 102.

29. Osama bin Laden, "From Somalia to Afghanistan" (March 1997), in *Messages to the World*, 50–51.

30. Osama bin Laden, "The Saudi Regime" (November 1996), in *Messages to the World*, 39.

31. Osama bin Laden, "The Invasion of Arabia" (c. 1995/1996), in *Messages to the World*, 15. See also Osama bin Laden, "The Betrayal of Palestine" (December 29, 1994), in *Messages to the World*, 3–14.

32. See, for example, bin Laden, "The Saudi Regime," 32–33.

33. Mohammed Bamyeh, "Global Order and the Historical Structures of *dar al-Islam*," in *Rethinking Globalism*, ed. Manfred B. Steger (Lanham, MD: Rowman & Littlefield, 2004), 225.

34. Bin Laden, "Betrayal of Palestine," 9.

35. Osama bin Laden, "A Muslim Bomb" (December 1998), in *Messages to the World*, 88.

36. Sayyid Qutb, "War, Peace, and Islamic Jihad," in *Modernist and Fundamentalist Debates in Islam: A Reader*, ed. Mansoor Moaddel and Kamran Talattof (New York: Palgrave Macmillan, 2002), 240.

37. Mary R. Habeck, *Knowing the Enemy: Jihadist Ideology and the War on Terror* (New Haven, CT: Yale University Press, 2006), 62.

38. Osama bin Laden, "Terror for Terror" (21 October 2001), in *Messages to the World*, 119.

39. Ayman al-Zawahiri, "I Am among the Muslim Masses" (2006), in *The Al Qaeda Reader*, 227–28.

40. Olivier Roy, *Globalized Islam: The Search for the New Ummah* (New York: Columbia University Press, 2006), 19.

41. For more on the nature and role of the corporations mentioned, see http://www.timex.com and http://kalashnikov.guns.ru. See also Manfred B. Steger, *Globalization: A Very Short Introduction*, 2nd ed. (Oxford: Oxford University Press, 2009).

42. Osama bin Laden, "Moderate Islam Is a Prostration to the West" (2003), in Ibrahim, *The Al Qaeda Reader*, 22–62. For a readable overview of the history and meanings of jihad, see David Cook, *Understanding Jihad* (Berkeley: University of California Press, 2005).

43. Osama bin Laden, "Among a Band of Knights" (February 14, 2003), in *Messages to the World*, 202; "Resist the New Rome" (January 4, 2004), in *Messages to the World*, 218; and "A Muslim Bomb," in *Messages to the World*, 69.

44. Osama bin Laden, "The World Islamic Front" (February 23, 1998), in *Messages to the World*, 61; "To the Americans" (October 6, 2002), 166; "The World Islamic Front" (February 23, 1998), in *Messages to the World*, 61.

45. Osama Bin Laden, "Depose the Tyrants" (December 16, 2004), in *Messages to the World*, 245–75; Ayman al-Zawahiri, "Jihad, Martyrdom, and the Killing of Innocents" (n.d.), in Ibrahim, *The Al Qaeda Reader*, 141–71.

46. Bin Laden, "A Muslim Bomb," 73, 87; and "The Winds of Faith," in *Messages to the World*, 105.

47. Bin Laden, "Moderate Islam Is a Prostration to the West," in Ibrahim, *The Al Qaeda Reader*, 51–52, 30–31.

48. Osama bin Laden, untitled transcript of the videotaped message (September 6, 2007).

49. Bin Laden, "To the Americans," 167–68, and "Resist the New Rome," in *Messages to the World*, 214.

50. Bin Laden, "Nineteen Students" (December 26, 2001), in *Messages to the World*, 150, and untitled transcript of September 6, 2007.

51. Bin Laden, "Terror for Terror," in *Messages to the World*, 112.

52. Bin Laden, "The Towers of Lebanon" (October 29, 2004), in *Messages to the World*, 242.

53. Faisal Devji, "Osama Bin Laden's Message to the World," *Open Democracy* (December 21, 2005), 2. See also Faisal Devji, *Landscapes of Jihad: Militancy, Morality, Modernity* (Ithaca, NY: Cornell University Press, 2005), 144.

54. Bin Laden, untitled transcript of September 6, 2007.

55. Bin Laden, "A Muslim Bomb," in *Messages to the World*, 91.

56. Roy, *Globalized Islam*, chapter 7.

57. Manfred Steger, *Globalism: Market Globalism Meets Terrorism*, 2nd ed. (Lanham, MD: Rowman & Littlefield, 2005).

58. Jagdish Bhagwati, *In Defense of Globalization* (New York: Oxford University Press, 2004), 30.

59. *The National Security Strategy of the United States* [*NSSUS*] (September 2002), https://www.globalsecurity.org/military/library/policy/national/nss -020920.pdf.

60. Robert Kagan, "The U.S.–Europe Divide," *Washington Post*, May 26, 2002.

61. *NSSUS*.

62. Claes G. Ryn, "The Ideology of American Empire," *Orbis* 47, no. 3 (June 2003): 384–85.

63. George W. Bush, "Securing Freedom's Triumph," *New York Times*, September 11, 2002.

64. Transcript of George W. Bush's Inaugural Address, *New York Times*, January 20, 2005.

65. Bush, cited in David Stout, "Bush Calls for World Bank to Increase Grants," *New York Times*, July 17, 2001. Bush's "Three Pillar Speech" is taken from a transcript of his address in London on Iraq and the Middle East, *New York Times*, November 19, 2003.

66. Richard Falk, "Will the Empire Be Fascist?" *The Transnational Foundation for Peace and Future Research Forum*, March 24, 2003, http://www.oldsite .transnational.org/SAJT/forum/meet/2003/Falk_FascistEmpire.html.

67. William H. Thornton, *New World Empire: Civil Islam, Terrorism, and the Making of Neoglobalism* (Lanham, MD: Rowman & Littlefield, 2005), 19.

68. Ryn, "The Ideology of American Empire," 384. In his article "Will the Empire Be Fascist?" Richard Falk, too, argues that the "American response to September 11 has greatly accelerated the drive for global dominance, although it has been masked beneath the banners of anti-terrorism."

69. Chalmers Johnson, *The Sorrows of Empire: Militarism, Secrecy, and the End of the Republic* (New York: Metropolitan Books, 2004), 24, 288.

70. Robert McFarlane and Michael Bleyzer, "Taking Iraq Private," *Wall Street Journal*, March 27, 2003.

71. Robert D. Kaplan, *Warrior Politcs: Why Leadership Demands a Pagan Ethos* (New York: Vintage, 2003).

72. Norman Podhoretz, *World War IV: The Long Struggle against Islamofascism* (New York: Doubleday, 2007).

73. Thomas P. M. Barnett, *The Pentagon's New Map: War and Peace in the Twenty-First Century* (New York: G. P. Putnam's Sons, 2004). The sequel to this book is *Blueprint for Action: A Future Worth Creating* (New York: G. P. Putnam's Sons, 2005).

74. A milder version of this argument can be found in Walter Russell Mead's advocacy of an "American project—a grand strategic vision of what it is that the United States seeks to build in the World." See *Power, Terror, Peace, and War: America's Grand Strategy in a World of Risk* (New York: Knopf, 2004), 7.

75. Barnett, *Pentagon's New Map*, 31–32, 294–302.

76. Barnett, *Pentagon's New Map*, chapters 3 and 4.

77. Barnett, *Pentagon's New Map*, 245.

78. Arundhati Roy, "The New American Century," *The Nation* (February 9, 2004): 11.

79. Thomas L. Friedman, *Longitudes and Attitudes: The World in the Age of Terrorism* (New York: Anchor Books, 2003), 222–23; see also Thomas L. Friedman, *The World Is Flat 3.0: A Brief History of the Twenty-First Century* (New York: Picador, 2007), esp. chapter 10.

CHAPTER 5: SECOND-WAVE
CHALLENGERS IN THE 2010s

1. John Ralston Saul, *The Collapse of Globalism and the Reinvention of the World* (London: Penguin, 2005), 270.

2. Heikki Patomäki, *Disintegrative Tendencies in the Global Political Economy: Exits and Conflicts* (London and New York: Routledge, 2018), 122.

3. Dani Rodrik, *The Globalization Paradox: Democracy and the Future of the World Economy* (New York: Norton, 2012).

4. See Karl Jackson, ed., *Asian Contagion: The Causes and Consequences of a Financial Crisis* (New York: Perseus, 1999).

5. David M. Kotz, "The Financial and Economic Crisis of 2008: A Systemic Crisis of Neoliberal Capitalism," *Review of Radical Political Economies* 41, no. 3 (2009): 307.

6. See Joseph Stiglitz, *Freefall: America, Free Markets, and the Sinking of the World Economy* (New York: Norton, 2010).

7. See David M. Kotz, *The Rise and Fall of Neoliberalism* (Cambridge, MA: Harvard University Press, 2015).

8. Stiglitz, *Freefall*.

9. See CNN Library, "Syrian Civil War Fast Facts," April 9, 2019, accessed April 21, 2019, https://www.cnn.com/2013/08/27/world/meast/syria -civil-war-fast-facts/index.html.

10. David Scott FitzGerald, *Refuge beyond Reach: How Rich Democracies Repel Asylum Seekers* (New York: Oxford University Press, 2019).

11. Eliot Dickinson, *Globalization and Migration: A World in Motion* (Lanham, MD: Rowman & Littlefield, 2016), 121–26.

12. See Pierre-André Taguieff, "The Revolt against the Elites, or the New Populist Wave: An Interview," *TelosScope*, June 25, 2016, accessed July 23, 2019, http://www.telospress.com/the-revolt-against-the-elites-or-the-new-populist-wave-an-interview; John Judis, *The Populist Explosion: How the Great Recession Transformed American and European Politics* (New York: Columbia Global Reports, 2016); Rogers Brubaker, "Why Populism?" *Theory and Society* 46 (2017): 357–85; and Barry Eichengreen, *The Populist Temptation: Economic Grievance and Political Reaction in the Modern Era* (New York: Oxford University Press, 2018).

13. Pierre-André Taguieff, "La rhétoric du national-populisme," *Mots: Les Langues du politique* 9 (1984): 113–39.

14. Anton Jäger, "The Semantic Drift: Images of Populism in Post-War American Historiography and Their Relevance for (European) Political Science," *Populismus Working Papers* no. 3 (2016), 16.

15. Jean-Yves Camus and Nicolas Lebourg, *Far Right Politics in Europe* (Cambridge, MA: Belknap, 2017), 13.

16. See, for example, Ruth Wodak, *The Politics of Fear: What Right-Wing Populist Discourses Mean* (London: Sage, 2015).

17. See, for example, Paolo Gerbaudo, *The Mask and the Flag* (Cambridge: Cambridge University Press, 2017); and Chantal Mouffe, *For a Left Populism* (London: Verso, 2018).

18. Benjamin Moffitt, *The Global Rise of Populism: Performance, Political Style, and Representation* (Stanford, CA: Stanford University Press, 2016).

19. Dani Rodrik, "Populism and the Economics of Globalization," *Journal of International Business Policy* 1, nos. 1–2 (2018): 13.

20. Guy Standing, *The Precariat: The New Dangerous Class* (London: Bloomsbury, 2011).

21. Pankaj Ghemawat, "Globalization in the Age of Trump," *Harvard Business Review* (July/August 2017), accessed July 11, 2018, https://hbr.org/2017/07/globalization-in-the-age-of-trump.

22. Colin Crouch, *The Globalization Backlash* (Cambridge: Polity, 2019), 1.

23. Pippa Norris and Ronald Inglehart, *Cultural Backlash: Trump, Brexit, and Authoritarian Populism* (Cambridge: Cambridge University Press, 2019), 12–13; 16.

24. W. B. Gallie, *Philosophy and the Historical Understanding* (London: Chatto & Windus, 1964).

25. Paul Taggart, *Populism* (Buckingham: Open University Press, 2000).

26. Cas Mudde and Cristobal Rovira Kaltwasser, *Populism: A Very Short Introduction* (Oxford: Oxford University Press, 2017), 6.

27. Mouffe, *For a Left Populism*, 11.

28. See, for example, Ghita Ionescu and Ernest Gellner, eds., *Populism: Its Meaning and National Characteristics* (London: Weidenfeld and Nicolson, 1969); Margaret Canovan, *Populism* (New York: Harcourt Brace Jovanovich, 1981); Francisco Panizza, ed., *Populism and the Mirror of Democracy* (London: Verso, 2005); Noam Gidron and Bart Bonikowski, "Varieties of Populism: Literature Review and Research Agenda," *Harvard University, Waterhead Center of International Affairs Working Paper* 13, no. 4 (2013): 1–38; and Manuel Anselmi, *Populism: An Introduction* (London and New York: Routledge, 2018).

29. Canovan, *Populism*, 299.

30. Ernesto Laclau, "Populism: What's in a Name?" in Panizza, *Populism and the Mirror of Democracy*, 5. See also Ernesto Laclau, *On Populist Reason* (London: Verso, 2006); and Francisco Panizza, "The Ambiguities of Populism," *Political Quarterly* 77, no. 4 (2006): 512.

31. Taggart, *Populism*; Paris Aslanidis, "Is Populism an Ideology? A Refutation and a New Perspective," *Political Studies* 64, no. 1S (2016): 88–104; and Brubaker, "Why Populism?"

32. Aslanidis, "Is Populism an Ideology?" 89.

33. Yves Mény and Yves Surel, eds., *Democracies and the Populist Challenges* (Basingstoke, UK: Palgrave Macmillan, 2002): 6.

34. For a useful distinction between "classical populisms" and "neo-populisms," see Manuel Anslemi, *Populism: An Introduction* (New York and London: Routledge, 2018), 39.

35. "Neither Left nor Right," *Southern Poverty Law Center Intelligence Report* (Winter 2000), accessed June 24, 2008, https://www.splcenter.org/intelligence-report. I want to thank Mark Potok, the editor of the *Southern Poverty Law Center Intelligence Report*, for his personal correspondence of January 25, 2001, clarifying my questions about the presence of the radical Right in Seattle.

36. For an enlightening discussion of the link between the American radical Right of the 1990s and the "alt-right" movement of the Obama years, see Lane Crothers, *Rage on the Right: The American Militia Movement from Ruby Ridge to the Trump Presidency*, 2nd ed. (Lanham, MD: Rowman & Littlefield, 2019).

37. Stephen K. Bannon, cited in Jason Horowitz, "Stephen Bannon Is Done Wrecking the American Establishment. Now He Wants to Destroy Europe's," *New York Times*, March 9, 2018. As Lane Crothers points out, the right-wing populist groups collectively labeled the "alt-right" are not a monolith. Still, at the heart of alt-right beliefs is the mixing of principles of white racial supremacy, anti-immigrant bias, assertive male dominance, and the victimization of white people and "Western civilization." In Europe, this worldview has become known by the umbrella designation of "Identitarianism." See Crothers, *Rage on the Right*, 157; and José Pedro Zuquéte, *The Identitarians: The*

Movement against Globalism and Islam in Europe (South Bend, IN: University of Notre Dame Press, 2018).

38. Patrick J. Buchanan, "The Global-Warming Hucksters" (blog), October 23, 2007, accessed June 1, 2008, http://buchanan.org/blog/2007/10/pjb -the-global-warming-hucksters.

39. Patrick J. Buchanan, *The Great Betrayal: How American Sovereignty and Social Justice Are Being Sacrificed to the Gods of the Global Economy* (Boston: Little, Brown, 1998), 97; "The Second Battle of NAFTA" (blog), March 8, 2008, http://buchanan.org/blog/2008/03/pjb-the-second-battle-of-nafta; "The 'Isms' That Bedevil Bush" (blog), March 25, 2008, accessed November 11, 2008, http://buchanan.org/blog/2008/03/pjb-the-isms- that-bedevil-bush.

40. Buchanan, "Second Battle of NAFTA."

41. Buchanan, *Great Betrayal*, 288.

42. Patrick J. Buchanan, *A Republic, Not an Empire: Reclaiming America's Destiny* (Washington, DC: Regnery Publishing, 1999), xi–xii.

43. Patrick J. Buchanan, "Address to the Chicago Council on Foreign Relations" (speech in Chicago, November 18, 1998).

44. Patrick J. Buchanan, *Day of Reckoning: How Hubris, Ideology and Greed Are Tearing America Apart* (New York: Thomas Dunne Books, 2007), 1.

45. Buchanan, "Second Battle of NAFTA," and "Subprime Nation" (blog), January 15, 2008, accessed November 12, 2008, https://buchanan.org/blog/ pjb-subprime-nation-919.

46. Patrick J. Buchanan, "The Decline of the Anglos" (blog), September 18, 2007, accessed March 23, 2008, https://buchanan.org/blog/?s=The+Decline+of +the+Anglos.

47. Patrick Buchanan, press release, July 2, 1999; Patrick J. Buchanan, *State of Emergency: The Third World Invasion and Conquest of America* (New York: Thomas Dunne, 2007).

48. Speech by Patrick Buchanan (May 28, 1999).

49. Stephen Bannon and many other "alt-right" activists are greatly influenced by a cyclical theory of history presented by William Strauss and Neil Howe, *The Fourth Turning: What Cycles of History Tell Us about America's Next Rendezvous with Destiny* (New York: Three Rivers Press, 1997). The "fourth turning" is alleged to be the last, crisis-ridden period in four historical phases that repeat themselves every eighty to one hundred years.

50. For short summaries of Stephen Bannon's ideological perspective, see Jeffrey C. Alexander, "Raging against the Enlightenment: The Ideology of Steven Bannon," *asaculturesection* (Spring/Summer 2017), https://ccs.yale .edu/sites/default/files/files/Alexander%20Articles/2017_Bannon_Culture.pdf; and Andrew Prokop, "Inside Steve Bannon's Apocalyptic Ideology: Like Karl Rove on an Acid Trip," *Vox*, July 21, 2017, accessed May 1, 2019, https://

www.vox.com/policy-and-politics/2017/7/21/16000914/steve-bannon-devils
-bargain-josh-green.

51. Taggart, *Populism*.

52. John R. Bolton, *How Barack Obama Is Endangering Our National Sovereignty* (New York: Encounter Books, 2010): 1. Similarly, the conservative writer Matthew Roberts identified, in 2008, what he called the "three basic tenets" of "the new religion of globalism": (1) interventionist foreign policies; (2) free trade; (3) mass immigration (illegal or legal). See Matthew Roberts, "The Archaeology of Globalism," *Taki's Magazine*, February 4, 2008, accessed May 1, 2019, https://www.takimag.com/article/the_archaeology_of_globalism/#
.XMZcBknQiII.email.

53. The MDA performed in this chapter draws on a data set of seventeen formal speeches made by then Republican Party candidate Donald J. Trump during the US electoral campaign between March and October 2016. These texts are supplemented by three additional public remarks delivered between 2016 and 2018 on American soil by Nigel Farage, the former leader of the United Kingdom Independence Party (UKIP) and driving force behind Britain's 2016 referendum in favor of the country exiting the European Union. The citations offered in this chapter are taken from transcripts accessible via the *Factbase* website: http://factba.se. A useful online source for the study of Trump's speeches, *Factbase* also contains a massive collection of his campaign-relevant tweets, deleted tweets, and video materials, including his deleted video log from 2011–2014. *Factbase* does not engage in news or interpretation, but focuses on the entire, available corpus of Donald Trump's public statements and recordings in unedited form.

54. Although this chapter does not focus on the racial and gendered aspects of Trumpism, these categories are crucial in its discursive drawing of exclusive boundaries toward racial and religious minorities, women, and other social groups that are seen as lower in the social pecking order and thus might not qualify as "real Americans." For such "boundary work" in Trump's discourse, see Michelle Lamont, Bo Yun Park, and Elena Ayala-Hurtado, "Trump's Electoral Speeches and His Appeal to the American White Working Class," *British Journal of Sociology* 68, no. S1 (2017): 153–80.

55. Donald J. Trump, "Remarks at a Rally in Fredericksburg" (speech in Fredericksburg, PA, August 20, 2016).

56. Donald J. Trump, "Remarks on American Economic Independence" (speech in Monessen, PA, June 28, 2016).

57. Trump, "Remarks on American Economic Independence"; "Address Accepting the Presidential Nomination" (speech at the Republican National Convention in Cleveland, OH, July 21, 2016); "Remarks at a Rally in Fredericksburg"; "Remarks at the Mississippi Coliseum" (speech in Jackson, MS,

August 21, 2016); and "Remarks at the South Florida Fair Expo Center" (speech in West Palm Beach, FL, October 13, 2016).

58. Donald J. Trump, "Remarks at Luedecke Arena" (speech in Austin, TX, August 23, 2016); and "Address Accepting the Presidential Nomination."

59. Mudde and Rovira Kaltwasser, *Populism*, 9–11.

60. Jan-Werner Müller, *What Is Populism?* (Philadelphia: University of Pennsylvania Press, 2016), 38.

61. Donald J. Trump, "Remarks at Trump SoHo" (speech in New York City, June 22, 2016).

62. Trump, "Remarks at Trump SoHo"; "Remarks at the South Florida Fair Expo Center"; and "Remarks on American Economic Independence."

63. Donald J. Trump, "Remarks Announcing Candidacy for President" (speech in New York City, June 16, 2015); and "Remarks at a Rally" (speech in Toledo, OH, September 21, 2016).

64. Trump, "Remarks Announcing Candidacy for President"; and "Remarks at the Mississippi Coliseum." As mentioned, Mudde and Rovira Kaltwasser identify the "general will" as the third and final core concept of populism.

65. Trump, "Remarks at the South Florida Fair Expo Center."

66. Nigel Farage, "Remarks at the Mississippi Coliseum" (speech in Jackson, MS, August 24, 2016).

67. Trump, "Remarks at the Mississippi Coliseum"; "Remarks at a Rally in Toledo, OH"; "Remarks on American Economic Independence"; and "Remarks at a Rally at Berglund Center" (speech in Roanoke, VA, September 24, 2016).

68. Trump, "Remarks at the South Florida Fair Expo Center."

69. Trump, "Remarks Announcing Candidacy for President."

70. Trump, "Remarks on American Economic Independence."

71. Trump, "Remarks on American Economic Independence"; "Remarks Introducing Governor Mike Pence as the 2016 Republican Vice-Presidential Nominee" (speech in New York City, July 16, 2016); "Address Accepting the Presidential Nomination"; "Remarks to the Detroit Economic Club" (speech in Detroit, MI, August 8, 2016); "Remarks at a Rally in Fredericksburg"; "Remarks at Luedecke Arena"; "Remarks at the Mississippi Coliseum"; and "Remarks to the American Legion" (speech in Cincinnati, OH, September 1, 2016).

72. Donald J. Trump, "Remarks on Foreign Policy at the National Press Club" (speech in Washington, DC, April 27, 2016).

73. Trump, "Remarks at a Rally in Toledo, OH"; "Remarks at Trump SoHo"; "Remarks at the South Florida Fair Expo Center"; and "Address Accepting the Presidential Nomination at the Republican National Convention."

74. Trump, "Remarks on American Economic Independence"; "Remarks at Trump SoHo"; and "Remarks at a Rally at Berglund Center."

75. Trump, "Remarks on American Economic Independence"; and "Remarks at Trump SoHo."

76. Trump, "Address Accepting the Presidential Nomination"; "Remarks at the South Florida Fair Expo Center"; "Remarks to the American Legion"; "Remarks at the Cleveland Arts and Social Sciences Academy" (speech in Cleveland, OH, September 8, 2016).

77. Trump, "Remarks on American Economic Independence."

78. Donald J. Trump, "Remarks at the AIPAC Policy Conference" (speech in Washington, DC, March 21, 2016); and "Remarks at a Rally at Berglund Center."

79. Trump, "Remarks at Trump SoHo."

80. Trump, "Remarks at a Rally at Berglund Center."

81. Trump, "Remarks at a Rally at Berglund Center."

82. Trump, "Remarks at the South Florida Fair Expo Center."

83. Donald J. Trump, "Remarks by Donald J. Trump to the United Nations General Assembly," September 25, 2018, accessed December 26, 2018, https://www.whitehouse.gov/briefings-statements/remarks-president-trump-73rd-session-united-nations-general-assembly-new-york-ny.

84. Trump, cited in Peter Baker, "'Use That Word'! Trump Embraces the 'Nationalist' Label," *New York Times*, October 23, 2018, https://www.nytimes.com/2018/10/23/us/politics/nationalist-president-trump.html. Similarly, Marine Le Pen argues that the real cleavage in French politics is not between the Left and Right, but between "nationalists" and "globalists."

85. Most current national-populist leaders share Trump's antiglobalist rhetoric. For example, RN's leader Marine Le Pen identifies "globalism" as the "second enemy" next to "Islamism." For Le Pen, globalism consists of two principal elements: transnational capitalism and multiculturalism. In fact, in a 2017 speech in Lyon that kicked off her presidential campaign, Le Pen went so far as to characterize "Islamic fundamentalism" as "another form of globalization." See William Galston, *Anti-Pluralism: The Populist Threat to Liberal Democracy* (New Haven, CT: Yale University Press, 2018), 56; and Nicholas Vinocur, "Marine Le Pen Makes Globalization the Enemy," *Politico*, February 6, 2017, accessed December 31, 2018, https://www.politico.eu/article/marine-le-pen-globalization-campaign-launch-french-politics-news-lyon-islam.

86. See, especially, Lamont, Park, and Ayala-Hurtado, "Trump's Electoral Speeches." The authors' computer-assisted qualitative analysis of seventy-three formal speeches made by Donald Trump during the 2016 electoral campaign identifies one of the central features of Trump's discourse as its emphatic description of workers as hardworking Americans who are victims of globalization: "By focusing on globalization as a source of deindustrialization,

Trump repeatedly framed the problems experienced by working-class Americans as structural and removed blame from them" (S165).

87. Nigel Farage, "Remarks at the Conservative Political Action Conference" (speech in Washington, DC, February 24, 2017).

88. Bart Bonikowski, "Ethno-Nationalist Populism and the Mobilization of Collective Resentment," *British Journal of Sociology* 68, no. S1 (2017): 202–3.

89. Brubaker, "Why Populism?," 369.

CHAPTER 6: GLOBALISMS IN THE 2020s

1. Karl Polanyi, *The Great Transformation: The Political and Economic Origins of Our Time* (1944; reprint, Boston: Beacon Press, 1957), 132.

2. For a concise explication of Polanyi's ethical theory, see Gregory Baum, *Karl Polanyi on Ethics and Economics* (Montreal: McGill-Queen's University Press, 1996).

3. Polanyi, *Great Transformation*, 237.

4. 2018 KOF Globalization Index, accessed May 25, 2019, https://www.kof .ethz.ch/en/forecasts-and-indicators/indicators/kof-globalisation-index.html; Ruchir Sharma, *The Rise and Fall of Nations: Forces of Change in the Post-Crisis World* (New York: Norton, 2016); and Finbarr Livesey, *From Global to Local: The Making of Things and the End of Globalization* (New York: Pantheon, 2017).

5. McKinsey Global Institute, "Digital Globalization: The New Era of Global Flows," February 2016, accessed April 2, 2019, https://www.mckinsey .com/business-functions/digital-mckinsey/our-insights/digital-globalization -the-new-era-of-global-flows.

6. See Pippa Norris and Ronald Inglehart, *Cultural Backlash: Trump, Brexit, and Authoritarian Populism* (Cambridge: Cambridge University Press, 2019).

7. Intergovernmental Panel on Climate Change, *Global Warming of 1.5°C*, 2018, accessed May 2, 2019, http://www.ipcc.ch/report/sr15.

8. Donald Trump, "Statement by President Trump on the Paris Climate Accord," June 1, 2017, accessed May 23, 2019, https://www.whitehouse.gov/ briefings-statements/statement-president-trump-paris-climate-accord.

9. Joseph Stiglitz has been insisting for years that the chief problem with neoliberal globalization is that it has been "mismanaged." To be fair, however, he has gradually radicalized his reformist approach by including part of the justice-globalist agenda. See Joseph E. Stiglitz, *Globalization and Its Discontents Revisited: Anti-Globalization in the Era of Trump* (New York: Norton, 2018); *The Price of Inequality: How Today's Divided Society Endangers Our Future* (New York: Norton, 2012); and *People, Power, and Profits: Progressive Capitalism for an Age of Discontent* (New York: Norton, 2019).

10. James H. Mittelman, "Ideologies and the Globalization Agenda," in *Rethinking Globalism*, ed. Manfred B. Steger (Lanham, MD: Rowman & Littlefield, 2004), 22.

11. Klaus Schwab, "The New Architecture for the Fourth Industrial Revolution," *Foreign Affairs*, January 16, 2019, accessed May 25, 2019, https://www.foreignaffairs/articles/word/2019-01-16/globalization-40.

12. Schwab, "New Architecture."

13. Klaus Schwab, "Climate Change—Arguably Humanity's Most Existential Challenge—Requires Urgent Global Action," *World Economic Forum*, January 22, 2019, accessed May 23, 2019, https://naturalcapitalcoalition.org/klaus-schwab-founder-executive-chairman-of-the-world-economic-forum-climate-change-is-arguably-humanitys-most-existential-challenge.

14. See, for example, the Dalai Lama, *Ethics for the New Millennium* (New York: Riverhead Books, 1999), and Pope Francis, *Laudato Si: On Care for Our Common Home* (New York: Our Sunday Visitor Publishing, 2015).

15. Hans Küng, *A Global Ethic for Global Politics and Economics* (New York: Oxford University Press, 1998), 111.

16. Dalai Lama, *Ethics for the New Millennium*, 197.

17. For the notion of a "global systemic shift," see Roland Benedikter, "Global Systemic Shift: A Multidimensional Approach to Understand the Present Phase of Globalization," *New Global Studies* 7, no. 1 (2015): 1–15.

GUIDE TO
FURTHER READING

There is a great deal of academic literature on globalization and its many dimensions, but many of these books are not easily accessible to those who are just setting out to acquire some knowledge of the subject. However, readers who have already digested the present volume on the ideological aspects of globalization may find it easier to approach some of the academic works listed below. While these books do not exhaust the long list of publications on the subject, they nonetheless represent what I consider to be the most appropriate sources for further reading. Indeed, some of them have influenced the arguments made in the present volume. I also wish to acknowledge my intellectual debt to the authors below, whose influence on this book is not always obvious from the text.

CHAPTER 1: IDEOLOGY AND THE
MEANING OF GLOBALIZATION

For the main arguments on the "end of ideology" debate, see Lyman Tower Sargent, *Contemporary Political Ideologies: A Comparative Analysis*, 14th ed. (Fort Worth, TX: Harcourt Brace College Publishers, 2008); Mostafa Rejai, ed., *Decline of Ideology?* (Chicago: Aldine-Atherton, 1971); and Chaim I. Waxman, ed., *The End of Ideology Debate* (New York: Funk & Wagnalls, 1968).

CHAPTER 2: THE ACADEMIC
DEBATE OVER GLOBALIZATION

Accessible academic introductions to the subject of globalization include Jan Aart Scholte, *Globalization*, 2nd ed. (Houndmills, UK: Palgrave Macmillan, 2005); George Ritzer and Paul Dean, *Globalization: A Basic Text*, 2nd ed. (Malden, MA: Wiley-Blackwell, 2015); Manfred B. Steger, *Globalization: A Very Short Introduction*, 4th ed. (Oxford: Oxford University Press, 2017); and Leo McCann, *A Very Short, Fairly Interesting and Reasonable Cheap Book about Globalization* (London: Sage, 2018).

For a book-length introduction to the scope and methods of global studies, see Manfred B. Steger and Amentahru Wahlrab, *What Is Global Studies? Theory and Practice* (London and New York: Routledge, 2017); and Eve Darian-Smith and Philip McCarty, *The Global Turn: Theories, Research Designs, and Methods for Global Studies* (Berkeley: University of California Press, 2017).

Influential attempts to distinguish between various camps in the globalization debates include David Held, Anthony McGrew, David Goldblatt, and Jonathan Perraton, *Global Transformations: Politics, Economics, and Culture* (Stanford, CA: Stanford University Press, 1999); and Luke Martell, "The Third Wave in Globalization Theory," *International Studies Review* 9 (2007): 173–96. These models of "waves of globalization" and their corresponding schools of thought are accessible metaphors that possess descriptive utility, especially for introductory surveys of major approaches to globalization such as the one offered in the present study. However, they have less value for the development of global theory beyond such entrenched typologies. For this reason, I have introduced an alternative framework that breaks down the existing camp mentality of the dominant three-wave "camp model" by presenting complementary insights drawn from multiple perspectives. See Manfred B. Steger and Paul James, *Globalization Matters: Engaging the Global in Unsettled Times* (Cambridge: Cambridge University Press, 2019), chapter 3.

For accounts of economic globalization from different ideological perspectives, see, for example, Jagdish Bhagwati, *In Defense of Globalization* (Oxford: Oxford University Press, 2007); Peter Dicken, *Global Shift: Mapping the Contours of the World Economy*, 7th ed. (New York: Guilford Press, 2015); Pietra Rivoli, *The Travels of a T-Shirt in the Global Economy*, 2nd ed. (Hoboken, NJ: Wiley, 2015); and Robert K.

Schaeffer, *Understanding Globalization*, 5th ed. (Lanham, MD: Rowman & Littlefield, 2016); and Joseph E. Stiglitz, *Globalization and Its Discontents Revisited:* (New York: Norton, 2018).

Sophisticated, yet accessible, books on the relationship between globalization and capitalism include William I. Robinson, *A Theory of Global Capitalism: Production, Class, and the State in a Transnational World* (Baltimore: Johns Hopkins University Press, 2004) and *Into the Tempest: Essays on the New Global Capitalism* (Chicago: Haymarket Books, 2019); Jeffry A. Frieden, *Global Capitalism: Its Rise and Fall in the Twentieth Century* (New York: Norton, 2007); and Robert Reich, *Saving Capitalism: For the Many, Not the Few* (New York: Vintage, 2016).

The most comprehensive book on political globalization is John Baylis, Steve Smith, and Patricia Ownes, *The Globalization of World Politics: An Introduction to International Relations*, 7th ed. (Oxford: Oxford University Press, 2017).

The classic work on cultural globalization is Roland Robertson, *Globalization: Social Theory and Global Culture* (London: Sage, 1992). The best introduction to the topic remains Jan Nederveen Pieterse, *Globalization and Culture: Global Mélange*, 4th ed. (Lanham, MD: Rowman & Littlefield, 2020). For an excellent discussion on the impact of American popular culture on globalization dynamics, see Lane Crothers, *Globalization and American Popular Culture*, 4th ed. (Lanham, MD: Rowman & Littlefield, 2018).

Accessible books on ecological globalization include Peter Newell, *Globalization and the Environment: Capitalism, Ecology and Power* (Cambridge: Polity, 2012); and Robyn Eckersley and Peter Christoff, *Globalization and the Environment* (Lanham, MD: Rowman & Littlefield, 2013).

CHAPTER 3: THE DOMINANCE OF MARKET GLOBALISM IN THE 1990s

For more in-depth discussions of neoliberalism, see David Harvey, *A Brief History of Neoliberalism* (New York: Oxford University Press, 2007); David Kotz, *The Rise and Fall of Neoliberal Capitalism* (Cambridge, MA: Harvard University Press, 2015); and Manfred Steger and Ravi Roy, *Neoliberalism: A Very Short Introduction*, 2nd ed. (Oxford: Oxford University Press, 2020).

For a comprehensive overview of Adam Smith's life and thought, see Ryan Patrick Hanley, ed., *Adam Smith: His Life, Thought, and Legacy* (Princeton, NJ: Princeton University Press, 2016). For a succinct explanation and critique of Ricardo's economic theories, see Theodore Cohn, *Global Political Economy: Theory and Practice* (New York: Longman, 2000). For a detailed exposition of Herbert Spencer's social and economic theories, see M. W. Taylor, *Men versus the State: Herbert Spencer and Late Victorian Individualism* (Oxford: Clarendon Press, 1992); and David Wiltshire, *The Social and Political Thought of Herbert Spencer* (Oxford: Oxford University Press, 1978). For a brief, but clear, introduction to John Maynard Keynes's life and thought, see Robert Sidelsky, *Keynes: A Very Short Introduction* (Oxford: Oxford University Press, 2010).

Two excellent books on the evolution of neoliberalism in the globalizing post–World War II context are Nicholas Wapshott, *Keynes Hayek: The Clash That Defined Modern Economics* (New York: Norton, 2011); and Quinn Slobodian, *Globalists: The End of Empire and the Birth of Neoliberalism* (Cambridge, MA: Harvard University Press, 2018).

For various approaches to critical discourse analysis, see Teun van Dijk, *Discourse and Power* (Basingstoke, UK: Palgrave Macmillan, 2008); Ruth Wodak and Michael Meyer, eds., *Methods for Critical Discourse Analysis*, 2nd ed. (London: Sage, 2009); and Norman Fairclough, *Critical Discourse Analysis: The Critical Study of Language* (New York and London: Routledge, 2010).

CHAPTER 4: FIRST-WAVE CHALLENGERS IN THE 2000s

For accessible accounts of the 1999 "Battle of Seattle," see Martin Khor, "Seattle Debacle: Revolt of the Developing Nations," in *Globalize This! The Battle against the World Trade Organization*, ed. Kevin Danaher and Roger Burbach (Monroe, ME: Common Courage Press, 2002), 48; and Mary Kaldor, "'Civilising' Globalisation? The Implications of the 'Battle in Seattle,'" *Millennium: Journal of International Studies* 29, no. 1 (2000): 105–15. For a useful collection of left positions taken by various antiglobalist groups, see Eddie Yuen, George Katsiaficas, and Daniel Burton Rose, eds., *The Battle of Seattle: The New Challenge to Capitalist Globalization* (New York: Soft Skull Press, 2002), and Robin

Broad, ed., *Global Backlash: Citizen Initiatives for a Just World Economy* (Lanham, MD: Rowman & Littlefield, 2002).

Notable examples of the overlapping literature on global civil society and transnational activism include, for example, Peter Funke, Gary Prevost, and Harry Vanden, eds., *The New Global Politics: Global Social Movements in the 21st Century* (London and New York: Routledge, 2017); Carew Boulding, *NGOs, Political Protest, and Civil Society* (Cambridge: Cambridge University Press, 2016); Valentine Moghadam, *Globalization and Social Movements: Islamism. Feminism, and the Global Justice Movement*, 2nd ed. (Lanham, MD: Rowman & Littlefield, 2012); Jan Aart Scholte, *Building Global Democracy? Civil Society and Accountable Global Governance* (Cambridge: Cambridge University Press, 2011); Geoffrey Pleyers, *Alter-Globalization: Becoming Actors in the Global Age* (Cambridge: Polity, 2011); Charles Lindblom and José Pedro Zúquete, *The Struggle for the World: Liberation Movements for the 21st Century* (Stanford, CA: Stanford University Press, 2010); Kevin McDonald, *Global Movements: Action and Culture* (Oxford: Blackwell, 2006); Donatella della Porta, Massimiliano Andretta, Lorenzo Mosca, and Herbert Reiter, *Globalization from Below: Transnational Activists and Protest Networks* (Minneapolis: University of Minnesota Press, 2006); and Donatella della Porta and Sidney Tarrow, eds., *Transnational Protest and Global Activism* (Lanham, MD: Rowman & Littlefield, 2005).

For an insightful analysis of the tribal, national, and global dimensions in jihadist globalist discourse, see Denis McAuley, "The Ideology of Osama Bin Laden: Nation, Tribe and World Economy," *Journal of Political Ideologies* 10, no. 3 (October 2005): 269–87. For a brilliant discussion of globalizing dynamics involving tribal identities, see Paul James, *Globalism, Nationalism, Tribalism: Bringing the State Back In* (London: Sage, 2006).

For insightful academic perspectives on the globalization of Islam, see Roel Meijer, *Global Salafism: Islam's New Religious Movement* (Oxford: Oxford University Press, 2014); Nevzat Soguk, *Globalization and Islamism: Beyond Fundamentalism* (Lanham, MD: Rowman & Littlefield, 2011); and Olivier Roy, *Globalized Islam: The Search for the New Ummah* (New York: Columbia University Press, 2006).

For a discussion of a link between jihadist Islamism and political forms of "totalitarianism," see, for example, Bassam Tibi, "The Totalitarianism of Jihadist Islamism and Its Challenge to Europe and to

Islam," *Totalitarian Movements and Political Religion* 8, no. 1 (March 2007): 35–54, and Hendrik Hansen and Peter Kainz, "Radical Islamism and Totalitarian Ideology: A Comparison of Sayyid Qutb's Islamism with Marxism and National Socialism," *Totalitarian Movements and Political Religion* 8, no. 1 (March 2007): 55–76.

CHAPTER 5: SECOND-WAVE CHALLENGERS IN THE 2010s

For two excellent studies of the GFC and the ensuing Eurozone Debt Crisis, see David M. Kotz, *The Rise and Fall of Neoliberal Capitalism* (Cambridge, MA: Harvard University Press, 2015); and Adam Tooze, *Crashed: How a Decade of Financial Crisis Changed the World* (New York: Viking, 2018).

For two different assessments of the origins and evolution of the Eurozone debt crisis with a special focus on Greece, see Costas Simitis, *The European Debt Crisis: The Greek Case* (Oxford: Oxford University Press, 2014); and Yanis Varoufakis, *Adults in the Room: My Battle with the European and American Deep Establishment* (New York: Farrar, Straus and Giroux, 2017).

For the best study on the rise of the US Tea Party, see Theda Skocpol and Vanessa Williamson, *The Tea Party and the Making of Republican Conservatism* (New York: Oxford University Press, 2012). In addition there are two other landmark studies on the evolution of the American right-wing and "alt-right" movements: Arlie Russell Hochschild, *Strangers in Their Own Land: Anger and Mourning on the American Right* (New York: The New Press, 2016); and Lane Crothers, *Rage on the Right: The American Militia Movement from Ruby Ridge to the Trump Presidency* (Lanham, MD: Rowman & Littlefield, 2019).

For a selection of books on the Occupy Movement and its ideological vision, see Todd Gitlin, *Occupy Nation: The Roots, the Spirit, the Promise of Occupy Wall Street* (New York: itBooks, 2012); Janet Byrne, *The Occupy Handbook* (New York: Back Pay Books, 2012); and Mark Bray, *Translating Anarchy: The Anarchism of Occupy Wall Street* (Laurel House, UK: Zero Books, 2013). For an insightful article about the (dis)continuities between the Global Justice Movement and the Occupy Movement, see Helma De Vries-Jordan, "The Global Justice

Movement and Occupy Wall Street: Spillover, Spillout, or Coalescence?" *Global Discourse* 4, nos. 2–3 (2014): 182–202.

Some of the most influential studies on the growing global socioeconomic inequality in the 2010s include Joseph E. Stiglitz, *The Price of Inequality: How Today's Divided Society Endangers our Future* (New York: Norton, 2012); Thomas Piketty, *Capital in the Twenty-First Century* (Cambridge, MA: Belknap, 2014); Branko Milanovic, *Global Inequality: A New Approach for the Age of Globalization* (Cambridge, MA: Belknap, 2016); and Elhanan Helpman, *Globalization and Inequality* (Cambridge, MA: Harvard University Press, 2018).

For arguments in favor of a supposed "end" or "failure" of market globalism, see Stephen D. King, *Grave New World: The End of Globalization and the Return of History* (New Haven, CT: Yale University Press, 2017); Finbarr Livesey, *From Global to Local: The Making of Things and the End of Globalization* (New York: Pantheon, 2017); and Ian Bremmer, *Us vs. Them: The Failure of Globalism* (New York: Portfolio/ Penguin, 2018).

For comprehensive studies on right-wing populism in the global context that represent different theoretical perspectives and methodological approaches, see Benjamin Moffitt, *The Global Rise of Populism: Performance, Political Style, and Representation* (Stanford, CA: Stanford University Press, 2016); Cristobal Rovira Kaltwasser, Paul A. Taggart, Paulina Ochoa Espejo, and Pierre Ostiguy, eds., *The Oxford Handbook of Populism* (Oxford and New York: Oxford University Press, 2018); Pippa Norris and Ronald Inglehart, *Cultural Backlash: Trump, Brexit, and Authoritarian Populism* (Cambridge: Cambridge University Press, 2019); and John Agnew and Michael Shin, *Mapping Populism: Taking Politics to the People* (Lanham, MD: Rowman & Littlefield, 2019).

CHAPTER 6: GLOBALISMS IN THE 2020s

For additional discussions of globalization future scenarios, see Colin Crouch, *The Globalization Backlash* (Cambridge: Polity, 2019); and Michael O'Sullivan, *The Levelling: What's Next After Globalization* (Washington, DC: PublicAffairs, 2019).

While generally sympathetic to the WEF's Globalization 4.0 agenda, Richard Baldwin, a trade economist at the Graduate Institute in Geneva, offers a more nuanced discussion of the advantages and shortcomings of digital globalization, especially with regard to what he calls "globotics"—the mixing of globalization with new kinds of job-killing robotics. See Richard Baldwin, *The Globotics Upheaval: Globalization, Robotics, and the Future of Work* (New York and Oxford: Oxford University Press, 2019); and *The Great Convergence: Information Technology and the New Globalization* (Cambridge, MA: Harvard University Press, 2016).

INDEX

About the Author

Manfred B. Steger is professor of sociology at the University of Hawai'i–Mānoa and global professorial fellow at the Institute of Culture and Society, Western Sydney University. He has served as an academic consultant on globalization for the US State Department and as an adviser to the PBS television series *Heaven on Earth: The Rise and Fall of Socialism*. He is the author or editor of twenty-seven books on globalization and social and political theory, including *The Rise of the Global Imaginary: Political Ideologies from the French Revolution to the Global War on Terror* (2008); *Globalization: A Very Short Introduction* (2017); and *Globalization Matters: Engaging the Global in Unsettled Times* (with Paul James, 2019).

GLOBALIZATION

Series Editors

Manfred B. Steger
*University of Hawai'i at Mānoa
and Western Sydney University*

and

Terrell Carver
University of Bristol

"Globalization" has become the buzzword of our time. But what does it mean? Rather than forcing a complicated social phenomenon into a single analytical framework, this series seeks to present globalization as a multidimensional process constituted by complex, often contradictory interactions of global, regional, and local aspects of social life. Since conventional disciplinary borders and lines of demarcation are losing their old rationales in a globalizing world, authors in this series apply an interdisciplinary framework to the study of globalization. In short, the main purpose and objective of this series is to support subject-specific inquiries into the dynamics and effects of contemporary globalization and its varying impacts across, between, and within societies.

Globalization and Sovereignty, 2nd ed.
John Agnew

Globalization and War
Tarak Barkawi

Globalization and Human Security
Paul Battersby and Joseph M. Siracusa

Globalization and the Environment
Peter Christoff and Robyn Eckersley

Globalization and American Popular Culture, 4th ed.
Lane Crothers

Globalization and Migration
Eliot Dickinson

Globalization and Militarism, 2nd ed.
Cynthia Enloe

Globalization and Law
Adam Gearey

Globalization and Feminist Activism, 2nd ed.
Mary E. Hawkesworth

Globalization and Postcolonialism
Sankaran Krishna

Globalization and Media, 3rd ed.
Jack Lule

Globalization and Social Movements, 2nd ed.
Valentine M. Moghadam

Globalization and Terrorism, 2nd ed.
Jamal R. Nassar

Globalization and Culture, 4th ed.
Jan Nederveen Pieterse

Globalization and Democracy
Stephen J. Rosow and Jim George

Globalization and International Political Economy
Mark Rupert and M. Scott Solomon

Globalization and Citizenship
Hans Schattle

Globalization and Money
Supriya Singh

Globalization and Islamism
Nevzat Soguk

Globalization and Urbanization
James H. Spencer

Globalisms, 4th ed.
Manfred B. Steger

Rethinking Globalism
Edited by Manfred B. Steger

Globalization and Labor
Dimitris Stevis and Terry Boswell

Globaloney 2.0
Michael Veseth

Globalization and Health
Jeremy Youde

Supported by the Globalization Research Center at the University of Hawai'i–Mānoa